Uncle John's

LISTS

THAT MAKE YOU GO

Hmmm...

By the
Bathroom Readers' Institute

Bathroom Readers' Press
Ashland, Oregon

6 READERS WHO LOVE UNCLE JOHN'S BOOKS

1 "As a trivia buff cursed with a short attention span, your books are tailor-made for me. You keep writing 'em, I'll keep buying 'em. And recommending them to my friends!"
—Deborah W.

2 "Before I found the Bathroom Readers' Institute, I was unpopular with the ladies; now that I'm a walking font of knowledge, they can't keep their hands off me. Thanks!"
—Dwayne R.

3 "I started reading your books after a colleague, ordinarily not much of a conversationalist, started to get smarter and smarter by the day. We couldn't figure out what was going on until we caught him reading an *Uncle John's Bathroom Reader*. I bought my first one that night."
—Ernie P.

4 "My husband and I are huge fans of your books. I can't imagine how we lived without them as long as we did."
—Nora P.

5 "You guys write the funniest, most informative books I've ever read! All my friends love the crazy facts!"
—Nathaniel Y.

6 "To you, dear Uncle John, I place full credit for everything I know."
—Lauren F.

Portable Press is an imprint of the Printers Row Publishing Group
A Division of Readerlink Distribution Services, LLC

"Bathroom Reader," "Portable Press," and "Bathroom Readers' Institute" are registered trademarks of Readerlink Distribution Services, LLC. All rights reserved

For information, write: The Bathroom Readers' Institute,
P.O. Box 1117, Ashland, OR 97520
www.bathroomreader.com

Cover design by Jon Valk

Interior design by Jeff Altemus

ISBN-13: 978-1-62686-361-3

Library of Congress Cataloging-in-Publication Data

Uncle John's lists that make you go hmmm...
    pages cm
  ISBN 978-1-62686-361-3 (hardcover)
1. American wit and humor. 2. Curiosities and wonders. I.
Bathroom Readers' Institute (Ashland, Or.)
  PN6165.U5373 2015
  081--dc23

                                2014033978

Printed in the United States of America
First Printing: March 2015
19 18 17 16 15 1 2 3 4 5

THANK YOU!

The Bathroom Readers' Institute sincerely thanks the people whose advice and assistance made this book possible.

Gordon Javna

Jay Newman

Tracy Vonder Brink

Trina Janssen

Jeff Altemus

Julie McLaughlin

Dan Mansfield

Jill Bellrose

J. Carroll

Kim Griswell

Brian Boone

Jon Valk

Rusty von Dyl

Michael Brunsfeld

Aaron Guzman

Blake Mitchum

Melinda Allman

Jennifer Magee

Peter Norton

Rick Vonder Brink

Susie Loaf Newman

Franz Liszt

8 HAIRY WORLD RECORDS

1 Longest ear hair: 7.12 inches

2 Heaviest vehicle pulled by hair: 20,690 pounds

3 Highest hairstyle: 8.73 feet

4 Most plastic straws put in hair at one time: 312

5 Largest gathering of natural redheads: 1,672 redeads

6 Most scissors used simultaneously during a haircut: 10

7 Priciest hair sold online: Elvis Presley's, for $115,120

8 Biggest ball of human hair: 4 feet high, 167 pounds

CONTENTS

MYTHS & LEGENDS

BC & AD

LIFE & DEATH

TRAVEL & LEISURE

SCIENCE & TECHNOLOGY

WINNERS & LOSERS

FOOD & DRINK

MONEY & POWER

TOYS & GAMES

MOVIES & SHOWS

SONG & DANCE

WORDS & LANGUAGE

THIS & THAT

1NTRODUCT1ON

It's the Age of the List!

Why the list? More than ever before, we as a society are being bombarded by information. It just keeps on coming! Clever informationalists (like us) have learned that by skillfully placing that information into lists, it becomes a lot easier to digest. A well-constructed list breaks down a big story to its most essential elements—or it cleverly strings together a bunch of little stories.

And that's where we come in. Lists have been a mainstay of the *Uncle John's Bathroom Reader* series ever since we started collecting them in the late 1980s. Our goal: to pique your curiosity by telling you things you didn't know. For example, did you know that Cher once dated Tom Cruise? If little-known celebrity flings isn't your cup of tea, we've included something for everyone in here: silly lists (like the court case names on the facing page), science lists ("10 Reasons Why Laughter Isn't the Best Medicine"), essential lists ("15 Lists that Changed the World"), and all sorts of random and surprising lists. If we thought it was interesting, we included it. And new for this book: We've incorporated our famous "running feet" facts into the page numbers!

So sit back, and have fun reading list after list that will make you go hmmm—or make you shake your head, roll your eyes, guffaw, suppress your gag reflex... One thing we can promise: After reading this book, you certainly won't feel listless! (I wouldn't be doing my job if I didn't use that pun at least once in here.)

Happy reading!

—Uncle John and the BRI staff

21 FUNNY-BUT-REAL COURT CASE NAMES

1 *Batman v. Commissioner*

2 *Easter Seals Society for Crippled Children v. Playboy Enterprises*

3 *United States v. Forty Barrels and Twenty Kegs of Coca-Cola*

4 *Demosthenes v. Baal*

5 *The California Coalition of Undressed Performers v. Spearmint Rhino*

6 *United States v. Forty-three Gallons of Whisky*

7 *Death v. Graves*

8 *United States v. Ninety-five Barrels (More or Less) Alleged Apple Cider Vinegar*

9 *One 1958 Plymouth Sedan v. Pennsylvania*

10 *United States v. 12 200-Foot Reels of Super 8MM Film*

11 *Schmuck v. United States*

12 *South Dakota v. Fifteen Impounded Cats*

13 *United States v. 11¼ Dozen Packages of Articles Labeled in Part Mrs. Moffat's Shoo-Fly Powders for Drunkenness*

14 *Robin Hood v. United States*

15 *Association of Irritated Residents v. United States Environmental Protection Agency*

16 *Terrible v. Terrible*

17 *Nebraska v. One 1970 2-Door Sedan Rambler (Gremlin)*

18 *Wang v. Poon*

19 *United States v. Approximately 64,695 Pounds of Shark Fins*

20 *United States v. Article Consisting of 50,000 Cardboard Boxes More or Less, Each Containing One Pair of Clacker Balls*

21 *Juicy Whip v. Orange Bang*

After *This Is Spinal Tap*, Marshall started making amplifiers that go up to 11.

3 LISTS OF SOUND ADVICE FROM YESTERYEAR

RUDYARD KIPLING'S 7 RULES FOR LIFE IN LONDON FOR HIS 12-YEAR-OLD DAUGHTER, 1908

1 Wash early and often with soap and hot water.

2 Do not roll on the grass of the parks. It will come off black on your dress.

3 Never eat penny buns, oysters, periwinkles, or peppermints on the top of a bus. It annoys the passengers.

4 Be kind to policemen. You never know when you may be taken up.

5 Never stop a motor bus with your foot. It is not a croquet ball.

6 Do not attempt to take pictures off the wall of the National Gallery or remove cases of butterflies from the National History Museum. You will be noticed if you do.

7 Avoid late hours, pickled salmon, public meetings, crowded crossings, gutters, water-carts, and over-eating.

F. SCOTT'S FITZGERALD'S ADVICE TO HIS DAUGHTER, 1933

Things to worry about:

1 Worry about courage.

2 Worry about cleanliness.

3 Worry about efficiency.

4 Worry about horsemanship.

Things not to worry about:

1 Don't worry about popular opinion.

2 Don't worry about dolls.

3 Don't worry about the past.

4 Don't worry about the future.

5 Don't worry about growing up.

6 Don't worry about anybody getting ahead of you.

7 Don't worry about triumph.

8 Don't worry about failure unless it is your own fault.

9 Don't worry about mosquitoes.

10 Don't worry about flies.

11 Don't worry about insects in general.

12 Don't worry about parents.

13 Don't worry about boys.

14 Don't worry about disappointments.

15 Don't worry about pleasures.

16 Don't worry about satisfactions.

Things to think about:

1 What am I really aiming at?

2 How good am I really in comparison to my contemporaries in regard to:

• Scholarship

• Do I really understand about people and am I able to get along with them?

• Am I trying to make my body a useful instrument or am I neglecting it?

BENJAMIN FRANKLIN'S 13 VIRTUES, 1726

1 **Temperance.** Eat not to dullness; drink not to elevation.

2 **Silence.** Speak not but what may benefit others or yourself; avoid trifling conversation.

3 **Order.** Let all your things have their places; let each part of your business have its time.

4 **Resolution.** Resolve to perform what you ought; perform without fail what you resolve.

5 **Frugality.** Make no expense but to do good to others or yourself; waste nothing.

6 **Industry.** Lose no time; be always employ'd in something useful; cut off all unnecessary actions.

7 **Sincerity.** Use no hurtful deceit; think innocently and justly, and, if you speak, speak accordingly.

8 **Justice.** Wrong none by doing injuries, or omitting the benefits that are your duty.

9 **Moderation.** Avoid extremes; forbear resenting injuries so much as you think they deserve.

10 **Cleanliness.** Tolerate no uncleanliness in body, cloaths, or habitation.

11 **Tranquility.** Be not disturbed at trifles or accidents common or unavoidable.

12 **Chastity.** Rarely use venery but for health or offspring, never to dullness, weakness, or the injury of your own or another's peace or reputation.

13 **Humility.** Imitate Jesus and Socrates.

World's largest gallstone: 13 pounds (removed from an 80-year-old woman).

7 EPIC CELEBRITY SMACKDOWNS

1 *Truman Capote* belittles playwright *Tennessee Williams*:
"Here's a dumpy little guy with a dramatic mind who, like one of his adrift heroines, seeks attention and sympathy by serving up half-believed lies to total strangers."

2 *Noel Gallagher* describes fellow rocker *Jack White*:
"He looks like Zorro on doughnuts."

3 *Joan Rivers* tweets about *Lindsay Lohan*'s legal troubles:
"She said she wouldn't mind being under oath because she thought Oath was a Norwegian ski instructor."

4 *Bette Midler* feels bad for *Princess Anne*:
"She loves nature in spite of what it did to her."

5 How much does *Robert Smith* of the Cure (a vegetarian) hate the singer *Morrissey*?
"If Morrissey says not to eat meat, then I'll eat meat—that's how much I hate Morrissey."

6 *Dorothy Parker*, when told that former president *Calvin "Silent Cal" Coolidge* was dead, asked:
"How can they tell?"

7 *Kathy Griffin* uses hindsight to describe *Angelina Jolie*:
"Her lips look like an inflamed anus."

Pillbugs (also called potato bugs and roly-polies) have 14 legs.

15 WAYS TO NOT LOOK LIKE A FOOL ABROAD

1 CHINA, INDIA, AND AFGHANISTAN. These three countries don't adhere to the "clean plate club." Finishing everything on your plate means you weren't given enough food in China (and could be insulting), while in India and Afghanistan, an empty plate signals that you want another helping.

2 GERMANY AND KENYA. On the other hand, if you don't finish everything on your plate in these two countries, your hosts may feel insulted that you didn't enjoy the dish.

3 GERMANY. Americans tend to smile a lot, even at strangers, but Germans primarily use their smiles to show affection to those close to them. So if you're attending a business meeting in Germany, keep things on the serious side. If you laugh during a meeting, they may frown even more.

4 SAUDI ARABIA. The men there stand much closer to one another than Americans do. Although it might feel like they're invading your "personal space," close proximity is the social norm for Saudis, so try not to back away.

5 GREECE. If you're invited to a dinner party, don't show up empty-handed. A small gift of flowers or wine is expected.

6 AUSTRALIA. Don't try to "speak Australian" to an Australian. "G'day, mate" won't go over well. A simple "hello there" will do. And don't mention that Australia was founded as a penal colony; that's how only a few immigrants arrived there.

7 CANADA. When discussing the indigenous population, avoid the terms "Indian," "Eskimo," and "tribe." Each is considered offensive. Instead, say "First Nations," "Inuit," and "bands" or "nations" for specific tribes.

8 MEXICO. Don't be insulted if you show up on time for a meeting and it takes an hour for everyone else to get there. Meeting times are approximate. For parties, however, you're expected to be punctual.

9 CHINA. If a Chinese businessman gives you his business card, you are expected to give yours in return. That holds true even if a group of them gives you their cards. They should all get one in return. So bring plenty.

10 JAPAN. Apologize frequently during conversation, even if you have nothing to apologize for.

11 MALAYSIA. Pointing your index finger at someone is considered rude. Instead, point with your right thumb, with the other fingers folded into your palm.

12 INDIA. Cows are considered sacred, so leave your leather at home. And don't make light of this custom (such as joking about how great cheeseburgers taste).

13 THAILAND. Thais consider the head to be the sacred seat of the soul, so unless you're a monk or a family member, don't touch anyone's head—especially a child's.

14 BELGIUM. A standard greeting is three kisses on the cheeks, alternating from one cheek to the other.

15 ITALY. When in Rome, do as the Romans do.

27 EDIBLE BOOK TITLES

At first glance, this may look like a typical list of classic books, but look closer—they're food puns! Not only that, but these are actual dishes that chefs have entered into the annual "Edible Book Festival." So have a good read and...bon appétit!

1 Anne of Green Bagels

2 Call of the Wild Rice

3 Olive R Twist

4 Chivanhoe

5 Chronicles of Naania

6 Grilled with a Dragon Tattoo

7 The Age of Raisin

8 The DaVinci Cod

9 Lord of the Fries

10 Lord of the Onion Rings

11 Harry Potter and the Prisoner of Marzipan

12 The Communist Can-of-Pesto

13 As I Lay Frying

14 Bridge over the River Chai

15 Cauliflowers for Algernon

16 The Decline and Fall of the Ramen Empire

17 Remembrance of Things Pasta

18 The Invisible Manwich

19 Tinker, Tailor, Soldier, Pie

20 Alice in Wonderbread

21 For Hummus the Bell Pepper Tolls

22 Kon Twinkie

23 Jurassic Tart

24 The Bundt for Red October

25 Treasure Pieland

26 A SweeTart Named Desire

27 Fifty Shades of Grape

10 DRAGONS FROM GREEK MYTHOLOGY

1 Ketos. Better known as the Kraken from Clash of the Titans, it was going to eat Andromeda (chained to a rock as a sacrifice) until Perseus saved her.

2 Python. Guarded the Oracle of Delphi's shrine, killed by Apollo.

3 Hesperios. The guard dragon of the Golden Apples. After Heracles slew it, the gods placed it in the heavens to become the constellation Draco.

4 Drakones of Medea. Two flying dragons that pulled the witch Medea's chariot.

5 Chimera. A lion's body with a dragon's tail and a goat head on its back, slain by Bellerophon.

6 Campe. This winged serpent was a woman from the waist up. Her feet were 1,000 vipers, and the heads of 50 animals protruded from her waist. Guarded the prison pit of Tartaros.

7 Kholkikos. This unsleeping dragon guarded the Golden Fleece until it was slain by the hero Jason.

8 Thespiakos. To save his city, Menestratos wore a breastplate covered in hooks and let Thespiakos eat him; the hooks slew the beast from within.

9 Kykhreides. Terrorized the island of Salamis until Kykhreus drove it away. Then it fled to the goddess Demeter and became her companion.

10 Hydra. When Heracles tried to remove her nine heads, two more popped up for every one he chopped off. So he cauterized the neck stumps so they couldn't regenerate and kept hack, hack, hacking away until Hydra was dead.

8 SCANDALS THAT GOT THE "GATE" TREATMENT

In 1974 President Richard Nixon resigned after he was implicated in a burglary of the Democratic National Committee offices at the Watergate Hotel. Ever since then, when the news media really wants to milk a scandal for ratings, they throw a "gate" at the end of it.

1 CAMILLAGATE

Gate Open: "Camillagate May Keep Charles Off Throne" wrote the *LA Times* in 1992 after the fairy tale marriage of Prince Charles and Princess Diana imploded. Why? British tabloids had leaked the transcript of a sexually explicit phone call between Charles and his mistress Camilla Parker-Bowles. The British public—who loved Diana—turned on Camilla (but a subsequent leak revealed that Diana had a lover of her own).

Gate Closed: The troubled royal marriage ended in divorce in 1996. Diana died a year later. Charles finally married Camilla in 2005, and to this day some Brits still dislike her.

2 NIPPLEGATE

Gate Open: Even if you don't remember who played in 2004's Super Bowl (the Patriots beat the Panthers in a nail-biter), you probably remember "Nipplegate." During the MTV-produced halftime show, Justin Timberlake yanked on Janet Jackson's top, and her breast (adorned with a decorative nipple shield) spilled out on live TV for 9/16ths of a second. Timberlake said it was an unplanned "wardrobe malfunction."

Gate Closed: The NFL booted MTV from future halftime shows, and FCC chairman Michael Powell fined everyone involved a lot of money. Jackson's career never rebounded. Ten years later, Powell admitted, "I had to put my best version of outrage on that I could put on. It was surreal." (Footnote: Jawed Karim, who worked at PayPal, tried to view Nipplegate online, but he couldn't find it, so he invented YouTube.)

3 FAJITAGATE
Gate Open: In 2002 three off-duty San Francisco cops confronted two men, one of whom was carrying a mysterious paper bag. The officers ordered the man to hand over the bag. He refused...and then suffered a beatdown by the cops. What was in the bag? Steak fajitas. So the press, of course, called the scandal "Fajitagate."

Gate Closed: The officers were acquitted of criminal charges (they said they had "probable cause" to search the bag). But they later lost a civil suit and had to pay $41,000 in damages.

4 TOWELGATE
Gate Open: "Toallagate" (as it was called in Mexico) rocked President Vicente Fox's administration in 2001 after reports surfaced that the presidential mansion underwent a $400,000 overhaul that included $400 monogrammed towels and $1,000 bedsheets. The dirty laundry didn't bode well for Fox, who had promised impoverished Mexicans he would put an end to government kickbacks. He denied any knowledge of the extravagances and apologized profusely. "If the towels have caused offense," he said, "I'll pay for them out of my own pocket."

Gate Closed: Three government officials resigned, and three others were suspended. (No word if Fox bought the towels.)

5 HAIRGATE
Gate Open: Early in his first term in 1993, President Bill Clinton was hammered by the press for a haircut he got on *Air Force One* while it was parked on a runway at LAX (Los Angeles International Airport). Reports said that approaching planes had to circle the airport for an hour while Clinton got a $200 trim from a stylist named Cristophe. "Hairgate" dominated the

headlines, causing headaches for Clinton's PR team.

Gate Closed: The reports were false...mostly. Clinton did get a haircut, but the FAA said that it caused no delays at LAX.

6 PASTAGATE

Gate Open: Quebec law dictates that businesses cannot use another language more than French. So in 2013 the *Office Québecois de la Langue Française* (Office of the Language Minister) sent the owner of an Italian restaurant an official notice to stop using the words "pasta" and "antipasto" on the menu.

Gate Closed: Pastagate went viral and embarrassed the government so much that the head of the office resigned.

7 FANGATE

Gate Open: Florida Democratic gubernatorial candidate Charlie Crist keeps an electric fan at the base of his podium during debates, but the venue rules at an October 2014 debate against incumbent Republican Rick Scott forbade their use. Crist's team plugged one in anyway; Scott refused to go on. The debate aired live, so viewers saw an empty stage for six minutes. Then Crist went to his podium to complain about Scott: "Are we really going to debate about a fan? Or are we going to talk about education and the environment and the future of our state? I mean, really." Scott hurried to his podium, and the two opponents traded barbs for an hour. Of course, the next day, all the press could talk about was "Fangate."

Gate Closed: Scott's image was tarnished by his refusal to take the podium, but he had enough fans to win reelection.

8 GATE-GATE

Gate Open: British MP Andrew Mitchell tried to ride his bike through the main gate at his Downing Street office, but the guard told him to use the pedestrian gate instead. Mitchell unleashed an expletive-laced tirade and called the guard a "pleb."

Gate Closed: Mitchell resigned from his post as chief whip.

6 WEIRDEST PLACES WHERE LIFE HAS BEEN FOUND

Michael Crichton wrote in his novel Jurassic Park, *"The history of evolution is that life escapes all barriers. Life breaks free. Life expands to new territories. Painfully, perhaps even dangerously. But life finds a way." As this list shows, he wasn't kidding.*

1 IN A CAN OF IRRADIATED MEAT

In the 1950s, scientists experimented with a new technique of sterilization: They pelted cans of meat with gamma radiation. To their amazement, the bacteria *Deinococcus radiodurans* not only survived the process but were thriving inside the cans.

2 IN RADIOACTIVE SOIL

Another place *D. radiodurans* lives: the Hanford Nuclear Reserve in Washington state, where 53 million gallons of radioactive waste left over from World War II weapons production are being stored in tanks...that leaked. In 2004 scientists studying the area discovered the bacteria living in what microbial ecologist Fred Brockman called "the most radioactive soil that's ever been looked at for microorganisms."

3 IN AN RIVER OF ACID

Spain's Rio Tinto is called the "River of Fire" for both its red color and the acidity of the water—it has a pH level between 1.5 and 3.1 (about the same as the acid in your stomach). Despite those extreme conditions, microorganisms called *acidophiles* thrive there. Scientists once thought nearby mines were making the river acidic, but the acidophiles themselves are the culprits; so many live in the water that they've changed its pH. Because similar conditions exist on Jupiter's moon Europa, astrobiologists are very interested in the Rio Tinto.

4 IN A SUBGLACIAL LAKE

Another Europa-like site that has scientists buzzing is Lake Whillans. This liquid water lake is located underneath the ice sheet in West Antarctica. Sunlight hasn't reached these waters in thousands of years. "The first time we went to Antarctica, and the first place we selected to drill a hole, we found life," boasted researcher Brent Christner in 2013. His team drilled through nearly half a mile of ice to sample the water and found 3,900 different types of microorganisms living there. Christner said, "So it's not much of a stretch that in similar conditions, like on the icy moon of Europa, life could exist there."

5 IN ONE OF THE DEEPEST, HOTTEST PLACES ON EARTH

Three miles beneath the surface of the Caribbean Sea lies the otherworldly Piccard vent field. Shifting tectonic plates there eject massive plumes of superheated water through vents in the seafloor. Water temperatures can reach an incredible 750°F. In spite of the depth and the heat, an expedition to the vent field in 2012 found a thriving ecosystem of fish, shrimp, crabs, snails, anemones, starfish, and tubeworms.

6 IN THE WORLD'S MOST ARID CLIMATE

Chile's Atacama Desert receives an average rainfall of 0.0004 inch per year. Some years it doesn't rain at all. In fact, there hasn't been a significant rainfall there in 400 years. In the Atacama's central region—the driest place in the world—biologists searched for but couldn't find any sign of life, animal or plant. But then, in 2004, a team decided to dig 8 to 12 inches below the desert's surface and take soil samples. Once back in the lab, the specimens were soaked in water and then spread on a Petri dish to grow. Result: Every sample turned out to contain bacteria. The microorganisms had survived without water for at least four centuries. The Atacama findings suggest that there might be life in the form of bacteria on another extremely arid place—Mars. And the search there has only just begun.

11 ITEMS ON HOUDINI'S SCENE AND PROP LIST

Think the dressing-room demands of today's stars are weird? Well, "no brown M&M's" is nothing compared to illusionist Harry Houdini's demands for a performance in the early 1900s. This list couldn't have made the theater manager happy.

1 "As I leave stage soaking wet in bathing suit, I require two dressing rooms nearest stage (6 in company). Couch in dressing room."

2 "Small trap in center of stage, not less than 8", 2' feet in rear of front cloth."

3 "Use of fire hose to reach from side of stage, about 3' past center stage, used in view of audience."

4 "Please see to it that the water in hose is run off. It must be clear, so that audience can see through it."

5 "100 gallons of boiling water (must be boiling)."

6 "We carry four brass tubs to hold this water, which must be filled ready on stage before each performance."

7 "Prepare a chute for 250 gallons of water, from the small 8x8' trap to most convenient spot under stage. The outlet in our water cloth is 6" in diameter."

8 "Water carpet must be flied after each show."

9 "Two small occasional tables (gold if possible, and four gold chairs) and 18 Bentwood Chairs."

10 "A run or stair case, so that committee from audience can come over footlights onto stage."

11 "A small, clean looking (mahogany colored if possible) step ladder about 3 feet 6 inches high."

"DO NOT PURCHASE ANYTHING AT MY EXPENSE!"

---

27 THINGS HUMANS HAVE LEFT ON THE MOON

We receive so much from our lunar neighbor—the tides, a light at night—that it's only fair we give something back. So in addition to the 70 spacecraft and satellites that were intentionally left or crashed on the Moon, future spacefarers will also find...

1 Several bags of urine

2 Several bags of feces

3 Several bags of vomit

4 "Defecation Collection Device"

5 American flags

6 Golf balls

7 TV cameras

8 Still cameras

9 Backpacks

10 Falcon feather (used in an experiment to see if it would fall faster than a hammer)

11 Hammer

12 Wet wipes

13 Towels

14 Javelins

15 Personal hygiene kits

16 Boots

17 Blankets

18 Space food packages

19 Three lunar rovers

20 Two mirrors that NASA uses to calculate the distance to the Moon

21 A photo of astronaut Charles Duke's family

22 A silver pin left by astronaut Alan Bean

23 An aluminum sculpture of fallen astronauts

24 A patch from the ill-fated *Apollo I* mission that killed three astronauts

25 A small disk with greetings from 73 countries

26 A medal honoring the first cosmonauts

27 A gold replica of an olive branch left by *Apollo 11* (the first manned Moon mission) printed with a message of "peace for all mankind."

9 MUSICIANS WHO SERVED IN THE MILITARY

1 PRIVATE JIMI HENDRIX, U.S. Army

The influential guitarist didn't enlist by choice in 1961: It was either join the army or serve two years in prison for stealing a car. Hendrix was assigned to the 101st Airborne Division in Fort Campbell, Kentucky. He was a poor shot, slept on duty, and made missing bed checks a habit. Hendrix also irritated his bunkmates by playing his guitar at all hours. He was signed up for three years, but his commanding officer had had enough after just one and let an ankle injury be the pretext for an honorable discharge, commenting, "Hendrix's mind cannot function properly while performing duties and thinking about his guitar."

2 CORPORAL TONY BENNETT, U.S. Army

Drafted into the U.S. Army in 1944, the crooner served in France and Germany in the 63rd Infantry, known as the "Blood and Fire" Division. Bennett's unit helped liberate the Nazi concentration camp at Landsberg, Germany. One evening Corporal Bennett was having dinner with an African American friend, and an officer told Bennett that his friend should take his meal in the kitchen. Bennett objected, and for that he was demoted to private and assigned to a unit that disinterred graves. He later got a job singing in a military band and finished the war touring Europe. Afterward, he used the GI Bill to study voice.

3 PRIVATE TRACY LAUREN "ICE-T" MARROW, U.S. Army

When the future rapper and Law & Order star became a dad in the late 1970s, he knew that it was time to stop selling drugs: "I was like, man, I'm going to go to jail, I got to do something. So I went to an enlistment office. Next thing you know,

I'm in the military." In 1979 Marrow was assigned to the 25th Infantry Division in Hawaii, where he served as squad leader at Schofield Barracks (and once went AWOL after being accused of stealing a rug). That's where he was introduced to hip-hop. Marrow bought a turntable, mixer, and speakers, and five years later—as Ice-T—he released his debut album, *Rhyme Pays*.

4 SERGEANT JOHNNY CASH, U.S. Air Force

Cash joined the U.S. Air Force a month after graduating high school in 1950. He served for four years—most of them stationed in Landsberg, West Germany. As part of the USAF Security Service, he worked as a Morse code intercept operator. His job: to eavesdrop on Soviet radio transmissions. During down time, Cash taught himself to play guitar and write songs. He even formed his first band there, the Landsberg Barbarians.

5 PRIVATE ORVILLE "SHAGGY" BURRELL, U.S. Marines

In 1988 the Jamaica-born reggae singer moved to the U.S. and joined the Marines. He became an artilleryman in the 5th Battalion, 10th Marines, and saw action during the liberation of Kuwait in 1991. Shaggy's highest rank was lance corporal, but he kept getting demoted for returning late to his barracks after recording sessions in New York. Even so, Shaggy credits his military experience for his success: "I honestly think it was destined to prepare me for what I had to do in music."

6 SERGEANT ELVIS PRESLEY, U.S. Army

"People were expecting me to mess up," recalled Presley, who was already a huge star when he announced his intentions to join the military. "They thought I couldn't take it, and I was determined to go to any limits to prove otherwise, not only to the people who were wondering, but to myself." Both the navy and the air force tried hard to recruit the King. The navy planned to start an "Elvis Presley company," and the air force wanted him at their recruitment centers. Instead, Elvis chose the army as a regular GI. Assigned to the 2nd Armored Division, he was stationed in Texas and Germany, eventually achieving the rank of sergeant. During his leave time, Elvis still made records and even starred in the film *G.I. Blues*.

7 CAPTAIN KRIS KRISTOFFERSON, U.S. Army

Raised an army brat, the future actor/country superstar was under constant pressure from his father to join the army. He finally relented in 1960...*after* he'd earned a master's degree in English literature at Oxford University. Once in the army, Kristofferson became a helicopter pilot, eventually earning the rank of captain. In 1965 he was assigned to West Point and offered a teaching position in literature. He turned it down and resigned his commission to pursue his music career—a decision that led to his family disowning him.

8 SERGEANT JASON EVERMAN, U.S. Army

Most musicians on this list became famous *after* serving; Everman went the opposite route. After the bassist was fired from Nirvana and then from Soundgarden, he was at a crossroads in 1994. So he joined the army and saw action in South America with the 2nd Ranger Battalion. Then he completed special forces training and served with distinction in Iraq and Afghanistan. (He was awarded the Combat Infantryman Badge.) Everman left the army in 2006 and used the GI Bill to attend Columbia University, earning a degree in philosophy.

9 LIEUTENANT JOSEPHINE BAKER, Free French Air Force

The American-born singer became a French citizen in 1937. While there, Baker did more than sing: Her fame served as the perfect cover as a secret agent for the French Resistance during World War II. She was able to smuggle classified documents to and from France, including messages written with invisible ink on her sheet music. Baker even concealed photos of German installations in her underwear.

4 TOYS THAT REALLY HURT

1 LAWN DARTS

Fun Toy! Remember this pointy toy from the 1980s? Played like horseshoes, kids threw plastic darts toward a target on the ground (or at each other). Lawn darts, or Jarts, were hugely popular, selling 1.5 million units per year...until the deaths.

Ouch! Why did the darts stick in the ground so easily? Each one was topped with a 1³/₄-inch metal tip that weighed a whole pound. Not surprisingly, lawn dart injuries sent more than 6,100 people (mostly children) to the ER in an eight-year period. In 1987, after a lawn dart killed seven-year-old Michelle Snow, her father David convinced the Consumer Product Safety Commission to launch an investigation. Once the commission saw the alarming statistics—three dead, one comatose, thousands injured—it went beyond a standard recall and issued an official ban. Lawn darts were removed from stores in December 1988. To this day, it's illegal to sell them.

2 CABBAGE PATCH KIDS SNACKTIME KIDS

Fun Toy! Cabbage Patch Kids—the soft, puffy dolls that you could "adopt"—sold 80 million units starting in 1982. In 1996 Mattel released a Cabbage Patch Kid that could be "fed" via a battery-powered mouth that "chewed" plastic carrots and French fries. Nearly half a million Snacktime Kids were sold within a few months of their release.

Ouch! The doll's mechanical jaws chomped whatever went into them—including little kids' fingers and hair. In one case, a seven-year-old girl's hair got tangled so severely in her doll's mouth that her parents called an ambulance. After nearly 100 reports of the dolls snacking on children, Mattel voluntarily recalled Snacktime Kids and offered $40 to replace them.

3 SKY DANCERS

Fun Toy! From Galoob, these winged ballerina dolls were placed feet-first into a launch pad shaped like a flower. When you pulled the cord, the doll shot out and "danced" through the air. Twenty million Sky Dancers were sold in the mid-1990s.

Ouch! The famous mom phrase "you'll put an eye out" was especially true when it came to these ballistic ballerina missiles. There were a reported 170 cases of the dolls striking people—150 of those resulting in broken teeth, broken ribs, concussions, face lacerations, and a few eyes out. In 2000 Galoob recalled 8.9 million Sky Dancers and stopped selling them.

4 AQUA DOTS

Fun Toy! Released by Spin Master in April 2007, Aqua Dots were craft kits consisting of colorful beads that "melted" together when sprayed with water. Because the bonding process didn't require heat, Aqua Dots was marketed as a creative toy for all ages. It was even named toy of the year in Australia (where it was called Bindeez).

Ouch! Aqua Dots were perfectly safe—if they stayed *outside* your body. When swallowed, the chemical coating that made the beads fuse together turned into *gamma hydroxybutyrate*, also known as GHB...also known as the "date rape drug" because it causes a comalike state—not to mention vomiting, seizures, flaccid muscles, memory loss, and potentially death. After two kids from the U.S. and one from Australia were hospitalized by the beads, Spin Master recalled Aqua Dots in November 2007. After that, the toy maker found some non-date-rapey chemicals to use to make the beads and reissued a new, safer version under the name PixOs.

> "I knew I was an unwanted baby when I saw that my bath toys were a toaster and a radio."
> **—Joan Rivers**

6 ROYALS AND THEIR STRANGE DELUSIONS

1 CHARLES VI: Made of Glass

He started out as "Charles the Well-Beloved" when he was crowned king of France in 1380 at age 11, but by his 20s, he was known as "Charles the Mad." During one of his psychotic episodes, Charles claimed that he was made of glass and was afraid of being "shattered." He refused to let anyone touch him and demanded that iron rods be put in his clothes so he wouldn't break.

2 MARIA I: Her Father's Spirit

In this tragic story, Maria ascended to the Portuguese throne in 1777, but she was stricken with grief after losing her husband, oldest son, and daughter within a few years. As Maria became more and more unhinged, she was constantly tormented by visions of her dead father, Joseph I, being taken to hell. She reported seeing her dad "in colour black and horrible, erected on a pedestal of molten iron, which a crowd of ghastly phantoms were dragging down."

3 JUSTIN II: Animal Sounds

Justin was a Byzantine emperor who grew increasingly unbalanced as his empire crumbled. He became emperor in AD 565, but by 568, he'd already lost land in Italy. More defeats followed on the Crimean Peninsula, and when the Persians captured vital cities in 573, Justin suffered a complete and permanent breakdown. He made animal sounds—barking, crowing, and mewing—and at other times he became so terrified that he'd hide under his bed or try to throw himself out the window. When his men tried to calm him down, he'd bite them.

"Se mettre sur son _31_" is the French version of "dressed to the nines."

4 GEORGE III: A "Prince" Pillow

Americans know George as the king of England during the American Revolution, but he ruled for 59 years...when he wasn't crazy, that is. George suffered from recurrent bouts of insanity that required him to be restrained in a straitjacket. He was usually able to recover for brief periods after months-long bouts of madness, but by 1810 George's mind was irrevocably gone. During one of his spells, he cradled a pillow, addressed it as his dead son Prince Octavius, and declared that his son/pillow "was to be new born this day!"

5 CHRISTIAN VII: A Changeling

Poor Christian was never fit to be king, but he was the only one available to take the throne of Denmark-Norway in 1766. He'd been mentally unstable from childhood (a condition possibly made worse by brutal beatings at the hands of his elders). While his ministers effectively ruled the country, Christian became increasingly insane: He complained of noises in his head, insisted that he'd killed people when he'd been alone, and sometimes claimed that he was the son of Catherine the Great (he wasn't) and that he was a fairy changeling (which he also wasn't).

6 CALIGULA: Just Plain Nuts

Here are a few of the awful things this Roman emperor did (so you don't have to watch that awful movie that was made about him in the 1970s). Emperor Caligula (full name: Gaius Caesar Augustus Germanicus) thought he was the Greek god Zeus, so he married his sister, whom he thought was the goddess Venus. Then—*turn the page now if you have a weak stomach*—fearing that their unborn child would one day try to kill him, Caligula cut it out of her and ate them both. The emperor did even worse things—*way* worse—but we'll just skip to the "funny" part where he declared his horse a senator (which he may have done simply to taunt his human senators).

33 LISTS OF 3s

3 PRIMARY COLORS
1 Red
2 Yellow
3 Blue

3 LITTLE PIGS (DISNEY'S VERSION)
1 **Fifer Pig** (straw)
2 **Fiddler Pig** (sticks)
3 **Practical Pig** (brick)

3 "THREEPEAT" CHAMPIONSHIP WINNERS
1 **Chicago Bulls** ('91–93)
2 **Oakland Athletics** ('72–74)
3 **Green Bay Packers** ('65–67)

3 TYPES OF UNEMPLOYMENT
1 **Structural:** More workers than jobs due to changing tastes and new tech
2 **Frictional:** People willfully moving between jobs and entering the workforce
3 **Cyclical:** Losing jobs due to shifts in the economy, especially a recession

THE ORIGINAL 3 STOOGES
And what they died of.
1 **Moe Howard**, lung cancer
2 **Larry Fine**, stroke
3 **Shemp Howard**, heart attack

3 BALTIC STATES
1 Estonia
2 Latvia
3 Lithuania

3 SPECIES OF HUMANS IN THE GENUS *HOMO*
1 *Homo habilis* (Latin "handy man"): 2.33 mya to 1.44 mya
2 *Homo erectus* (Latin "upright man"): 1.9 mya to 143,000 ya
3 *Homo sapiens* (Latin "wise man"): 200,000 ya to now

3 MUSKETEERS
From Alexandre Dumas's 1844 novel The Three Musketeers.
1 Athos
2 Porthos
3 Aramis

3 MEN DON McLEAN ADMIRES THE MOST

From his 1971 folk song "American Pie."

1 Father
2 Son
3 Holy Ghost

THE 3 AMIGOS (1986)

1 **Lucky Day** (Steve Martin)
2 **Dusty Bottoms** (Chevy Chase)
3 **Ned Nederlander** (Martin Short)

THE 3 AXIS POWERS (WWII)

1 Germany
2 Italy
3 Japan

3 "AXIS OF EVIL" NATIONS

Named by President George W. Bush in 2002.

1 Iran
2 Iraq
3 North Korea

3 "AXIS OF TERROR" NATIONS

Named by Israel's UN ambassador, Dan Gillerman, in 2006.

1 Iran
2 Syria
3 The Hamas-run Palestinian government

HORSE RACING'S TRIPLE CROWN

1 Kentucky Derby
2 Preakness Stakes
3 Belmont Stakes

BASEBALL'S TRIPLE CROWN

When a hitter leads the league in...

1 Batting average
2 Home runs
3 Runs batted in

3 TYPES OF DISTRACTED DRIVING

According to the National Transportation Safety Board.

1 **Cognitive:** Caused by fatigue, drugs and alcohol, even listening to your favorite song
2 **Visual:** Taking your eyes off the road to look at your kids or read a text message
3 **Manual:** Taking your hands off the wheel to sip your coffee or send a text message

SIGMUND FREUD'S 3 PARTS OF PERSONALITY

1 **Id:** Unconscious mind, acts on instincts
2 **Ego:** Conscious mind, keeps the id in check
3 **Superego:** The moral center, distinguishes between right and wrong

THREEFOLD OF AUSTERITY

From the Hindu scripture Bhagavad Gita.

1 Thought
2 Word
3 Deed

DESTINY'S CHILD

1 Beyoncé Knowles
2 Kelly Rowland
3 Michelle Williams

THE JIMI HENDRIX EXPERIENCE

1 **Jimi Hendrix**, guitar and vocals
2 **Noel Redding**, bass, vocals
3 **Mitch Mitchell**, drums

THE 3 TENORS

1 Placido Domingo
2 José Carreras
3 Luciano Pavarotti

3 TYPES OF TEARS

1 **Basal:** Continual tearing that lubricates the eye and protects it from bacteria
2 **Reflex:** Created in response to eye irritants like onions, tear gas, and bright light
3 **Weeping:** Created by strong emotions, including sadness, happiness, and physical pain

3 BRANCHES OF U.S. GOVERNMENT

1 **Legislative:** Congress, which drafts laws
2 **Judicial:** the Supreme Court, which ensures laws are constitutional
3 **Executive:** the cabinet, vice president, and president, who signs or vetoes laws and pardons turkeys

3 BONES IN THE HUMAN EAR

1 **Malleus** (hammer)
2 **Incus** (anvil)
3 **Stapes** (stirrup)

3 ORIGINAL VOWS MADE BY BENEDICTINE MONKS

1 To **remain** at the monastery
2 To **labor** until death in order to attain perfection
3 To **obey** one's superiors

3 BODILY FUNCTIONS THAT BRIEFLY TAKE OVER YOUR AWARENESS

1 Sneezing
2 Laughing
3 Climaxing

3 MAIN HUMAN BODY TYPES

1 **Ectomorph:** Tall, thin
2 **Endomorph:** Short, round
3 **Mesomorph:** Athletic

3 TYPES OF PARENTS

According to American education guru Jim Fay.

1 Consultant
2 Helicopter
3 Drill sergeant

3 TYPES OF FOOD CONTAMINATION

1 **Biological:** Insects, fungus
2 **Chemical:** Oil, detergents, pesticides
3 **Physical:** Glass, sediment, hair

3 POINTS OF VIEW IN LITERATURE

1 **First person** (I, we)
2 **Second person** (you)
3 **Third person** (he, she, they)

IN SHOWBIZ, A TRIPLE THREAT IS ONE WHO CAN

1 Act
2 Dance
3 Sing

3 BROWNIE B'S (GIRL SCOUTS)

1 Be discoverers.
2 Be ready helpers.
3 Be friend-makers.

"THE ONLY 3 SPORTS"

According to Ernest Hemingway.

1 **Bullfighting**
2 **Motor racing**
3 **Mountaineering**

"All the rest are merely games."

8 THINGS THEY CALL THE UNDEAD ON *THE WALKING DEAD*

1 Walkers
2 Biters
3 Rotters
4 Roamers
5 Lurkers
6 Lame-brains
7 Decays
8 Geeks

(Strangely, no one uses the word "zombie.")

In the cross-dressing 1982 film *Tootsie*, Dustin Hoffman wore a size 36C bra.

40 ODD VERSIONS OF MONOPOLY

The first themed Monopoly was a San Diego edition in 1994. Hasbro has since licensed dozens more versions, including....

1 Chocolate
2 Worms
3 Dog Artist
4 Bass Fishing
5 Night Sky
6 World Cup France '98
7 Stock Exchange
8 Dale Earnhardt
9 Toys 'R' Us Times Square
10 World Dredging
11 *Coronation Street*
12 UPS
13 U Build
14 Blackberry Phone
15 *Star Trek: The Next Generation*
16 Uniquely Singapore
17 James Bond 007
18 Inflatable
19 *Doctor Who*
20 Deep Sea Adventure
21 Duel Masters
22 FedEx
23 My Disney Villains
24 Reading
25 Sephora
26 Planet Earth
27 Klingon
28 Century of Flight
29 Alaska's Iditarod
30 *Ultraman*
31 Option One Mortgage Corporation
32 Tutankhamun and the Golden Age of the Pharaohs
33 *Rudolph the Red-Nosed Reindeer*
34 *Only Fools and Horses*
35 Cricket Australia
36 John Deere
37 Heinz Ketchup
38 QVC (Shopping Channel)
39 *Powerpuff Girls*
40 Metallica

Longest time between #1 albums: **37** **years, for Johnny Cash (1969 to 2006).**

8 OF THE MOST NOTORIOUS M.I.T. "HACKS"

At the Massachusetts Institute of Technology in Boston, a "hack" is an elaborate practical joke conducted by anonymous students. Here are some of the all-time greats from the MIT's "Gallery of Hacks."

1 THAT'S THE DROID YOU WEREN'T LOOKING FOR

The 150-foot-high Great Dome sits atop MIT's Maclaurin Building. In May 1999, to celebrate the release of *Star Wars: The Phantom Menace*, the Great Dome was given the R2-D2 treatment via colored fabric panels that mimicked the look of the droid's head. In the tradition of MIT hacks, which students define as "harmless and ethical pranks," the perpetrators left detailed instructions for removing the giant pieces of fabric.

2 ARMS RACE

On March 26, 2006, a "moving company" showed up at Caltech—home of NASA's Jet Propulsion Laboratory in Pasadena, California—and told security they were there to remove the large cannon from in front of the Fleming House. The movers hoisted the cannon onto a truck and drove it all the way back to Boston. It took a couple of weeks before Caltech tracked down their cannon and retrieved it—with one addition: a 24-karat gold-plated MIT class ring bolted around its barrel.

3 HATS OFF

In 1996 MIT's Great Dome became the Great Beanie Hat, complete with a red stripe and a moving propeller. As workers climbed the dome to remove it, hackers dressed up their truck like an ambulance with the words "MIT Hack Removal Team."

4 WRITTEN IN "STONE"

In 1994 hackers altered a stone building inscription that read "Established for Advancement and Development of Science its Application to Industry the Arts Agriculture and Commerce" to end instead with "...the Arts Entertainment and Hacking." To match the look of the original lettering, the clever students engraved Styrofoam panels and painted them to resemble stone. The hack was so subtle that university police didn't even notice it for a few days.

5 COP ON TOP

Hackers painted a Chevy Cavalier to look like a police car, then removed its metal body and attached it to a wooden frame. The fake cop car was then hoisted atop the Great Dome. It even had flashing lights and a dummy inside dressed as a police officer (along with a box of doughnuts).

6 TOOL TIME

In MIT-speak, "tool" refers to students who constantly study. In 1992 hackers transformed a dorm lobby into the "Cathedral of Our Lady of the All-Night Tool." The windows were covered in cellophane that resembled stained glass. Hackers brought in pews, a confessional, an altar, and an organ. A wedding was performed in the cathedral the next morning.

7 JUST HAZING THE NEWBIE

When MIT president Charles Vest showed up for his first day of work in 1996, he couldn't find his office, so he asked students if he was in the right place. He was. Only later did he find out his office door had been hidden behind a bulletin board.

8 THE SHAPES OF THINGS TO COME

In 2012 hackers turned MIT's 21-story Green Building into a Tetris game by placing colored lights in 153 windows. A wireless controller on the ground let passersby play the game.

10 STRANGE THINGS THE GOVERNMENT SPENDS YOUR MONEY ON

During his time in the U.S. Senate, fiscal conservative Tom Coburn (R-OK) produced an annual "Wastebook" that called out the "100 most blatant examples of unnecessary government grants." Here are a few of the oddest entries from recent years.

1 AMERICA'S SWANKIEST BUS STOP

In 2013 Arlington County, Virginia, received federal funding to build a luxury "SuperStop" bus stop complete with Wi-Fi, heated benches and sidewalks, and "a wall made of etched glass that opens the rear vista to newly planted landscaping." Too bad the slanted glass roof doesn't do much to keep out rain and snow, or provide shade in the summertime.

Cost to taxpayers: $1 million

2 BEGONIAS IN BRUSSELS

The U.S. ambassador to NATO's residence in Brussels, Belgium, is lavishly decorated with "960 violets, 960 tulips, 960 begonias, 72 Japanese evergreen shrubs, 504 ivy geraniums, 168 hybrid heath evergreen shrubs, 204 American wintergreens, and 60 English ivy shrubs."

Cost to taxpayers: $704,000

3 SILLY SOLAR PANELS

A federal grant was used to install solar panels on the parking garage at the Manchester-Boston airport. One problem: The reflective panels were blinding the pilots, so 25 percent of them had to be removed (the panels, not the pilots). But the

remaining panels, say airport officials, will generate "$2 million in savings over 25 years."
Cost to taxpayers: $3.5 million

4 CLANDESTINE CREATIVE CONSULTANTS
The sole purpose of the FBI's "Investigative Publicity and Public Affairs Unit" is to answer any questions that writers and filmmakers might have to ensure that any film, TV, or book that features the FBI will get the details right.
Annual cost to taxpayers: $1.5 million

5 INDIE ROCK IN RIO
Several executives from various independent music labels received a government-funded, all-expenses-paid trip to Rio de Janeiro and São Paulo, Brazil, in 2013. Reason: "to compare the record stores, club districts, and facial expressions of locals at the mention of their bands." While the execs reportedly enjoyed their trip, one of them said he "didn't ink any deals."
Cost to taxpayers: $284,300

6 GIVING ROMANCE NOVELS THE SERIOUS STUDY THEY DESERVE
In 2010 the National Endowment of the Humanities funded the Popular Romance Project, establishing a website to "explore the fascinating, often contradictory origins and influences of popular romance as told in novels, films, comics, advice books, songs, and Internet fanfiction." Topics on the website include "The Romance of British Secret Service Agent James Bond" and "Team Edward or Team Jacob?"
Cost to taxpayers: $914,000

7 WINE GLASSES THAT SING
The State Department uses taxpayer money to pay for hand-blown crystal wine glasses for U.S. embassies around the world. This is no ordinary glassware—it must be purchased only

from high-end retailers, and each glass "has to make a sharp high-pitched resonant sound when tapped with a metal object, such as a fork or spoon."

Cost to taxpayers: $5 million

8 WATCHING MARRIED COUPLES BICKER

A study conducted by the National Institutes of Health observed 82 married couples to determine what factors make them happy. The conclusion? "The marriages that were the happiest were the ones in which the wives were able to calm down quickly during marital conflict."

Cost to taxpayers: $325,525

9 ANTI-SOCIAL MEDIA

State Department officials wanted to increase traffic on the agency's various Facebook pages and Twitter accounts, so they spent lavishly on in-site advertising. What did they get in return? Not much. Less than 2 percent of visitors to their pages "liked" or "favorited" any of their posts or tweets.

Cost to taxpayers: $630,000

10 DUCKY NAUGHTY BITS

In 2005 biologists at Yale University were awarded a research grant to study the reproductive anatomy of the duck. Specifically, the researchers studied the unique corkscrew-like shape of the male duck's genitalia. After the study was show-cased in Coburn's Wastebook and lambasted by cable news pundits, lead researcher Patricia Brennan defended her work. "This is basic science," she said. "The headlines reflect outrage that the study was about duck genitals, as if there is something inherently wrong or perverse with this line of research. Imagine if medical research drew the line at the belt! Genitalia, dear readers, are where the rubber meets the road, evolutionarily."

Cost to taxpayers: $384,989

16 ANIMALS ON THE VERGE OF EXTINCTION

1 **Amur Leopard:** Russia; population 30

2 **Black Rhino:** Namibia, coastal East Africa; pop. 4,848

3 **Cross River Gorilla:** Congo Basin; pop. 200 to 300

4 **Hawksbill Turtle:** Mesoamerican Reef, coastal East Africa, Coral Triangle; pop. unknown

5 **Javan Rhino:** Indonesia; pop. 35

6 **Leatherback Turtle:** Mesoamerican Reef, coastal East Africa, Gulf of California, the Galápagos, Coral Triangle; pop. unknown

7 **Mountain Gorilla:** African Congo, pop. 880

8 **Saola:** Vietnam; it's unknown how many of these antelope-like animals are left.

9 **South China Tiger:** southeast China; believed to be extinct in the wild, approximately 20 left in zoos

10 **Sumatran Elephant:** Borneo, Sumatra; pop. fewer than 3,000

11 **Sumatran Orangutan:** Borneo, Sumatra; pop. 7,000

12 **Sumatran Rhino:** Borneo, Sumatra; pop. fewer than 200

13 **Sumatran Tiger:** Borneo, Sumatra; pop. fewer than 400

14 **Vaquita:** Gulf of California; pop. fewer than 100

15 **Western Lowland Gorilla:** Congo Basin, pop. unknown

16 **Yangtze Finless Porpoise:** Yangtze River; fewer than 2,000 remain

10 WORDS PEOPLE SAY AREN'T WORDS BUT ARE

Good news: These are all words! Bad news: Language snobs will scoff if you use them—so you'll have to politely correct them.

1 FIRSTLY

First things first: Why would anyone still say *firstly* instead of *first*? Ordinal numbers such as *first, second,* and *third* serve as both adjectives and adverbs, making the adverbs *firstly, secondly,* and *thirdly* redundant. Most grammarians agree with *Garner's Modern American Usage*: "*Firstly* is considered inferior to *first*." But it is a word that people use, even if the best example given in the *Merriam-Webster Dictionary*—"Firstly, gather all the ingredients together"—sounds a bit awkward.

2 IRREGARDLESS

Merriam-Webster says "the most frequently repeated remark about *irregardless* is that 'there is no such word.' There is such a word, however." It has been used (mistakenly) in place of *regardless* since the early 1900s and has now been admitted into dictionaries. So even though it is a word, *irregardless* is still far from being widely accepted. And judging by the scorn it receives online, it won't be widely accepted anytime soon. *Merriam-Webster*'s advice: "Use *regardless* instead."

3 PROLLY

Prolly is taking over for *probably* in text messages, but its origin goes back much earlier—to the 1940s. Considered a "relaxed pronunciation contraction" (like *gonna* and *outta*), *prolly* even shows up in the *Oxford English Dictionary*. But you should definitely only use *prolly* informally, as in: "U prolly don't like that I said prolly when u asked me to marry u."

4 LITERALLY

How long does it take for a word to be used incorrectly before linguists give up and alter its meaning? It's happening to *literally*, which literally means "in a literal way or sense." So many speakers are using it in place of *virtually* that the *Oxford English Dictionary* has redefined *literally* to say it can be "used for emphasis rather than being actually true, such as, 'We were literally killing ourselves laughing.'" Meanwhile, English is left with no word reserved to mean "in a literal sense." Result: Language purists refuse to use *literally* figuratively.

5 FUNNER

If a tough day can get tougher, and weird house guests can get weirder, why can't a fun drink get funner after they're gone? Actually, it can. *Merriam-Webster* states that *funner* and *funnest* are "sometimes" permissible. Although *fun* has long been accepted as a noun, it is considered informal when used as an adjective, and therefore—some people claim—it shouldn't be inflected like other adjectives, but those people are no fun.

6 ANYWAYS

Dating back to the 13th century, *anyways* was gradually shortened to *anyway*. Today, it's only used colloquially, as in: "I've been blabbing about myself for hours. Anyways, why are you leaving?" The word is considered superfluous—most dictionaries list it as an informal synonym for *anyway*. The *Oxford English Dictionary* goes a step further—it identifies *anyways* as being of North American origin and gives this snobbish example: "You wouldn't understand all them long words anyways."

7 ORIENTATE

Like *irregardless* and *anyways*, *orientate* can be used but shouldn't. The word originated in British English in the 1840s as a variant of *orient* (both mean "to determine bearings"). Yanks stuck with *orient*, which is still the preferred usage—*orientate* is considered nonstandard in most American dictionaries. Even so, many people use it interchangeably with *orient* (and *disorientated* for *disoriented*). A *Collins Dictionary* entry reads, "We've taken so many turns I'm completely disorientated."

8 SNUCK

The past tense of *sneak* is *sneaked*, so why have people stuck with *snuck* since the 1800s? It's a mystery; no English verb that ends in the *-eek* sound has a past tense ending in *-uck*. But dictionaries have adopted the made-up word. *Random House Dictionary* explains, "*Snuck* has occasionally been considered nonstandard, but it is so widely used by professional writers and educated speakers that it can no longer be so regarded." In response, grammarian James J. Kilpatrick lamented that *Random House*'s "tolerant view has not snuck up on me; it has sneaked up on me. I will have none of it."

9 MADDED

Word snobs may get mad if you say *madded*, but it is in fact a verb. *Merriam-Webster* gives this example: "Her endless excuses for not doing the work madded her overburdened coworkers." Less cringeworthy, and also recognized by dictionaries, is the adjective *maddish*. For example, when Uncle John gets sent to Acapulco in the dead of winter for a "business trip," we're happy for him but also maddish.

10 IMPACTFUL

Impactful was invented by advertising agencies in the 1960s to describe their campaigns as "having a big impact." (These are the same "mad men" who coined *lite* and *signage*.) All three words are detested by grammarians; *impactful* even made it onto *Harvard Business Review* blogger Bryan A. Garner's list of "65 Forbidden Buzzwords." But it's now in the dictionary, so it's a word. Anyways, we hope you found our list of despised words to be impactful. We'd literally die if you didn't.

14 SPECIALTY CASKETS FOR THE DEAD HOBBYIST

There's no need to go into the afterlife in a boring urn or casket. Here are actual descriptions—from the manufacturers of "signature vessels"—that will prove to your loved ones that you'll be just as fascinating in death as you were in life.

1 Return to Sender. "The casket is designed to look like an old-school brown bag package wrapped in string being shipped. The phrase 'Express Delivery' and 'Return to Sender' are stamped onto the wrapping paper for that special touch."

2 The Capsula Mundi Eco Coffin. "The body is placed within this egg-shaped biodegradable coffin in a fetal position and is planted in the ground like a bulb. Then a tree is planted on the surface to mark the grave as a living memorial."

3 Ghost-shaped Urn. "Why should cremation be so somber? And why should your eternal resting place be some giant flower pot? Ghost Urns are perhaps the only way to be certain you'll become a ghost after you pass away."

4 Cruisin Caskets. "We are a casket fabricating company that creates custom car designs for the car lover that wants to leave this world in style."

5 KISS Kasket. "The 'KISS® Kasket' is completely covered with a specially laminated photomural that features the KISS® logo and the images of the band members."

6 Camo Casket. "The camo casket offers a custom camouflage material surrounding the whole casket."

Uh-oh: The flag of Mozambique has a picture of an AK-47 assault rifle.

7 Do It Yourself. "Make your own casket with our easy to assemble kit."

8 Sports Bag. "A luxurious sports bag coffin in homage to Louis Vuitton."

9 Cattle King Casket. "Handcrafted solid alder wood, genuine Brazilian cowhide panels, concho accents, hand-carved twist and carrying bar, hand-forged custom hardware. Choice of exotic brindle, speckled, or Hereford cowhide."

10 Head-shaped Urn. "These urns are created from one or two photographs with exceptional attention to details. With advances in facial analysis and the advent of state of the art 3D imaging, these high tech urns can be made to look like anyone."

11 Red Tractor Casket. "This casket features a Red Case IH tractor plowing the fields in a spring sunset. Also available with John Deere Green!"

12 Fairway to Heaven. "A golfer's paradise, the Fairway to Heaven Art casket is for the truly devoted golf fan. Deep green and sky blue on top of rolling hills."

13 Holy Smoke! "For the shotgunner, 250 shotshells (with your loved one's ashes loaded into each shell) shipped in fifty-round, labeled, plastic shotshell carriers with handles."

14 The Rings of Time Hourglass Keepsake Urn: "This hourglass-shaped urn is a wonderful way to reflect on the sands of time and the time that you and your loved one shared."

20 COUNTRIES BIG AND SMALL

10 SMALLEST COUNTRIES

1 **Vatican City:** 0.17 sq miles; pop.: 824 (Italy)

2 **Monaco:** 0.76 sq miles; pop.: 33,000 (Mediterranean Sea)

3 **Nauru:** 8.1 sq miles; pop.: 13,700 (western Pacific)

4 **Tuvalu:** 10 sq miles; pop.: 12,000 (southern Pacific)

5 **San Marino:** 24 sq miles; pop.: 30,000 (southern Europe)

6 **Liechtenstein:** 62 sq miles; pop.: 35,000 (central Europe)

7 **Marshall Islands:** 70 sq miles; pop.: 62,000 (Pacific Ocean)

8 **St. Kitts and Nevis:** 104 sq miles; pop.: 63,000 (Caribbean Sea)

9 **Maldives:** 115 sq miles; pop.: 350,000 (Indian Ocean)

10 **Seychelles:** 174 sq miles: pop.: 81,000 (Indian Ocean)

10 LARGEST COUNTRIES

1 **Russia:** 6,592,846 sq miles; pop.: 142 million (Europe/Asia)

2 **Canada:** 3,602,707 sq miles; pop.: 34 million

3 **China:** 3,600,947 sq miles; pop.: 1.326 billion (Asia)

4 **United States:** 3,539,242 sq miles; pop.: 305 million

5 **Brazil:** 3,265,075 sq miles; pop.: 188 million (South America)

6 **Australia:** 2,941,283 sq miles; pop.: 21 million (South Pacific)

7 **India:** 1,147,949 sq miles; pop.: 1.13 billion (southern Asia)

8 **Argentina:** 1,056,636 sq miles; pop.: 40 million (South America)

9 **Kazakhstan:** 1,049,150 sq miles; pop.: 15 million (Asia)

10 **Sudan:** 917,374 sq miles; pop.: 39 million (Africa)

NBA legend Michael Jordan was on the cover of *Sports Illustrated* **49 times.**

15 BASEBALL ONE-AND-ONLYS

More than 200,000 Major League Baseball games have been played since the late 1800s—which makes it amazing that these feats have only happened once and (so far) never again.

1 A SLAMMING INNING. It's rare that a batter comes to the plate twice in one game with the bases loaded—it's almost unheard of for it to happen twice in *one inning*. But on April 23, 1999, Fernando Tatis of the St. Louis Cardinals, playing against the L.A. Dodgers, came up twice in the third with the sacks full. Both times Tatis hit it out of the park, making him the only player in MLB history to hit two grand slams in one inning.

2 ROLE REVERSAL. Pitchers aren't expected to put up good numbers at the plate, so it was big news in 1966 when Atlanta Braves ace Tony Cloninger, playing against the San Francisco Giants, hit two grand slams in one game. No pitcher has done it since.

3 BACK AT YOU. On September 17, 1968, the Giants' Gaylord Perry pitched a no-hitter against St. Louis. On September 18, the Cardinals' Ray Washburn no-hit the Giants. It's the only time two teams have no-hit each other on consecutive days.

4 FLYDAY. Four homers by one team in one inning is rare but not unheard of. What was unheard of—until May 2, 2002—was two players hitting two homers each in a single inning. Seattle's Mike Cameron and Bret Boone hit two each out of the park in the first inning of a game against the Chicago White Sox.

5 LOSING COUNT. An April 2000 game between the Minnesota Twins and the Kansas City Royals saw another one-and-only: Both teams had three players each hit back-to-back-to-back home runs.

6 SEXTUPLE PLAY. During a tough 1–0 loss to the Boston Red Sox in July 1990, the Minnesota Twins' defense turned two triple plays (wherein all three outs are recorded in one at bat). Unbelievably, it's the only time that one team has completed two triple plays in one game.

7 SUPER SOUTHPAW. Only once has a left-handed pitcher struck out 20 batters in a game. The Arizona Diamondbacks' Randy Johnson did it in 2001 against the Cincinnati Reds. No pitcher of either handedness has done it since.

8 A TALE IN TWO CITIES. On August 4, 1984, New York Mets outfielder Joel Youngblood drove in two runs against the Chicago Cubs in the third inning of a day game. A little later, he was told he'd been traded to the Montreal Expos, who were playing that night a few hundred miles away against the Phillies. Youngblood cleared out his locker, took a plane to Philadelphia, put on an Expos uniform, entered the game in the sixth, and singled in the seventh. He's the only player to get a hit for two different teams in two different cities on the same day.

9 FOUR ON THE FLOOR. In 1895 New York Giants third baseman Mike Grady tried to field a routine ground ball, but bobbled it (error #1). Then he threw the ball to first, but it sailed over the head of the first baseman (error #2), who retrieved it and threw it back to Grady as the runner rounded second. Grady missed the catch (error #3), ran to the dugout, picked up the ball, threw it...and it sailed over the catcher (error #4), allowing the runner to score. Never before and never since (outside of Little League) has one player committed four errors on a single play.

10 HERO AND GOAT. Since 1909, only 15 players have turned an unassisted triple play. (Two runners are on base with no outs, and a line drive is hit to an infielder who catches it for out #1; then he steps on second base, getting the lead runner for out #2, and then tags the other runner for out #3.) On August 23, 2009, Phillies second baseman Eric Bruntlett helped himself to a record when he bobbled a hit ball, allowing the man to reach base. One batter later, Bruntlett became the only big league player in history to turn an unassisted triple play... after committing an error in the same inning.

11 KEEP DREAMING. Every hitter's dream is to step up to the plate in game 7 of the World Series with two outs in the bottom of the ninth with his team trailing and the bases loaded...and then hit a walk-off home run for the championship. So far, it's never happened. In fact, the only come-from-behind, postseason, series-winning hit in MLB history occurred in the seventh game of the 1992 National League Championship Series when the Braves' Francisco Cabrera drove in two runs against the Pittsburgh Pirates to take his team to the World Series. (Also close: Pittsburgh's Bill Mazeroski's 1960 World Series–winning homer in the bottom of the ninth of game 7, but the score was tied at the time.)

12 FREE SHIPPING. On August 10, 2004, the Cincinnati Reds' Adam Dunn hit a ball so far out of Great American Ball Park that it landed in the Ohio River, which is in Kentucky, marking the only time a batter ever hit a ball into another state. A new deck has since been added to Great American, ensuring that this feat will (most likely) never happen again.

13 BONK! Jose Canseco is the only player who ever hit a homer with his head. Sort of. The Texas Ranger was playing right field in a 1993 game when he ran to catch a deep fly ball, which he missed. The ball landed on his noggin and bounced over the fence for a home run.

14 **FAN-TASTIC.** Only once has a pitcher fanned (struck out) 10 batters in a row. The New York Mets' Tom Seaver blanked the final 10 San Diego Padres on April 22, 1970, en route to a 2–1 victory.

15 **WHAT A LONG, STRANGE TRIP.** The Pittsburgh Pirates' Dock Ellis may not be the only pitcher to ever throw a no-hitter while tripping on LSD, but he's the only pitcher to ever *admit* to throwing a no-hitter on LSD. (Nolan Ryan has remained surprisingly silent on the subject.) Ellis performed the dubious feat in a 1970 game against the San Diego Padres (he said took the acid because he thought he had the day off). Despite giving up eight walks and loading the bases twice, Ellis didn't allow a hit. He later attempted to describe the experience: "The ball was small sometimes, the ball was large sometimes. Sometimes I saw the catcher, sometimes I didn't. I chewed my gum until it turned to powder. I remember diving out of the way of a ball I thought was a line drive. I jumped, but it wasn't hit hard and never reached me."

---

7 WEALTHIEST AMERICANS NAMED GEORGE

1 **George Soros,** worth $20 billion (hedge funds)

2 **George Kaiser,** worth $10 billion (oil/gas/banking)

3 **George Roberts,** worth $4.4 billion (investments)

4 **George Lucas,** worth $4.2 billion (Jar-Jar Binks)

5 **George Lindemann,** worth $2.8 billion (investments/pipelines)

6 **George Argyros,** worth $2.1 billion (real estate)

7 **George Joseph**, worth $1.3 billion (insurance)

---

5 WORST "PARENT OF THE YEAR" CANDIDATES

1 FAST & FURIOUS

In 2014 Tracy Waihape of Wairoa, New Zealand, sped past a police checkpoint. A high-speed chase ensued. When the cops finally caught her, she shoved an officer and told him to "f*ck off." Why didn't she stop at the checkpoint? She didn't want to get a ticket for the seven unrestrained children (most of them hers) in the car, ranging in age from two to fourteen...including three little kids who were riding in the trunk.

2 HU'S THERE

A dad in Cascavel, Brazil, took his son to the zoo, where he let him pet a tiger named Hu—even though there was a fence several feet in front of the cage and a big sign that read "DANGER: DO NOT ENTER." Ignoring the warning, the dad let his 11-year-old boy climb the fence and pet Hu through the cage...and feed him meat. Had the kid only stayed there for a few seconds (and not *fed the tiger meat!*), he would probably have escaped unscathed. But he lingered too long, and the tiger tore off his hand.

3 SPOILED ROTTEN

Ann Lampe, a 34-year-old mom from Springfield, Missouri, included her 13-year-old daughter in her favorite hobby—meth. Mother and daughter smoked it in the car and in her apartment, and they even "hot railed" (smoking meth through a glass pipe) it together. After the methy-mom was arrested, she told the judge she knew what she did was wrong, but if her daughter didn't get what she wanted (which apparently was meth), she would "throw a fit."

4 OKAY, HOW ABOUT "BUTTCRACK"?

In 2013 a mom and dad from New Zealand wanted to name their newborn baby boy "Anal." Good news for the kid: Government officials rejected the name.

5 TOYING WITH HER DAUGHTER

Sarah Burge, a 51-year-old British mom who calls herself "the human Barbie," achieved her plastic look by spending nearly $250,000 on cosmetic surgery. (She earned the money by organizing "plastic surgery parties" and writing erotic novels.) Now, Burge is trying to pass along her, umm...good looks to her daughter Poppy. When Poppy turned six years old, Burge taught her how to pole dance. When Poppy turned seven, she got a $9,950 voucher for breast augmentation that can be redeemed when she actually has them. (The birthday party took place at a Botox clinic.) For Christmas, Poppy got an $11,600 voucher for liposuction. "I see these vouchers as investing in her future," brags Burge, "like saving money for her education."

AND TO RESTORE YOUR FAITH IN HUMANITY...

Yu Xukang, a 40-year-old dad from rural China, takes his 12-year-old son Xiao to school every day, which isn't easy because Xiao is disabled—he has a severe hunchback that makes it impossible for him to walk or ride a bike. But the school is 4½ miles away, the family doesn't own a car, and there's no bus service. So Yu built a special harness that allows him to carry Xiao on his back to school each morning. Then he walks home and works all day (to afford the school), and walks back and carries Xiao home. That's a total of 18 miles that Yu walks every day just so his son can get an education...which is far more valuable than a liposuction voucher.

---

40 STRANGE BUT TRUE PURITAN NAMES

In the 16th and 17th centuries, the Puritans believed that to be godly, their children's names should come from the Bible. A few names—like Grace, Hope, and Felicity—have stayed with us. Here are some names that didn't.

1 Abuse-not
2 Accepted
3 Aholiab
4 Be-strong
5 Be-thankful
6 Discipline
7 Dust
8 Faint-not
9 Fear-not
10 Fly-fornication
11 Forsaken
12 Free-gift
13 From-above
14 Hate-evil
15 Humiliation
16 Job-rakt-out-of-the-ashes
17 Joye-again
18 Lamentation
19 Mahershalalhashbaz
20 Melchisadeck

21 More-fruite
22 More-triale
23 Obedience
24 No-merit
25 Pentacost
26 Posthumus
27 Praise-God
28 Preserved
29 Rejoice
30 Repentance
31 Safe-on-high
32 Search-the-Scriptures
33 Standfast-on-high
34 Sin-denie
35 Sorry-for-sin
36 Thankful
37 The-Lord-is-near
38 Tribulation
39 What-God-will
40 Zeal-of-the-Land

Shirley Temple's hair had exactly 56 pin curls in every movie she made.

10 WAYS TO KEEP YOUR FOOD FROM ROTTING

1 **Don't cram veggies** together when you store them. The closer they are, the faster they'll spoil.

2 **Take "one bad apple"** to heart and keep fruits away from vegetables. Fruit gives off a ripening chemical that will start the veggies on the path to ripeness, even if it's not their time.

3 **Cut the greens** from the carrots before you put them in the fridge. Otherwise, the carrots will go limp faster.

4 **Apples keep better** if they're stored between 30 and 35°F, so the crisper drawer is a good place for them. They also like humidity, so put a slightly damp paper towel over their tops.

5 **Stop storing your tomatoes** in the fridge: It damages the membranes inside and robs the tomato of flavor. A better spot: on the countertop at room temperature.

6 **Treat your fresh herbs** like flowers and put their stems in a glass of water in the fridge.

7 **Don't store onions and potatoes** together; they'll spoil faster. Onions can be stored in an open container and potatoes somewhere dark and cool, like a basement.

8 **Keep that celery crisp** in the fridge by cutting off the bottom of the stalk and placing it upright in a pitcher of water.

The lowest known note, emitted by a black hole, is **57** octaves below middle C.

9 **Keep cherries** in a plastic bag in the fridge. Don't wash them until you're ready to eat them—moisture makes them spoil faster.

10 **Avocados ripen slower** in the fridge. So store them in there if you're not going to use them for a couple of days. Then put the avocados on the counter when you're ready for them to ripen again.

20 WORDS THAT GAIN A SYLLABLE WITH ONE LETTER CHANGE

1 quilt—quiet
2 leopard—leotard
3 onion—Orion
4 baseline—Vaseline
5 quick—Buick
6 waive—naive
7 boing—doing
8 picked—wicked
9 Tania—mania
10 detour—devour
11 soldier—moldier
12 dilate—Pilate
13 priest—driest
14 bait—Baio
15 ration—ratios
16 matte—latte
17 baked—naked
18 headdress—readdress
19 bisque—risque
20 mature—manure

20 CHEMICAL ELEMENTS: YOU VS. EARTH

You have more in common with the planet you reside on than you might realize—chemically speaking. Here's the breakdown.

YOUR BODY	THE EARTH'S CRUST
1 Oxygen: 65%	1 Oxygen: 46.71%
2 Carbon: 18%	2 Silicon: 27.69%
3 Hydrogen: 10%	3 Aluminum: 8.07%
4 Nitrogen: 3%	4 Iron: 5.05%
5 Calcium: 1.5%	5 Calcium: 3.65%
6 Phosphorus: 1%	6 Sodium: 2.75%
7 Sulfur: 0.25%	7 Potassium: 2.58%
8 Potassium: 0.2%	8 Magnesium: 2.08%
9 Chlorine: 0.15%	9 Titanium: 0.62%
10 Sodium: 0.15%	10 Hydrogen: 0.14%
11 Magnesium: 0.05%	11 Phosphorus: 0.13%
12 Iron: 0.006%	12 Carbon: 0.094%
13 Fluorine: 0.0037%	13 Manganese: 0.09%
14 Zinc: 0.0032%	14 Sulfur: 0.052%
15 Silicon: 0.002%	15 Barium: 0.05%
16 Zirconium: 0.0006%	16 Chlorine: 0.045%
17 Rubidium: 0.00046%	17 Chromium: 0.035%
18 Strontium: 0.00046%	18 Fluorine: 0.029%
19 Bromine: 0.00029%	19 Zirconium: 0.025%
20 Lead: 0.00017%	20 Nickel: 0.019%

First woman to drive across the U.S.: Alice Ramsey, in 1909. It took her **59** days.

9 DISTINCTIONS: TERMS & MEASUREMENTS EDITION

1 MASS VS. WEIGHT. Weight is a term used to measure the force of gravity upon an object. That means an object's weight can change depending on the gravity—which is why we weigh less in space. Mass, however, is constant. It is the "measurement of an object's resistance to being accelerated."

2 ILLEGAL VS. UNLAWFUL. For an act to be considered illegal, there must be a law specifically written that says it's illegal. It's illegal to drive the wrong way on a road. You can look it up in law books. An unlawful act is more vague: It means that the act in question—say, driving in reverse on a highway—is against the law because it's dangerous...even though there's no specific law that says you can't.

3 LAWYER VS. ATTORNEY. The difference between these terms has lessened in recent years, but technically speaking, an attorney-at-law is a member of the legal profession who is licensed to represent a client in court. A lawyer is versed in the law and can thus give legal advice to people and do research on their behalf but can't represent someone in court until he or she has passed the bar exam. So an attorney is always a lawyer, but a lawyer doesn't necessarily have to be an attorney.

5 CARAT VS. KARAT. A carat is a unit of weight used for precious gems and is equal to 200 milligrams (about the weight of a small vitamin tablet). A karat is a unit of purity for gold; 24-karat gold is 100% (actually 99.9%) pure gold, 20-karat gold is 83.3% pure, 18-karat gold is 75% pure, and so on. Confusion reigns: "karat" can also be spelled as "carat."

4 BANK VS. CREDIT UNION. Banks are for-profit, and credit unions are not-for-profit. That's why you're a "member" or "owner" of a credit union but a "customer" of a bank. Credit union members vote for the board of directors, and the profits go toward keeping interest rates low and serving the community. Banks' profits primarily go to their shareholders.

6 REVOLVE VS. ROTATE. A rotation is the movement of a body around a point within that body; Earth rotates on its axis. A revolution is the movement of a body around a point outside that body; Earth revolves around the Sun.

7 HEMP VS. MARIJUANA. Marijuana gets you high; hemp doesn't. They both come from the *Cannabis sativa* plant; the difference is in how they're cultivated. Hemp stalks are grown much tougher, making them great for use in textiles, plastics, and paper production. Hemp can also be used in food production—it can even be made into beer. But because of hemp's similarity to its druggy cousin, it is very difficult to obtain the necessary permits to grow it in the U.S.

8 INFECTIOUS VS. CONTAGIOUS. If a disease can be spread from human to human via direct or indirect contact, it's considered contagious. If it's spread by microscopic germs (in the air, water, food, or even humans), it's infectious. So a disease that's infectious can also be contagious. Malaria, for example, is an infectious disease, but it's not contagious.

9 DISC VS. DISK. Spelled with a c, it describes removable optical media, such as a compact disc or DVD. Spelled with a k, it describes read-only magnetic disks, such as those inside hard drives or floppy disks. The reason: When IBM created the hard disk in the 1950s, they used the "disk" spelling; when Sony created the compact disc in 1979, they chose the "disc" spelling to differentiate their new product from magnetic disks.

14 MOVIE STARS WHO PAID DEARLY FOR ROLES

1 Bruce Willis, permanent hearing damage in one ear (*Die Hard*, 1989)

2 Ellen Burstyn, broken tailbone, spine damage (*The Exorcist*, 1973)

3 Buster Keaton, broken neck (*Sherlock, Jr.*, 1924)

4 Margaret Hamilton, severe burns to hands and face (*The Wizard of Oz*, 1939)

5 Linda Hamilton, permanent hearing damage (*Terminator 2*, 1991)

6 George Clooney, fractured spine (*Syriana*, 2005)

7 Jaimie Alexander, slipped disk, chipped vertebrae, dislocated shoulder (*Thor: The Dark World*, 2013)

8 Charlize Theron, herniated disk (*Aeon Flux*, 2005)

9 Joseph Gordon-Levitt, 31 stitches in his arm (*Premium Rush*, 2012)

10 Jim Caviezel, dislocated shoulder, hypothermia, pneumonia, struck by lightning (*The Passion of the Christ*, 2004)

11 Harrison Ford, broken leg (*Star Wars: The Force Awakens*, 2015)

12 Halle Berry, broken arm (*Gothika*, 2003)

13 Nicole Kidman, knee injury, two fractured ribs (*Moulin Rouge*, 2001)

14 Jackie Chan's numerous on-set injuries include: broken cheekbone, broken nose (three times), fractured skull, brain bleed, spine damage, lacerated arm, broken ankle, dislocated pelvis, and many more!

Sigmund Freud was afraid of train travel, ferns, and the number **62**.

8 ODD KICKSTARTERS INVOLVING ANIMALS

Wild requests found on the Web's weirdest funding site.

1 DUCKY DIAPERS

"Have you ever dreamed of having a pet duckling but are concerned about all the pooping? Here is a solution to help solve that issue."

2 PET PHONE

"It's the world's first personal music player designed especially for pets."

3 MONKEY PHONE CALL

"I will call your phone number and make monkey noises that sound like 'eeee eee eeeeeee EEEEEE!'"

4 KITTY ON KITTY: PURRFECT CAT UNDIES

"Kitty on Kitty began when two University of Arizona students observed that cat enthusiasts were an underserved community amongst women's undergarments consumers."

5 WOOFLER, A DATING SITE FOR PETS

"Pets can meet other pets in their local area."

6 RUNNING THROUGH BIRDS IN A SPEEDO

"I'm going to spread cracker crumbs all over the beach, wait till a lot of birds show up, then film myself running through them in a Speedo."

7 DOG POWERED BEER CART

"It occurred to me that a backpack of beers on the dog was a good idea—until the running shook up the beer. Then it occurred to me that some dogs pull sleds..."

8 SUPER AMAZING 100% AWESOME CAT CALENDAR

"Do you enjoy photos of cats dressed up as magical creatures? Then this is the calendar for you."

20 PEOPLE ON NIXON'S "ENEMIES LIST"

During Richard Nixon's tumultuous years in office (1969-74), he made a list of his political enemies. Here are some excerpts.

1 ARNOLD M. PICKER. "United Artists Corp., N.Y. Top [Dem. VP candidate Edmund] Muskie fund raiser. Success here could be both debilitating and embarrassing to the Muskie machine. If effort looks promising, both Ruth and David Picker should be programmed and then a follow-through with United Artists."

2 ALEXANDER E. BARKAN. "National director of A.F.L.-C.I.O.'s committee on Political Education, Washington D.C.: Without a doubt the most powerful political force programmed against us in 1968 ($10 million, 4.6 million votes, 115 million pamphlets, 176,000 workers—all programmed by Barkan's C.O.P.E.—so says Teddy White in 'The Making of the President 1968'). We can expect the same effort this time."

3 ED GUTHMAN. "Managing editor, *Los Angeles Times*: Guthman, former Kennedy aide, was a highly sophisticated hatchetman against us in '68. It is obvious he is the prime mover behind the current Key Biscayne effort. It is time to give him the message."

4 MAXWELL DANE. "Doyle, Dane and Bernbach, N.Y.: The top Democratic advertising firm—they destroyed Goldwater in '64. They should be hit hard starting with Dane."

5 CHARLES DYSON. "Dyson-Kissner Corp., N.Y.: Dyson and Larry O'Brien were close business associates after '68. Dyson has huge business holdings and is presently deeply involved in the Businessmen's Educational Fund which bankrolls a national radio network of five-minute programs—anti-Nixon in character."

6 HOWARD STEIN. "Dreyfus Corp., N.Y.: Heaviest contributor to [Eugene] McCarthy in '68. If McCarthy goes, will do the same in '72. If not, Lindsay or McGovern will receive the funds."

7 ALLARD LOWENSTEIN. "Long Island, N.Y.: Guiding force behind the 18-year-old 'Dump Nixon' vote campaign."

8 MORTON HALPERIN. "Leading executive at Common Cause: A scandal would be most helpful here. (A consultant for Common Cause in February-March 1971) [On staff of Brookings Institution]"

9 LEONARD WOODCOCK. "United Auto Workers, Detroit, Mich.: No comments necessary."

10 S. STERLING MUNRO JR. "Sen. [Henry M.] Jackson's aide, Silver Spring, Md.: We should give him a try. Positive results would stick a pin in Jackson's white hat."

11 BERNARD T. FELD. "President, Council for a Livable World: Heavy far left funding. They will program an 'all-court press' against us in '72."

12 SIDNEY DAVIDOFF. "New York City: [NYC Mayor John V.] Lindsay's top personal aide: A first class S.O.B., wheeler-dealer, and suspected bagman. Positive results would really shake the Lindsay camp and Lindsay's plans to capture youth vote. Davidoff in charge."

13 JOHN CONYERS. "Congressman, Detroit: Coming on fast. Emerging as a leading black anti-Nixon spokesman. Has known weakness for white females."

14 **SAMUEL M. LAMBERT.** "President, National Education Association: Has taken us on vis-a-vis federal aid to parochial schools—a '72 issue."

15 **STEWART RAWLINGS MOTT.** "Mott Associates, N.Y.: Nothing but big money for radic-lib candidates."

16 **RONALD DELLUMS.** "Congressman, Calif.: Had extensive [Edward M. Kennedy] EMK–Tunney support in his election bid. Success might help in California next year."

17 **DANIEL SCHORR.** "Columbia Broadcasting System, Washington: A real media enemy."

18 **S. HARRISON DOGOLE.** "Philadelphia, Pa.: President of Globe Security Systems—4th largest private detective agency in U.S. Heavy [Dem. Senator Hubert] Humphrey contributor. Could program his agency against us."

19 **MARY McGRORY.** "Washington columnist: Daily 'Hate Nixon' articles."

20 **PAUL NEWMAN.** "Calif.: Radic-lib causes. Heavy McCarthy involvement '68. Used effectively in nation wide TV commercials. '72 involvement certain."

NIXON ON REAGAN

Nixon didn't just dislike hippies and Democrats. Some of his fellow Republicans rubbed him the wrong way, too—such as the governor of California (who would be president in less than a decade). Said Nixon: "Reagan is a man of limited mental capacity...He is not one that wears well. On a personal basis, he is terrible...He's just an uncomfortable man to be around."

---

9 SCIENCE FACTS THAT SOUND LIKE SCIENCE FICTION

1 EYEBOTS. A scientist carefully places a tiny robot into a syringe...and then injects it into an eyeball. Sound like a futuristic horror movie? Not quite. A research team at Switzerland's Institute of Robotics and Intelligent Design did just that in 2011—although the eyeball they used was a dead pig's. The researchers were testing a more effective way to deliver medication to patients suffering from macular degeneration, a retinal condition that causes blindness. The current treatment involves regular injections into the eye, but the microbot, when perfected, could be injected once and then move around the eye, delivering medicine for months at a time.

2 I THINK IT CAN. In 2010 a swimming accident left 19-year-old Ian Burkhart paralyzed from the elbows down; he couldn't even move his fingers. Four years later, doctors at Ohio State's Wexner Medical Center implanted a chip into Burkhart's brain designed to "read" his thoughts. Then a cable was plugged into his head that was hooked up to a computer, which was hooked up to an electronic stimulation sleeve around his forearm. Burkhart thought very hard, and then...his fingers moved. The device completely bypassed his broken spinal cord, and for the first time since the accident, he could open and close his hand.

3 FACE THE FUTURE. Remember that scene in *Minority Report* when Tom Cruise walks into a store and a computer knows who he is? That's a real thing now. Retail giant Tesco has installed facial recognition scanners at its gas stations around the UK: When a customer pays, his or her face is scanned to identify age and gender. Then an advertisement plays, specifically targeted to sell to the customer's demographic. Expect to see the scanners everywhere in the near future... unless they see you first.

4 A WALKING TANK. Looking like something that Tony "Iron Man" Stark might wear, the TALOS, or Tactical Assault Light Operator Suit, is the U.S. Army's newest toy. The suit has bulletproof armor, 360-degree cameras capable of night vision, and even sensors that can detect wounds and apply injury-sealing foam. The army hopes to have the suits in the field by 2018. (No flight capabilities are included. Yet.)

5 YOU CAN HEAR ME NOW. *Star Trek* introduced the concept of a universal translator for storytelling purposes, but scientists are hard at work making it a reality. In fact, the first one designed for commercial use might hit the shelves before this book does. Microsoft's Skype Translator can provide real-time translation between languages as people speak. The app was demonstrated at a conference in 2014: An English-speaking woman in California chatted with a German-speaking woman in London. The app still has some bugs to work out (it is Microsoft, after all), but expect universal translators to be a common sight before the end of the decade.

6 BLAST 'EM! Dr. Evil (from the Austin Powers movies) had one simple request: "sharks with frickin' laser beams attached to their heads." Now his dream is a reality (minus the sharks). In 2014 the U.S. Navy demonstrated its LaWS (Laser Weapons System). The prototype—installed on the USS *Ponce*—has a targeting, tracking, and firing system that is operated via a "video game–like controller." According to an ominous military press release: "The weapons officer manages the laser's power to accomplish a range of effects against a threat, from disabling to complete destruction." (Add maniacal laughter here.)

7 ANOTHER YOU. A printer that can replicate the human body? Sure, why not. Advanced 3-D scanners will scan you, and then organic ink and special plastics will "bioprint" made-to-order body parts. So far, skulls, eyes, skin, noses, ears, bones, and limbs have all been reproduced by 3-D printers. In 2014 doctors in Holland replaced a woman's damaged skull with a 3-D printed plastic version. According to the lead doctor, brain surgeon Dr. Bon Verweij, it was a resounding success: "There are almost no traces that she had any surgery at all."

8 RESISTANCE IS FUTILE. The demilitarized zone between North and South Korea requires constant surveillance, but South Korea has 655,000 troops to North Korea's 1.2 million. So South Korea's military is turning to the Samsung Techwin SGR-A1 for help. This stationary robot is equipped with a camera and a high-speed machine gun. The camera scans the area and sends images to a control room; if there's trouble, the robot can be ordered to fire 40-mm rounds. The first SGR-A1 prototype is already in place. South Korea plans to put one in every guard post along the border.

9 SITH HAPPENS. Do the names Mikhail Lukin and Vladan Vuletic sound like *Star Wars* characters? They're actually Earth-based physicists (Lukin from Harvard, and Vuletic from MIT) who announced in 2014 that they found a way to "bounce" photons off each other. That's right—photons are light particles that have no mass. But when the physicists placed two photons into a special type of vacuum chamber, where they interacted with "laser beams and a cloud of rubidium atoms cooled to near absolute zero," the light particles suddenly took on very different properties. "What we have done," said Lukin, "is create a special type of medium in which photons interact with each other so strongly that they begin to act as though they have mass, and they bind together to form molecules." Or, in other words, "It's not an in-apt analogy to compare this to light sabers."

3 BRONTË SISTERS

In their short, tragic lives, these three sisters penned some of the most influential novels of the English language.

1 CHARLOTTE

"I write because I cannot help it," said Charlotte Brontë. She started out with poems, as did her sisters, and it was Charlotte's discovery of Emily's poetry that began their literary careers. Charlotte—born in Yorkshire, England, in 1816—had worked as a teacher and a governess. But an unrequited crush on a married professor drove her back to the family home, where she stumbled upon Emily's poetry in 1845. Charlotte suggested the three sisters combine their poems into one volume and self-publish them using men's names as pseudonyms. Result: *The Poems of Currer, Ellis, and Acton Bell*. It sold two copies. Undeterred, the sisters tried their hands at novels, which they sent to the publishing house of Smith, Elder & Co. of London; Charlotte's *The Professor* was rejected, but the publisher asked to see another work. That was *Jane Eyre*, published in 1847. The ahead-of-its-time novel was told from the perspective of a strong woman who'd endured terrible abuse and had the gall to criticize English social norms. The book was so popular that the sisters were forced to reveal their true identities to their publisher: "Currer" was Charlotte, "Ellis" was Emily, and "Acton" was Anne.

Charlotte published two more novels, *Shirley* in 1849 and *Villette* in 1853. She married in 1854 but died soon after, just three weeks before her 39th birthday. She was thought to have died from tuberculosis, but modern scholars suspect that Charlotte may have died because of complications from a pregnancy.

Famous *Jane Eyre* quote: "I am no bird; and no net ensnares me: I am a free human being with an independent will."

2 EMILY

Born in 1818, shy Emily was also going to be a teacher, but she couldn't stand to be away from the family home and was horrified when Charlotte discovered her "private poems." But Emily's writing career prospered. Her novel *Wuthering Heights*—a sordid tale of jealousy and vengeance in an English farmhouse—was published in 1847 under the pseudonym Ellis Bell. Emily clung to anonymity and refused to go with Charlotte and Anne to their publisher to reveal that they were women. The following year, Emily fell ill but refused to see a doctor. She died from tuberculosis at only 30 years old.

Famous *Wuthering Heights* quote: "I gave him my heart, and he took and pinched it to death; and flung it back to me. People feel with their hearts, Ellen, and since he has destroyed mine, I have not power to feel for him."

3 ANNE

Anne also started out with poetry. Born in 1820, she worked as a governess like her sister Charlotte. Getting fired from a job inspired her to pen her 1847 novel *Agnes Grey*—yet another story of a strong woman facing a difficult life head-on. Anne's next novel, *The Tenant of Wildfell Hall*, was published in 1848 and sold well. But Anne had just as poor health as her sisters—she died five months after Emily, also of tuberculosis, at 29.

Famous *Agnes Grey* quote: "It is foolish to wish for beauty. Sensible people never either desire it for themselves or care about it in others. If the mind be but well cultivated, and the heart well disposed, no one ever cares for the exterior."

Bonus: There were two more sisters, Maria and Elizabeth, who both died in childhood. Their deaths deeply affected the other children, which explains their dark themes. There was a brother, too—Branwell—who also published a book of poetry. But his tragic life was marred by alcoholism before he succumbed to tuberculosis in 1848. Thankfully for us, his three sisters lived just long enough to change the face of English literature.

14 PARTS OF A HARDCOVER BOOK

Ever since the BRI formed, almost all of our books have been softcover. This book has a lot more parts!

1 **Front board:** The technical name for the front cover

2 **Top edge:** The top edge of the front board (also called the head)

3 **Tail:** The bottom of the book (the part that touches the table when standing upright)

4 **Endsheet:** The piece of paper that is pasted to the inside of the front board and makes up what constitutes the "first page" of a book. (There's another endsheet found at the back of the book.)

5 **Pastedown:** The pasted side of the endsheet

6 **Flyleaf:** A blank page, sometimes several, following the front free endpaper or at the end of a book where there isn't sufficient text to fill out the last few pages

7 **Hinge:** The inside portion of the flexible area where the book cover meets the book spine

8 **Spine:** The hinged back of the book

9 **Headband:** The visible top and bottom edges of the cloth (often striped) covering the spine

10 **Headcap:** The top of the spine, boards, and block when the book is standing upright (the tailcap is on the bottom)

11 **Back board:** The technical name for the back cover

12 **Square:** The top edge of the back board

13 **Fore edge:** The part opposite the spine

14 **Book block:** The inside pages (also called the text block)

5 TALES ABOUT THE DARK SIDE OF TOILET PAPER

Not literally the dark side of TP—that would be way too gross.

1 GRAND THEFT TP

Chaos nearly ensued at a 1995 Philadelphia Eagles home game when it was discovered that Veterans Stadium only had 13 rolls of toilet paper in its inventory—not quite enough for the 65,000 fans who would soon be showing up. Stadium officials made an emergency order, which arrived just in time to avoid a messy situation. An investigation later revealed that the stadium's stores manager, Ricardo Jefferson, had stolen $35,000 worth of TP. Philadelphia city spokesman Tony Radwanski quipped, "He really wiped the stadium clean."

2 PATTERN RECOGNITION

British mathematician Sir Roger Penrose sued bathroom products manufacturer Kimberly-Clark in 1997. His claim: Back in 1974, he created and patented a five-fold polygon design (for math, not for TP). But then, two decades later, Penrose was none too pleased when he found out that his patented design was being used for rolls of Kleenex Quilted bathroom tissue. So he filed suit. Kimberly-Clark settled out of court and hired Penrose as a consultant.

3 SIBLING RIVALRY

In 2013 a Brooklyn brother and sister—Howard and Bernice Meltzer—got into an argument in the house they shared (despite having a restraining order against each other). When things got heated, Bernice, 72, grabbed the last roll of TP and locked herself in the bathroom. Howard, 67, shouted through the door: "I want the toilet paper back by 1 a.m. or else I'm calling the police!" Bernice stayed in there for five hours, forcing Howard (who really had to go) to call 911. But his plan backfired: Cops showed up and arrested them both.

4 THE PRICE IS WRONG

Ever complained about the high cost of TP? Florida attorney general Bob Butterworth did. And he did something about it, too: In 1997 Butterworth filed a lawsuit accusing toilet paper makers of price fixing. His main argument: The cost of wood pulp had gone down by 18 percent, but the price of bathroom tissue had risen by 41 percent. That suit was settled quietly, but a class action suit filed a year later had toilet paper companies paying out $56 million.

5 ONCE AND FOR ALL: PAPER TOWELS ARE *NOT* TOILET PAPER!

In 2014 a New York City man named Burton Sultan filed a lawsuit against his upstairs neighbor Stephane Cosman Connery for clogging the toilets in their upscale Manhattan apartment building. Burton claimed that Connery (who happens to be actor Sean Connery's middle-aged son) had been flushing paper towels down the toilet instead of TP, causing more than $123,000 in damage to the building's plumbing. The outcome of the suit was still pending at press time, but Sultan and Connery have been suing each other back and forth since 2002, so don't expect this lawsuit to clear the foul air between them.

---

6 CLOSEST STARS TO EARTH

1 **The Sun** (0.000016 light-years)
2 **Proxima Centauri** (4.2 light-years)
3 **Alpha Centauri A** (4.3 light-years)
4 **Alpha Centauri B** (4.3 light-years)
5 **Barnard's Star** (5.96 light-years)
6 **Wolf 359** (7.6 light-years)

---

7 HORROR FILMS INSPIRED BY "TRUE" STORIES

1 *THE AMITYVILLE HORROR* FILMS (1979–2015), 2 *THE CONJURING* FILMS (2013–16), 3 *ANNABELLE* (2014)

In 1952 Ed Warren, a self-described "demonologist," and his wife Lorraine, a "trance medium," founded the New England Society for Psychic Research. Twenty years later, the Warrens investigated the Lutz family home on Long Island, New York, where six murders had occurred. That case inspired *The Amityville Horror* franchise. The Warrens' investigation of similar ghostly events involving the Perron family home in 1971 became *The Conjuring*. And the movie *Annabelle* came from a "haunted doll" case that the Warrens investigated in 1970.

4 *THE BLOB* (1958)

Steve McQueen became a star in this classic film about alien goo that grows and grows and swallows a small Pennsylvania town. Writer Irving H. Millgate got the idea from a story in the *Philadelphia Inquirer*: On the night of September 26, 1950, two cops reported a flying saucer approximately six feet in diameter. After it landed, they shined their flashlights at it, and it glowed purple. When one of the men tried to pick it up, it dissolved, leaving him with sticky hands. Within a half hour, the rest of the object had dissolved. That's basically how the movie starts (except in real life the alien didn't eat the town).

5 *JAWS* (1975)

Peter Benchley, who wrote the 1974 novel *Jaws*, got the idea for a killer shark story after chartering boat rides with a fisherman named Frank "Monster Man" Mundus (who claimed he was the inspiration for the gruff character Captain Quint).

The book's plot was inspired in part by the summer of 1916 when a rogue great white shark (da-dum) lurking in the waters (da-dum da-dum) off the Jersey shore (da-dum da-dum da-dum da-dum) killed five unlucky swimmers.

6 *PSYCHO* (1960)

When a sheriff visited Ed Gein's Wisconsin farm in 1957, he was expecting to find a robbery suspect. Instead, he stumbled upon a true house of horrors: There was a bowl made from a human skull—and a chair, lampshade, and a suit made out of skin. After Gein was arrested, investigators discovered the remains of 10 women at his farm. He was committed to a mental institution for the rest of his life. In 1959 author Robert Bloch used Gein as the model for Norman Bates in his novel *Psycho* (including Gein's unhealthy fascination with his domineering mother), and then Alfred Hitchcock turned it into a movie.

Bonus: Gein also inspired Leatherface from *The Texas Chain Saw Massacre*, Buffalo Bill from *The Silence of the Lambs*, and Bloody Face from the TV show *American Horror Story*.

7 *A NIGHTMARE ON ELM STREET* (1984)

Writer-director Wes Craven was creeped out by a story in the *L.A. Times* about three immigrants who died in their sleep. In one case, the man's family begged him to go to sleep, but he insisted that his nightmares were different from anything he'd ever experienced and was terrified he'd die if he went to sleep. When he finally did fall asleep...he died. Craven also said that the villain Freddy Krueger was based on a real-life creep:

> The hat was the kind worn by men when I was a kid, and there was one particular man who scared me. He was a drunk that came down the sidewalk and woke me up when I was sleeping. I went to the window to look...He looked right into my eyes. I went back and hid for what I thought was hours. I finally crept back to the window, and he was still there! Then he started walking almost half-backwards so that he could keep looking at me.

7 RANDOM LISTS OF 7'S

THE 7 HABITS OF HIGHLY EFFECTIVE PEOPLE

From the 1989 best-selling business and self-help book by Stephen R. Covey.

Habit 1: Be Proactive

Habit 2: Begin with the End in Mind

Habit 3: Put First Things First

Habit 4: Think Win-Win

Habit 5: Seek First to Understand, Then to Be Understood

Habit 6: Synergize

Habit 7: Sharpen the Saw

7 HOLES IN YOUR HEAD

1 Left eye

2 Right eye

3 Left ear

4 Right ear

5 Left nostril

6 Right nostril

7 Pie hole

7 CHAKRAS

Hindus and Buddhists believe these are the "centers of spiritual power in the body."

1 **Root** (tailbone)

2 **Sacral** (lower abdomen)

3 **Solar plexus** (upper abdomen)

4 **Heart**

5 **Throat**

6 **Third eye** (forehead between the eyes)

7 **Crown** (top of the head)

7 PLEASURES

From humorist Allan Sherman's 1963 book The Rape of the American Puritan Ethic, *there are seven basic pleasures we have in common with other animals.*

1 Eat

2 Drink

3 Sleep

4 Sh*t

5 Piss

6 F*ck

7 Play

7 DEADLY SINS

...and the SpongeBob SquarePants characters supposedly based on each one.

1 **Sloth:** Patrick, the lazy starfish

2 **Wrath:** Squidward, the angry squid

3 **Gluttony:** Gary, the ever-hungry snail

4 **Pride:** Sandy, the proud Texas squirrel

5 **Envy:** Plankton, the jealous...plankton

6 **Greed:** Mr. Krabs, the money-hungry crustacean

7 **Lust:** SpongeBob, the sponge who loves everyone... even Squidward

MILEY CYRUS'S "7 THINGS" SHE HATES ABOUT AN EX-BOYFRIEND

Who may or may not have been singer Nick Jonas.

1 "You're vain"

2 "Your games"

3 "You're insecure"

4 "You love me"

5 "You like her"

6 "You make me laugh"

7 "You make me cry"

7 AGES OF MAN

According to Spanish writer Baltasar Gracian (1601–58).

"At 20, a man is a peacock, at 30 a lion, at 40 a camel, at 50 a serpent, at 60 a dog, at 70 an ape, at 80 nothing."

3 ELEMENTAL FACTS

1 The cost of **carbon** depends on its form. As soot, it's free. As a diamond, it costs up to $75,000 per gram.

2 **Osmium** is the densest element. A six-inch cube is as heavy as an adult human.

3 **Gallium** will melt in your hand, and joke spoons that dissolve in hot coffee are made out of it. **Cesium** will also melt in hot liquid, but since it explodes on contact with water, it's not recommended that you put it in your coffee. (Cesium also burns on contact with air.)

5 STRANGE PLACES PEOPLE HAVE BEEN STRUCK BY LIGHTNING...IN JULY

The moral of this list: There's no safe place to be in July—inside or outside—so just try to enjoy yourself and have fun. Because at any second, a mighty flash of electrically charged air could come out of the sky and really ruin your day.

1 IN A GARAGE

"It blew me back a little bit. I got either a fork of the bolt or a ground travel," said Chad Greenlees of Arvada, Colorado, about the bolt of lightning that somehow managed to find its way into his garage on July 7, 2014. He thought he'd be safe in there while he took video of a hailstorm. But the lightning found him anyway. Greenlees suffered a concussion.

2 WHILE SCUBA DIVING

Stephen Wilson was scuba diving off Deerfield Beach, Florida, on July 22, 2007, when a thunderstorm rolled in. The divers all scrambled to get out of the water, but a bolt of lightning hit Wilson's oxygen tank just before he surfaced. His fellow divers radioed for help and rushed him to the beach, where paramedics were waiting for him. Sadly, he didn't survive.

3 ON A SUNNY DAY

No clouds could be seen as 11-year-old Britney Wehrle was walking with her friend in North Strabane Township, Pennsylvania, on July 25, 2011. Several miles away, a thunderstorm was brewing. All of a sudden, a bolt of lightning shot out of the clear blue sky and struck Britney's left arm, breaking it.

4 ON THE COUCH

At around 1:30 p.m. on July 30, 2014, Theresa Szelest was sitting on her sofa in Wheatfield, New York. "My mother was sitting right in front of me," she recalled. "My leg was on her lap and, great mom she is, she was rubbing my feet for me, 'cause I had a stressful day." Her day was about to get even more stressful. It started pouring outside, and then lightning struck the backyard. "That was close," Theresa said to her mother. Then came an even closer bolt: It tore a hole in the roof, pierced the ceiling, and struck Szelest on the couch. "I saw my head go back," she said. "And then the plaster was falling." Because the house took the brunt of the strike, Szelest wasn't seriously injured, but she couldn't stop shaking for several minutes, and her feet and toes turned purple. Mom was unscathed.

5 WHILE RUNNING A RACE

The Hardrock 100 is a grueling running race that traverses the trails of Colorado's San Juan Mountains. On July 11, 2014, runner Adam Campbell was at the highest point of the race when a thunderstorm rolled in. He lay flat on the ground hoping he would avoid getting struck. He didn't. Luckily, the lightning bolt only "fried" his headlamp; he was unhurt. What's so odd about getting struck by lightning on top of a mountain? Not much. Here's the odd part: After Campbell was struck, he got back up and actually finished the race. He came in third place. "Wow, that was hard," he said afterward. "That course is legit—even without the lightning."

---

7 MAFIA NICKNAMES

1 Philip Testa: "Chicken Man"

2 William Aloisio: "Smokes"

3 Alphonse Sisca: "Funzie"

4 John Zancocchio: "Porky"

5 Gaetano Vastola: "Corky"

6 Salvatore Maranzano: "Little Caesar"

7 Albert Anastasia: "Lord High Executioner"

---

7 THOUGHTS ON WHY LISTS MATTER

1 "The human animal differs from the lesser primates in his passion for lists."
—**H. Allen Smith**

2 "The list is the origin of culture. It's part of the history of art and literature. What does culture want? To make infinity comprehensible. It also wants to create order."
—**Umberto Eco**

3 "Breaking something big into its constituent parts will help you organize your thoughts, but it can also force you to confront the depth of your ignorance and the hugeness of the task. That's OK. The project may be the lion, but the list is your whip."
—**Adam Savage**

4 "Lists are anti-democratic, discriminatory, elitist, and sometimes the print is too small."
—**David Ives**

5 "One of the secrets of getting more done is to make a to-do list every day, keep it visible, and use it as a guide to action as you go through the day."
—**Jean de la Fontaine**

6 "Americans are good with to-do lists; just tell us what to do, and we'll do it. Throughout our history, we have proven that. Colonize. Check. Win our independence. Check. Form a union. Check. Expand to the Pacific. Check. Settle the West. Check. Keep the Union together. Check. Industrialize. Check. Fight the Nazis. Check."
—**Marianne Williamson**

7 "The only thing more important than your to-do list is your to-be list. The only thing more important than your to-be list...is to be."
—**Alan Cohen**

Esther 8:9 is the longest verse in the Bible at **81** words.

9 KILLER MAN-MADE DISASTERS

1 UNION CARBIDE GAS LEAK (India, 1984)

In the worst industrial accident since the Industrial Revolution began, 40 tons of toxic methyl isocyanate gas leaked from a pesticide plant in Bhopal, India. The lung-damaging gas immediately killed 3,800 people, and thousands more got sick and didn't recover. Even more developed terminal respiratory illnesses. Final death toll: 15,000.

2 CHERNOBYL REACTOR EXPLOSION (Ukrainian SSR, 1986)

The explosion and fire that followed were nothing compared to the radioactive cloud that leaked out of a blown reactor at the Chernobyl nuclear power plant on April 26, 1986. Workers, cleanup crews, and millions of people in the area received varying doses of radiation, so it's uncertain how many people died from cancers and other health problems. Estimated death toll: from 10,000 to 1 million.

3 SINKING OF TROOP TRANSPORT (China, 1948)

A ship evacuating Chinese troops exploded and sank off the coast of southern Manchuria. China's government didn't report the sinking until nearly a month later. Final death toll: 6,000.

4 GREAT SMOG (England, 1952)

On the morning of December 5, 1952, a thick layer of fog 30 miles wide settled over London for five long days. This was no ordinary fog: It was polluted with heavy concentrations of soot and sulfur. The noxious air proved fatal to the elderly, young children, and people with respiratory diseases. Final death toll: from 4,000 to 12,000.

5 PONTE DAS BARCAS DISASTER (Portugal, 1809)

When France's army invaded Porto, Portugal, on March 29, 1809, thousands of civilians tried to escape the city by crossing the Ponte das Barcas bridge. The center collapsed under the weight, but the thousands of people trying to cross it didn't know that until it was too late. Final death toll: 4,000.

6 SINKING OF THE DOÑA PAZ (Philippines, 1987)

The *Doña Paz* ferry was overloaded with passengers when it ran into an oil tanker south of Manila on December 20, 1987. The ship caught fire and then sank. Final death toll: 4,000.

7 CHONGQING TUNNELS (China, 1941)

On June 5, 1941, the Japanese bombed the city of Chongqing, China. Its people took shelter in a cave, but there were too many of them and not enough air. The bombing went on for so long—three hours straight—that the war refugees suffocated in the tunnels they thought would keep them safe. Final death toll: 4,000.

8 CHURCH OF THE COMPANY OF JESUS FIRE (Chile, 1863)

A gas lamp set fire to a wall hanging on the altar of the church during a December mass. Attempts to smother the fire had the opposite effect, and the conflagration quickly spread throughout the congregation. A stampede ensued, but there was only one exit. Then the church tower collapsed. Final death toll: nearly 3,000.

9 THE GREAT HALIFAX EXPLOSION (Nova Scotia, 1917)

During World War I, the *Mont Blanc* was carrying highly explosive cargo when it collided with another ship in Nova Scotia's Halifax harbor. As the vessel drifted toward the shore, thousands of locals gathered to watch it burn. That's when the fire ignited 200 tons of TNT. It was the largest man-made explosion of the pre-nuclear age. Final death toll: 1,800.

12 WEIRD EXAMPLES OF RECYCLING

1 AIRPLANES → SHOULDER PADS. In 2014 Russell Athletic teamed with Boeing to turn the airline manufacturer's extra composite material—which is used to make 787 Dreamliners—into CarbonTek football shoulder pads. Although the shoulder pads cost hundreds of dollars, they're the only ones that can claim to be "aerospace-grade."

2 MISSILES → GOLF CLUBS. Entrepreneurs John Lisanti and Cary Schuman were golfing one day when Lisanti mentioned that Schuman "hits the ball like a rocket." That sparked an idea: "Wouldn't it be great if we could melt down discarded Russian nuclear missiles and make some fabulous golf clubs out of them?" So they made golf clubs out of unused American A-3 Polaris and Soviet SS-23 nuclear missiles and sold them as the Peace Missile II Putter and Driver.

3 PLASTIC BOTTLES → MULTI-USE UNDERWEAR. It's called the "NO! Reji-Bukuro Bra." English translation: "No! Shopping Bag Bra." It was created by Triumph International Japan in response to a strict new environmental law that discourages the use of disposable plastic shopping bags. The bra's easily removable padding—made from polyester fiber recycled from plastic bottles—can be pulled out and used as a sturdy shopping bag.

4 DISCARDED ELECTRONICS → OLYMPIC MEDALS. In the 2012 Winter Olympic Games in Vancouver, British Columbia, the winning athletes received "green medals" made out of reclaimed electronics garbage. In a nod to the Olympic spirit of community, medal designer Corrine Hunt created a giant "patchwork quilt" of all the medals put together. Each unique gold, silver, and bronze medal is a piece of that artwork.

5 TOAD VENOM → SNAKE VENOM. The tiger keelback is a snake native to Asia with an amazing adaptation: The toads that it eats have a gland that dispenses toxic venom to ward off predators. After eating the toad, the snake extracts the toxin and stores it inside a protective gland. Later, the snake releases the toad toxin to kill other prey...including more toads.

6 SHIPPING CONTAINERS → HOMES AND SHOPS. Because Western countries import more goods than they export, there's a huge surplus of shipping containers piling up at the nations' ports. These metal boxes—45' long, 8' wide, and 9½' high—are usually crushed and sold for scrap (because shipping them back is too expensive). Seeing an opportunity, an English company called Urban Space Management has recycled hundreds of these shipping containers into small homes for the homeless and even shops and office buildings. Want to see them yourself? Check out "Container City" in East London.

7 WOOL SWEATERS → BASEBALLS. A baseball gets most of its volume and weight from the 900 feet of yarn that's wound around the pill. In the past, the yarn was 100 percent wool, but today it's allowed to contain up to 15 percent synthetic fibers. The yarn was once recycled from old wool carpeting, but now that carpets are primarily made from synthetic fibers, most of the wool used for baseball comes from old wool sweaters. Why wool? It has good "memory"—it returns to its original shape quickly after being hit by a bat.

8 HUMAN FAT → FUEL. In 2008 news outlets reported about a Beverly Hills cosmetic surgeon named Craig "Dr. Lipo 90210" Bittner. He boasted that he saved all of the globs of fat he removed from his patients' butts and bellies and then recycled that fat into biodiesel fuel. (Fat contains triglycerides, which can be extracted and turned into diesel.) "Not only do they get to lose their love handle," he said, "they get to take part in saving the Earth." He even drove his SUV to work every day, powered by his former patients. One problem: It's illegal in California to use human medical waste to power vehicles, so the state's public health department started an investigation. Result: Bittner lost his medical license, closed his practice, and, according to his website, moved to South America to do some "important work."

9 MUMMIES ⟶ PAPER. During a rag shortage in the 19th century—when paper was made from cloth fibers, not wood fibers—an unscrupulous Canadian paper manufacturer found a new source of cloth: Egyptian mummies. He imported them, ordered his workers to unwrap them, and then made the wraps into sturdy brown paper...which he then sold to butchers and grocers for use as a food wrap. The scheme died out after only a few months, when the workers who unwrapped the mummies started coming down with cholera.

10 AN ELECTRIC CHAIR ⟶ A ROYAL THRONE. Menelik II, the emperor of Ethiopia from 1889 until 1913, got excited when he heard about a new invention being used in New York: Criminals were getting executed via a device called an "electric chair." Eager to modernize, Menelik ordered three electric chairs. However, it wasn't until the devices arrived and were unpacked that the emperor realized they were useless for killing anyone. Why? Back then, Ethiopia had no electricity. Menelik tossed two of the chairs, but frugally recycled the third by converting it into his royal throne.

11 PIG BLOOD ⟶ CIGARETTES. Did you know that processed pig blood has been used in the manufacture of cigarette filters? It's true. In 2010 Dutch researchers released a report that concluded, "The pig's hemoglobin was found to be a fairly effective filter for cigarettes, but this information was not printed on cigarette labels because the tobacco industry was not required by law to disclose the ingredients of their products." The news caused outrage, particularly among Muslim and Jewish smokers, who are proscribed from ingesting pig products in any form.

12 AN OBSCURE SOUND EFFECT → HUNDREDS OF HOLLYWOOD DEATH WAILS.

In an industry known for recycling plots, the most recycled thing of all is the "Wilhelm Scream." Sound designer Ben Burtt first noticed it as a child in the 1950s: "Every time someone died in a Warner Bros. movie, they'd scream this famous scream." (It's a high-pitched wail that goes kind of like "ahhHHHUHH!") When Burtt became a sound designer in the 1970s, he tracked down the original recording and found it on an old studio reel marked "Man Being Eaten by an Alligator." No one knew who originally recorded it (it was first used in the 1951 western *Distant Drums*), so Burtt jokingly named it after a character named Wilhelm from the 1953 movie *Charge at Feather River* who screams the scream after he's struck in the leg by an arrow. Burtt first used it in *Star Wars* when a stormtrooper falls off a ledge, and then again in every other movie he's worked on. And he's not the only one: The Wilhelm Scream has become a Hollywood tradition. So far, it's been used in more than 300 movies.

FIRST 10 DOMAIN NAMES EVER REGISTERED

1 *symbolics.com* (3-15-1985)	6 *northrop.com* (11-7-85)
2 *bbn.com* (4-24-85)	7 *xerox.com* (1-9-86)
3 *think.com* (5-24-85)	8 *sri.com* (1-17-86)
4 *mcc.com* (7-11-85)	9 *hp.com* (3-3-86)
5 *dec.com* (9-30-85)	10 *bellcore.com* (3-5-86)

8 REASONS PEOPLE DON'T LIKE JUSTIN BIEBER

1 HE'S MEAN. While the 19-year-old pop star was hanging out by a hotel pool in Perth, Australia, in December 2013, he was overheard berating a female fan. According to a witness: "There were four girls in bikinis. One of the girls was gorgeous, with long dark hair and would have been about a size 14. Justin looked over at her and said, 'What are you, Hawaiian or something?' She said, 'No, I'm not.' Then he said, 'You look like a beached whale.' The girl said, 'Are you serious?' And he said, 'You should go on *The Biggest Loser*.' Everyone heard. And there was silence. It was almost like his security were used to it." Then the girl left in tears as Bieber and his entourage laughed.

2 HE'S A "NEIGHBOR FROM HELL." Don't you just hate it when some jerky pop star speeds through your gated community in his red Ferrari? Bieber's wealthy neighbors in Calabasas, California, sure did. NFL star Keyshawn Johnson even tried chasing him down one day, but the singer sped away at over 100 mph (in a 25-mph zone). Later, another neighbor confronted him and said, "You can't drive like this!" Bieber replied, "I'm gonna f***ing kill you!" And then he allegedly spit at the man. After an altercation with yet another unhappy neighbor, Bieber got revenge by throwing eggs "and other things" at the neighbor's house, causing $20,000 damage.

3 HE'S LAZY. While visiting the Great Wall of China, two of Bieber's brawny bodyguards carried him on their shoulders from viewpoint to viewpoint. A few months later, Bieber got pushed around in a wheelchair at Disneyland, prompting accusations that he was using it to cut to the front of long lines.

But since Bieber already receives VIP treatment at the park, he only rode in the wheelchair so he didn't have to walk from ride to ride.

4 HE'S AN INCONSIDERATE STONER.

In January 2014, Justin and his dad Jeremy Bieber both smoked lots of marijuana on a private jet from Canada to New Jersey to see the Super Bowl. It was so smoky in the plane that the pilots had to wear oxygen masks so they wouldn't get a contact high (or fail a drug test). It was also reported that Daddy and Junior Bieber were "extremely abusive" to the flight attendant; she had to spend most of the flight locked in the cockpit with the pilots.

5 HE'S A MILLIONAIRE CHEAPSKATE.

Why did Bieber and his entourage get banned for life from an indoor skydiving facility in Las Vegas? For one, they all showed up shortly before closing time so they could fly in private. Between flights, they reportedly "trashed" the rest room. The owner agreed to waive the $1,600 flying fee if Bieber took a photo with him and then posted it on his popular Instagram page. Bieber allowed the photo to be taken and then pretended to post the photo...but didn't. Then he and his pals left without paying—they didn't even tip the staff, who had to stay late and clean up the bathroom.

6 HE SPITS AND PEES WHEREVER HE PLEASES.

In addition to the spitting-at-his-neighbor incident, according to the gossip site TMZ, Bieber has also spit on "members of the paparazzi, a lady at the gym, and a deejay." Worse yet, the pop star was photographed "hocking a lugi" from a Toronto hotel balcony onto a throng of screaming fan girls below. No word if the Biebs has urinated on anyone yet, but in Colorado, he pulled over in an upscale neighborhood and "wrote his name" in the snow on someone's lawn. In another incident in a restaurant kitchen, Bieber peed into a mop bucket while his friends filmed it and laughed at him.

7 HE'S A MENACE TO SOCIETY. Bieber's most notorious incident (so far) took place in Miami in early 2014 when he was arrested for reckless driving and DUI after police pulled him over for speeding through the city in a rented yellow Lamborghini. According to the police report, Bieber had been drinking, smoking marijuana, and popping Xanax pills...while driving at speeds of over 130 mph. The arrest sparked so much outrage that fed-up Americans submitted a petition to the White House to get the Canadian crooner deported. Despite amassing more than 100,000 signatures, Bieber wasn't deported. Nor did he go to jail. (He was sentenced to an anger management class.)

8 HE SAID THIS: "So remember, this is Bieber's world. You're just living in it. Bieber or die."

---

10 MENU ITEMS FROM MONTY PYTHON'S FAMOUS "SPAM" SKETCH

1 Egg and bacon

2 Egg, sausage, and bacon

3 Egg and Spam

4 Egg, bacon, and Spam

5 Egg, bacon, sausage, and Spam

6 Spam, bacon, sausage, and Spam

7 Spam, egg, Spam, Spam, bacon, and Spam

8 Spam, Spam, Spam, egg, and Spam

9 Spam, Spam, Spam, Spam, Spam, Spam, baked beans, Spam, Spam, Spam, and Spam

10 Lobster thermidor aux crevettes with a Mornay sauce garnished with truffle pâté, brandy, and with a fried egg on top and Spam

---

Oliver Wendell Holmes Jr. retired at 90, the oldest Supreme Court justice to date.

5 THINGS YOU DIDN'T KNOW ABOUT SAUSAGE

We try to steer away from the recent list-naming fad of "10 Things You Didn't Know About Blank." It's a bit presumptuous. But we're going to guess that, unless you're a sausagologist yourself, you don't know a whole lot about this popular break-fast food. So let's just call it "5 Things You May Not Have Known About Sausage." (See? That's why we don't like these kind of list titles.)

1 SAUSAGE IS ANCIENT.

The simple definition of sausage: ground and seasoned meat, stuffed into a casing traditionally made from an animal intestine. The first recorded mention of such a food goes back to 589 BC, when the ancient Chinese referred to a semidried sausage called *lup cheong*, made from pork, salt, sugar, green onions, pepper, wine, and soy sauce. Some food historians claim that sausage is even older than that, possibly dating back to 5,000 years ago in ancient Sumeria.

2 SAUSAGE HAS A STORIED PAST.

The Greek poet Homer mentioned sausage in *The Odyssey*:

> There are some goats' paunches down at the fire,
> which we have filled with blood and fat, and set
> aside for supper; he who is victorious and proves
> himself the better man shall have his pick of the lot.

The Romans in turn learned to make sausage from the Greeks, and they spread it throughout Europe and North Africa, with different regions developing their own sausage recipes and traditions over the centuries. The modern word "sausage" is derived from the Latin *salsus*, meaning "salted," and dates to the 15th century.

3 SAUSAGE IS VERSATILE.

This meaty staple comes in five main categories:

• **Fresh:** This type of sausage is made of raw meat, uncooked and uncured; it must be refrigerated and cooked before eating. *Examples:* most pork breakfast sausage.

• **Cooked:** The sausage is cooked during the manufacturing process. It should be kept refrigerated, and then reheated before serving. *Examples:* braunschweiger, liver sausage.

• **Cooked, smoked:** It's cooked and then smoked (smoking is a kind of slow cooking in which the food is exposed to smoke, usually from smoldering wood). It too should be kept refrigerated and can be eaten cold or heated. *Examples:* kielbasa, wieners.

• **Fresh-smoked:** Uncooked and lightly smoked, it should be kept refrigerated and then fully cooked before eating. *Examples:* mettwurst, Romanian sausage.

• **Dry sausage:** The meat is put through a complicated "drying" process that gives it a "hard" texture and very long shelf life. It can be eaten hot or cold. *Examples:* pepperoni, Genoa salami.

4 SAUSAGE HAS QUITE THE WARDROBE.

Most sausage meat is squirted into natural casings made from hog, sheep, or beef intestines. Sometimes the skins are stomachs, or even actual skin. (Eww.) Artificial casings are made from collagen (from the connective tissues of animals), cellulose (from cotton fibers), muslin (woven cotton fabric), or thick, inedible synthetic casings that make refrigeration unnecessary. They're often color-coded, like bright red for bologna (or baloney, if you prefer).

5 SAUSAGE WAS ONCE ON THE "NO-EAT LIST."

The Catholic Church banned the food in the fourth century, claiming it was a sin to eat. Why? Because sausage was "linked" to pagan festivals.

7 THEORIES ABOUT BOXING DAY

Boxing Day is observed in the UK, Canada, and other countries on December 26, but who started it and why? (Uncle John figured it was named for the Rocky movie marathons they used to show on cable TV the day after Christmas.) Truth is, no one knows for sure. Here are seven theories.

THEORY #1. It was begun by British aristocrats who rewarded their servants with boxed holiday leftovers and gifts on December 26.

THEORY #2. British estate lords handed out sundries and supplies to their staff on December 26, which they carried home in boxes.

THEORY #3. It was named for the day when Europeans traditionally boxed up their unwanted presents and exchanged them at stores.

THEORY #4. It's called Boxing Day because people spend the day getting rid of their empty Christmas boxes.

THEORY #5. Churches in England had "alms boxes," where parishioners would donate money for the poor. On the 26th, clergy would distribute the contents of the boxes.

THEORY #6. Special boxes were kept on ships during long voyages. Sailors placed donations in the boxes to help reimburse a priest who was supposedly praying for their safe return.

THEORY #7. The one most likely to be true: Dating back to 18th-century England, where it's also known as Saint Stephen's Day, the upper classes spent the day doling out cash to the poor. Servants carried ceramic boxes to work on the 26th, and their employers would fill them with money, then smash them later like a piggy bank.

6 GENIUS GOOFS

1 ARISTOTLE. The "father of logical reasoning" thought that lower forms of life were spontaneously created from inanimate matter (like maggots appearing on rotting meat).

2 THOMAS EDISON. The famous inventor proposed that houses—including stairs, mantels, decorations, and fixtures—should be made entirely out of concrete, which he called "practically indestructible and perfectly sanitary."

3 ISAAC NEWTON. The man who "discovered" gravity also studied alchemy and believed other metals would become gold if they stayed in the ground long enough.

4 PYTHAGORAS. The Greek philosopher deemed "the first pure mathematician" believed the Earth was the center of the universe (but so did most everyone else back then).

5 PERCIVAL LOWELL. The astronomer who founded the Lowell Observatory that led to the discovery of Pluto also believed in intelligent life on Mars. He was convinced that Mars's linear topography was hundreds of canals constructed by Martians.

6 ALBERT EINSTEIN. Einstein may have been the 20th century's most renowned physicist, but he was terrible with numbers. He hired mathematicians to check his work, which was often riddled with errors. Einstein couldn't even deal with basic numbers—one time, he had to find a phone booth to look up his phone number, and then call home to get his address.

10 USES FOR VINEGAR AROUND THE HOUSE

1 Garden not growing? Check if the dirt is alkaline by pouring ½ cup of white vinegar over a handful of soil. If it bubbles or fizzes, it's alkaline, and you might need to add lime or sulfur to balance the pH.

2 Kill dandelions by spraying them with undiluted apple cider or white vinegar.

3 Got a stiff paintbrush? Soak it in undiluted white vinegar until the bristles are soft, and then wash it in hot, soapy water.

4 If you take the hem out of a garment and want to get rid of the holes left behind by the thread, moisten a cloth with white vinegar, lay the hem on top, and iron.

5 Smelly lunch box? Soak a slice of bread in distilled white vinegar, let it sit in the lunch box overnight, then wash.

6 Keep cut flowers fresh. Add two tablespoons of apple cider vinegar plus two tablespoons of sugar to the vase's water. Change the water and vinegar/sugar mixture every few days for best results.

7 Wooden cutting board need disinfecting? The acids in full-strength vinegar will do it. Just wipe it down and let dry.

8 Spray bird poop with apple cider vinegar to get rid of it.

9 Soak a rusty tool in full-strength white vinegar for several days to remove the rust.

10 Clogged drain? Before you pull out the Drano, try this: Pour in ½ cup of baking soda and then 1 cup of vinegar. When it stops foaming, flush it with hot water. After five minutes, flush again with cold water. (This technique will remove bad smells, too!)

The white Swany rose has 95 petals.

5 OF THE LEAST BLOODY BATTLES EVER

1 FORT SUMTER, THE UNION vs. THE CONFEDERACY, 1861

In the opening days of the American Civil War, South Carolina had seceded, but U.S. troops still occupied Fort Sumter. Confederate troops did not want a Union stronghold in the middle of Charleston Harbor, so 43 mortars and guns bombarded the fort with nearly 4,000 cannonballs, setting it on fire. As the flames threatened to spread to the ammunition and gunpowder storage room, garrison commander Major Robert Anderson surrendered the fort 34 hours after the attack began. Despite the heavy shelling and the fires it caused, the only casualty of the battle was a mule.

2 FORT TICONDEROGA, AMERICAN COLONISTS vs. ENGLAND, 1775

As the Revolutionary War began, Americans Ethan Allen and Benedict Arnold (before he became a traitor) realized the strategic importance of New York's Fort Ticonderoga: If the colonists held it, they would control the waterway between Canada and the colonies, thus stopping an English invasion. Allen, Arnold, and members of the Vermont militia, the Green Mountain Boys, launched a predawn raid on the fort. The sleeping British troops were awoken at gunpoint, and "America's first victory" was achieved without a single loss of life.

3 THE CAPTURE OF THE BAHAMAS, SPAIN vs. ENGLAND, 1782

While England's attention and resources were focused on the American Revolution, the Spanish navy took advantage and invaded Nassau in the Bahamas. The British governor watched as 1,800 Spanish troops descended on the island, and he quickly realized that he was vastly outnumbered. He surrendered.

There were 96 "official industrial fatalities" during Hoover Dam's construction.

4 THE CAPTURE OF THE BAHAMAS, ENGLAND vs. SPAIN, 1783

A year after Spain took the Bahamas, England's Colonel Andrew Deveaux gathered a force of 200 mercenaries: He ordered the men to land on the beach, then sneak back out, reboard their ships, and land again. This subterfuge was designed to fool the Spanish into believing that thousands of troops were invading. Did it work? The Spanish gave the Bahamas back to the British without putting up a fight.

5 THE HORATII AND THE CURIATII, ROME vs. ALBA LONGA, 672–642 BC

Roman historian Livy describes an early clash between Rome and rival city Alba Longa. Legend has it that the two cities were about to go to war over a land dispute when it was decided that two sets of brothers would settle the conflict via hand-to-hand combat: The Horatii were triplets and represented Rome, and the Curiatii were triplets and stood for Alba Longa. The first two Horatii were killed quickly, and the third pretended to flee but then returned and killed the three Curiatii one by one. Rome had won its land with the loss of only two men.

10 FOODS ON THE MENU AT JAPANESE BASEBALL GAMES

1 Curry rice

2 Gyoza (fried dumplings)

3 Edamame (steamed or boiled soybeans in the pod)

4 Shrimp-flavored chips

5 Fried mashed potato balls

6 Yakitori (chicken grilled on skewers)

7 Takoyaki (dough balls filled with octopus)

8 Ebi burger (fried shrimp burger)

9 Mandarin oranges over shaved ice

10 Bento boxes (rice, sushi, tofu, eel, vegetables)

33 NEW YEAR'S RESOLUTIONS WOODY GUTHRIE MADE FOR 1943

The legendary folk singer ("This Land Is Your Land") influenced everyone from Bob Dylan to Rage Against the Machine. This list gives a little insight into why Guthrie was so admired.

1 Work more and better

2 Work by a schedule

3 Wash teeth if any

4 Shave

5 Take bath

6 Eat good—fruit, vegetables, milk

7 Drink very scant if any

8 Write a song a day

9 Wear clean clothes— look good

10 Shine shoes

11 Change socks

12 Change bed clothes often

13 Read lots of good books

14 Listen to radio a lot

15 Learn people better

16 Keep rancho clean

17 Don't get lonesome

18 Stay glad

19 Keep hoping machine running

20 Dream good

21 Bank all extra money

22 Save dough

23 Have company but don't waste time

24 Send Mary and kids money

25 Play and sing good

26 Dance better

27 Help win war— Beat Fascism

28 Love Mama

29 Love Papa

30 Love Pete [his brother]

31 Love everybody

32 Make up your mind

33 Wake up and fight

7 TIMES WHEN MUSIC IS MORE THAN MUSIC

1 WHEN IT REDUCES CRIME

What deters loiterers and vandals? The soothing sounds of classical music. (Or, at one theater in Seattle, "It's a Small World.") How it works: When we're around something we find unpleasant, our brains shut off the production of dopamine, one of the chemicals that makes us feel happy. So unscrupulous shoppers who don't care for Chopin may get Straussed out and take a step Bach when confronted with classical music.

2 WHEN IT MOTIVATES FACTORY WORKERS

Up-tempo music is pumped into factories to help line workers stay efficient as they perform the same task over and over. According to studies, up-tempo music works even better if it doesn't have lyrics and if it's turned off and on periodically.

3 WHEN IT SOOTHES LITTLE BABIES

Moms have been singing lullabies for millennia, and now science backs them up. A 2009 study found that music in neonatal units helps preemies eat better and gain weight faster.

4 WHEN IT HELPS PHELPS

Swimmer Michael Phelps was on to something when he listened to Young Jeezy's "Go Getta" before winning eight gold medals at the 2008 Olympics. According to several studies, music helps athletes (or people exercising) stay motivated, helps them enjoy their activity, and can increase their performance. In fact, in 2007 USA Track and Field officials banned the use of portable music players during races in part because they felt it gave the music-listening runners an edge.

According to the Qur'an, Allah has 99 names.

5 WHEN IT HELPS PLANTS GROW

In 2007 South Korean scientists played classical music across rice fields, which grew faster than the fields without music. Their conclusion: Music played at certain frequencies—125 Hz and 250 Hz—activates certain plant genes, which increases their growth rate and can even make them flower early.

6 WHEN IT SCARES BIRDS AWAY

Officials at England's Gloucestershire Airport tried everything to keep birds off the runways. What finally worked? Pumping music onto the tarmac. (Tina Turner works the best.)

7 WHEN IT'S WEAPONIZED

"Joshua's army used horns to strike fear into the hearts of the people of Jericho," retired U.S. Air Force Lieutenant Colonel Dan Kuehl said about using music to "intimidate and interrogate." But not everyone likes what they hear: In 2008 the Zero Decibels Project was launched to protest using music as a weapon. So far, the feds show no sign of stopping the practice.

5 "INTIMIDATING" SONGS ON THE U.S. GOVERNMENT'S PLAYLIST

1 **"These Boots Were Made for Walking"** (Nancy Sinatra) FBI, 1993, used against a cult in Waco, Texas

2 **"Panama"** (Van Halen) U.S. armed forces, 1989, used against Manuel Noriega in Panama

3 **"Slim Shady"** (Eminem) U.S. armed forces, 2005, used against prisoners in Afghanistan

4 **"Hell's Bells"** (AC/DC) U.S. armed forces, 2004, during the taking of Fallujah (Iraq)

5 **"I Love You"** (Barney the dinosaur) U.S. armed forces, 2003, used against prisoners in Iraq

9 MUSEUMS NOBODY WANTS TO VISIT

Disclaimer: Lots of people probably love these museums—any one of them could certainly make for a fun afternoon with the kids (especially if the kids are really into barbed wire or Spam).

1 THE SALT AND PEPPER SHAKER MUSEUM
Where: Gatlinburg, TN
On Display: More than 20,000 sets of salt and pepper shakers
From the Website: "One of our main purposes is to show the changes in a society that can be represented in shakers."

2 THE NATIONAL MUSTARD MUSEUM
Where: Middleton, WI
On Display: 5,676 mustards from all 50 states and 70 countries
From the Website: "The Mustard Museum has been featured on *The Oprah Winfrey Show* and *Jeopardy!*"

3 THE IDAHO POTATO MUSEUM
Where: Blackfoot, ID
On Display: History, trivia, and a giant baked potato out front
From the Website: "Discover the world of potatoes®!"

4 THE SPAM MUSEUM
Where: Austin, MN
On Display: 16,500 square feet of Spam history, trivia, and vintage advertising—plus lots and lots of Spam
From the Website: "Few experiences in life are as meaningful and meaty-filled as those at the magnificent Spam Museum."

There are 6,469,952 spots in Disney's 1961 classic *101 Dalmatians.*

5 DEVIL'S ROPE BARBED WIRE MUSEUM
Where: McLean, TX
On Display: More than 2,000 variations of barbed wire
From the Website: "Get hooked on barbed wire."

6 THE WORLD FAMOUS MUSEUM OF DEATH
Where: Los Angeles, CA
On Display: The world's largest collection of serial murderer artwork, a body bag and coffin collection, replicas of full-size execution devices, pet death taxidermy, and more!
From the Website: "The Museum began in 1995 when J.D. Healy and Cathee Schultz realized the void in death education in this country and decided to make death their life's work."

7 THE WOODEN NICKEL MUSEUM
Where: San Antonio, TX
On Display: Over 1 million wooden nickels
From the Website: "We also now offer custom printed coasters, Yo-Yo's, and laser-engraved nickels and jumbos!!!"

8 BEER CAN MUSEUM & BEER CAN HALL OF FAME
Where: East Taunton, MA
On Display: 5,000 beer cans from more than 50 countries
From the Website: "These little steel and aluminum vessels are a wonder to behold."

9 LEILA'S HAIR MUSEUM
Where: Independence, MO
On Display: 600 hair wreaths and over 2,000 pieces of hair jewelry
From the Website: "You will find hair from Queen Victoria, four presidents, and celebrities from Michael Jackson to Marilyn Monroe."

15 WORDS THAT CHANGED MEANING

WORD	DATES TO	TODAY'S MEANING	ORIGINAL MEANING
1 **Cute**	1731	pretty in a youthful way	clever, shrewd
2 **Bully**	1538	someone cruel to those weaker	sweetheart
3 **Prestigious**	1546	honored	involving trickery
4 **Matrix**	1555	pattern of lines and spaces	female breeding animal
5 **Garble**	1400s	cause something to be confusing	sift, separate out impurities
6 **Nervous**	1300s	jumpy	sinewy
7 **Assassin**	1200s	killer of a VIP	hashish eater
8 **Silly**	1300s	foolish	innocent
9 **Nice**	1300s	kind, good	foolish, wanton
10 **Backlog**	1684	large number of jobs to be done	largest log in the hearth
11 **Dapper**	1400s	stylish	brave
12 **Girl**	1300s	young female	young person, either gender
13 **Fantastic**	1300s	exceptional	existing only in the imagination
14 **Buxom**	1100s	large-breasted	compliant
15 **Fizzle**	1598	fail weakly	fart quietly

Gene Kelly had a 103°F fever when he danced to "Singin' in the Rain."

4 HIGH-PRICED IN-GAME VIDEO GAME PURCHASES

1 A CHARACTER. In 2007 an anonymous *World of Warcraft* player from England managed to make one of his characters among the highest-leveled and best-geared in the Massively Multiplayer Online Role-playing Game (MMORPG). One of the world's tens of millions of *WoW* players sent the player a message asking if he'd be interested in selling the character. He was, and the buyer shelled out 7,000 euros ($9,000) for it.

2 A SWORD. In 2011, two years prior to the release of the game *Age of Wulin*, an auction was held for exclusive in-game items. A sword was sold for $16,000, and two special sheaths went for $2,500 and $1,600. That's real cash for stuff that only existed inside a game that hadn't even been released yet.

3 AN EGG. *Planet Calypso* is an MMORPG where players deposit real money that gets converted into "Project Entropia Dollars," the in-game currency. Players can earn more PEDs and then withdraw them as real money. In 2006 a player purchased a special egg for $10,000. He then sold it in 2010...for $69,696. What made this egg so special? No one knew—it didn't even "hatch" until 2013. What came out? "The creature that emerged killed everyone in its path and escaped."

4 A SPACE STATION. The most expensive item ever sold in a *Planet Calypso* auction: the Crystal Palace Space Station, purchased in 2009 by a player as an investment; he earns PEDs when other players visit the station—which happens to be the only place in the game to find certain kinds of armor. Hopefully, he's getting a lot of visitors so he can make back his $330,000.

9 REASONS TO TAKE THE BUS INSTEAD

Come to think of it, most of these scary airplane tales could happen on a bus, too—so maybe it's best to just stay home.

1 YOUR PILOT MIGHT GET "DISARMED"

In 2014 a plane approaching Belfast, Northern Ireland, landed hard on the runway. The 47 passengers were shaken up but otherwise okay. According to BBC News, the pilot's "prosthetic limb became detached, depriving him of control of the aircraft." He was able to regain the controls with his other hand just in time. The pilot promised that in the future, he will be more careful to make sure his arm stays attached.

2 YOUR PILOT MIGHT GET LOST

"Welcome to Branson," announced the pilot of a Southwest flight, followed by, "I'm sorry, ladies and gentlemen, we have landed at the wrong airport." Apparently, the pilot mistook the lights of the much smaller M. Graham Clark Downtown Airport for those of Branson, about seven miles away. It almost ended in tragedy because the Clark runway is half the length of Branson's, so the plane had to brake hard to avoid going off the end of the runway, down an embankment, and onto a highway.

3 THE AIR TRAFFIC CONTROLLERS MIGHT DOZE OFF

At around 3:00 a.m. during an April 2013 flight, a China Eastern Airlines plane was approaching Wuhan Airport when the pilot requested permission to land. There was no response from the tower, so the pilot tried again. Still no response. Then he tried a third time...still no response. So he circled the airport for ten minutes, calling again and again until the air traffic controllers finally woke up and cleared him for landing.

4 YOUR PILOTS MIGHT DOZE OFF

Halfway through an Air India flight in 2013, the copilot asked a flight attendant to take his seat while he took a bathroom break. Then the pilot said he needed a break and asked another flight attendant to take his place, but first he showed them how to fly the plane. Then he went to business class and took a nap...not far from the copilot, who was also napping. Forty minutes later, one of flight attendants accidentally switched off the autopilot. They woke the pilots, who groggily returned to the cockpit and regained control. Air India apologized and suspended the pilots and the flight attendants.

5 THERE MIGHT ACTUALLY BE SNAKES ON THE PLANE

Snakes are not acceptable carry-on items—cobras even less so. That didn't stop a Jordanian reptile dealer from smuggling one of the venomous serpents on to an Egypt Air flight from Cairo to Kuwait in 2012. Passengers watched in terror as the man tried to keep the slithering snake from escaping its bag. Good news: The cobra didn't escape. Bad news: It bit his handler on the hand. The plane was diverted to a nearby airport, where the cobra was confiscated and the man arrested. He refused medical attention, calling his wound "superficial."

6 THE WALLS MIGHT COME A-TUMBLIN' DOWN

The wall panels on an American Airlines flight started to pop off mid-flight, alarming passengers. A failure in the air duct system had caused the panels to pop, but because the plastic covers aren't part of the plane's skin, there wasn't any danger to the aircraft. Still, the pilot made an emergency landing. "It was very scary, really weird," said passenger Joan Denney.

7 YOUR FLIGHT MIGHT GET RAINED OUT...FROM THE INSIDE

Shortly after a Qantas Airlines flight took off from Los Angeles bound for Melbourne, the ceiling of the main cabin started leaking water. As the passengers covered up with blankets, the pilot had a decision to make: Continue the 14-hour flight to Australia, or return to LAX. On the plus side, the pipe burst didn't seem to be affecting the plane's flying abilities (although the in-flight entertainment was turned off as a precaution). On the down side, there was no potable water and the toilets were inoperable due to the leak. So the prudent pilot decided to turn the plane around. What had happened? A mop head in the upper galley got tangled in a drain pipe and unlatched it.

8 YOUR FELLOW PASSENGERS MIGHT START A RIOT

A Ryanair flight from Morocco to Paris was only supposed to take two and a half hours. But when a passenger got sick, the plane was diverted to Madrid, and the rest of the passengers waited on board for the plane to take off again. When it finally did, the pilots were told they couldn't land in Paris due to nighttime flying restrictions, so—seven hours after takeoff—the plane landed in western France...where the passengers were told they'd have to spend the night. Fed up and unfed, they disobeyed orders to disembark, and several started raiding the carts, stealing food and alcohol. A baggage handler described the looters as "barbaric." One of the looters saw it differently: "We compensated ourselves."

9 YOUR PILOT MIGHT BE A BIT TOO TALKY

In 2013 a Southwest Airlines flight was flying over North Carolina when the intercom crackled for a second. Then the pilot said, "We're in trouble. We're going down." Some of the passengers thought it was a joke...until the Boeing 737 went into a steep nosedive. "So this is how I'm going to die," said passenger Grace Stroud to herself. "At least it will be quick." Luckily, the pilot was able to regain control and make an emergency landing near Raleigh. A Southwest Airlines spokesman later explained that pilot was speaking to his copilot about a sudden pressure loss...and didn't realize the intercom was on. "We sincerely regret any confusion caused by the relay of the information."

13 QUESTIONABLE USES FOR LEFTOVER TURKEY

In the 1930s, author F. Scott Fitzgerald (The Great Gatsby) jotted down this list of post-Thanksgiving "recipes" to ease the "refrigerators of the nation overstuffed with large masses of turkey." But be warned: "Not one has been tried and proven—there are headstones all over America to testify to the fact."

1 Turkey Cocktail. "To one large turkey add one gallon of vermouth and a demijohn of angostura bitters. Shake."

2 Turkey à la Francais. "Take a large ripe turkey, prepare as for basting and stuff with old watches and chains and monkey meat. Proceed as with cottage pudding."

3 Turkey and Water. "Take one turkey and one pan of water. Heat the latter to the boiling point and then put in the refrigerator. When it has jelled, drown the turkey in it. Eat. In preparing this recipe it is best to have a few ham sandwiches around in case things go wrong."

4 Turkey Mongole. "Take three butts of salami and a large turkey skeleton, from which the feathers and natural stuffing have been removed. Lay them out on the table and call up some Mongole in the neighborhood to tell you how to proceed from there."

5 Turkey Mousse. "Seed a large prone turkey, being careful to remove the bones, flesh, fins, gravy, etc. Blow up with a bicycle pump. Mount in becoming style and hang in the front hall."

6 Stolen Turkey. "Walk quickly from the market, and, if accosted, remark with a laugh that it had just flown into your arms and you hadn't noticed it. Then drop the turkey with the white of one egg—well, anyhow, beat it."

7 Turkey à la Crême. "Prepare the crême a day in advance. Deluge the turkey with it and cook for six days over a blast furnace. Wrap in fly paper and serve."

8 Turkey Hash. "This is the delight of all connoisseurs of the holiday beast, but few understand how really to prepare it. Like a lobster, it must be plunged alive into boiling water, until it becomes bright red or purple or something, and then before the color fades, placed quickly in a washing machine and allowed to stew in its own gore as it is whirled around. Only then is it ready for hash. To hash, take a large sharp tool like a nail-file or, if none is handy, a bayonet will serve the purpose—and then get at it! Hash it well! Bind the remains with dental floss and serve."

9 Feathered Turkey. "To prepare this, a turkey is necessary and a one-pounder cannon to compel anyone to eat it. Broil the feathers and stuff with sage-brush, old clothes, almost anything you can dig up. Then sit down and simmer. The feathers are to be eaten like artichokes (and this is not to be confused with the old Roman custom of tickling the throat)."

10 Turkey à la Maryland. "Take a plump turkey to a barber's and have him shaved, or if a female bird, given a facial and a water wave. Then, before killing him, stuff with old newspapers and put him to roost. He can then be served hot or raw, usually with a thick gravy of mineral oil and rubbing alcohol. (Note: This recipe was given me by an old black mammy.)"

11 **Turkey Remnant.** "This is one of the most useful recipes for, though not, 'chic,' it tells what to do with the turkey after the holiday, and how to extract the most value from it. Take the remnants, or, if they have been consumed, take the various plates on which the turkey or its parts have rested and stew them for two hours in milk of magnesia. Stuff with mothballs."

12 **Turkey with Whiskey Sauce.** "This recipe is for a party of four. Obtain a gallon of whiskey, and allow it to age for several hours. Then serve, allowing one quart for each guest. The next day the turkey should be added, little by little, constantly stirring and basting."

13 **For Weddings or Funerals.** "Obtain a gross of small white boxes such as are used for bride's cake. Cut the turkey into small squares, roast, stuff, kill, boil, bake, and allow to skewer. Now we are ready to begin. Fill each box with a quantity of soup stock and pile in a handy place. As the liquid elapses, the prepared turkey is added until the guests arrive. The boxes delicately tied with white ribbons are then placed in the handbags of the ladies, or in the men's side pockets."

15 ANIMAL HEART RATES

1 **Human:** 60 beats/minute	9 **Canary:** 1,000 bpm
2 **Cat:** 150 bpm	10 **Cow:** 65 bpm
3 **Small dog**: 100 bpm	11 **Pig:** 70 bpm
4 **Large dog:** 75 bpm	12 **Rabbit:** 205 bpm
5 **Hamster:** 450 bpm	13 **Elephant:** 30 bpm
6 **Chicken:** 275 bpm	14 **Giraffe:** 65 bpm
7 **Horse:** 40 bpm	15 **Blue whale:** 20 bpm
8 **Monkey:** 192 bpm	

8 LISTS OF 1

1 ANN HODGES
The One and Only... Person known to get hit by a meteorite

Story: In 1954 Hodges was sitting on her couch when a grapefruit-sized meteorite came through the roof of her Alabama home, ricocheted off a radio, and hit her in the thigh. (Hodges was uninjured other than a meteorite-shaped bruise.)

2 OSCAR HAMMERSTEIN II
The One and Only... Oscar winner named Oscar

Story: The songwriter won Academy Awards for Best Original Song for "The Last Time I Saw Paris" (1941) and "It Might as Well Be Spring" (1945). No other Oscar has won an Oscar.

3 STEPHEN HAWKING
The One and Only... Person to play himself on *Star Trek*

Story: In a 1993 episode of *Star Trek: The Next Generation*, Commander Data plays poker against the holograms of Hawking (playing himself), along with Albert Einstein and Sir Isaac Newton (who weren't playing themselves).

4 TSUTOMU YAMAGUCHI
The One and Only... Official survivor of the atomic bomb attacks on both Hiroshima and Nagasaki

Story: Yamaguchi was in Hiroshima on business when the first bomb was dropped on August 6, 1945. His eardrums were ruptured and his upper body burned, but he went home to Nagasaki on August 7 and returned to work two days later... when the second bomb was dropped. He lived until 2010.

5 ADAM RAINER
The One and Only... Dwarf and a giant

Story: Rainer, from Austria, measured 4 feet, 6.3 inches when he was 18 in 1917, classifying him as a dwarf. A tumor in his pituitary gland caused accelerated growth—by 1930 he was nearly 8 feet tall, classifying him as a giant.

6 JOSEPH BEYRLE
The One and Only... World War II soldier to fight for both the U.S. Army and the Soviet army

Story: Beyrle, a demolitions expert, parachuted into Normandy on D-Day and was captured by the Germans. He spent time in seven Nazi prison camps before escaping to the nearest allies—the Soviets. Despite speaking only two words of Russian ("American comrade"), Beyrle showed his demolitions skills to a Soviet tank brigade. They let him fight beside them for three weeks until he was wounded. He later received medals from both countries.

7 SAM HOUSTON
The One and Only... Governor two U.S. states

Story: Houston was the governor of Tennessee, but a failing marriage and rumors of alcoholism forced him to flee the state in 1829. After leading the attack against Mexican forces that secured Texas for the U.S., he was elected governor of Texas in 1836. The city of Houston was later named in his honor.

8 BOBBY KEYS
The One and Only... Musician who played with Elvis Presley, the Rolling Stones, and all four solo Beatles

Story: Keys, a session musician, played saxophone on hundreds of songs from 1956 to 2014—including several for the Rolling Stones and all four former Beatles. And he played sax on the 1962 Elvis hit "Return to Sender."

9 WITTY RETORTS

1 DISS-INVITED. In the 1940s, British playwright George Bernard Shaw sent a backhanded invitation to Prime Minister Winston Churchill: "I am enclosing two tickets to the first night of my new play. Bring a friend...if you have one."

Churchill's response: "Cannot possibly attend the first night. Will attend second...if there is one."

2 FATHER KNOWS BEST? "Caroline's very bright," said Joseph Kennedy to his son, President John Kennedy, as they both watched JFK's young daughter playing on the White House lawn. Then Joseph added, "Smarter than you were at that age."

"Yes, she is," responded the president, "but look who she has as a father."

3 PUT THAT THING AWAY! According to Hollywood legend, silent film star John Barrymore was drinking in a bar one night when he accidentally walked into the ladies' room and started peeing in the toilet. A woman walked in and scolded him: "How dare you! This is for ladies!"

Without zipping up, Barrymore turned around and said, "And so, madame, is this!"

4 VERBAL KRYPTONITE. During the height of his fame in the 1970s, heavyweight boxing champ Muhammad Ali was on an airplane when a flight attendant told him to fasten his seat belt. Ali declared, "Superman don't need no seat belt!"

The sassy stewardess shot back, "Superman don't need no airplane, either."

The "A113" in Pixar films refers to the animators' college classroom number.

5 NO LOVE LOST. In 2010 British singer Lily Allen tweeted an "unflattering" photo of Hole frontwoman Courtney Love, who responded with a barely coherent Twitter rampage: "oh @ lilyroseallen tweeted that pic? thats just baby brat nonsense we are NOT having a 'FUED' WOULDNT DEIGN TO post a pic of her thighs." Love wasn't done: "I reserve my bile (dont worry shell slag me off cos we got into a BIG fight) for someone who NOONE i know likes calls herself relevant."

Allen's reply: "I would never fight with her, as a rule I don't pick on crazy old ladies."

6 PUNCH-LINED. Maligned comedian Dane Cook (notorious for stealing jokes) tweeted: "I just got in a fight with myself over something I have no business being involved in."

Fellow stand-up Eli Braden replied, "Comedy?"

7 SILENCED. Welsh poet Lewis Morris was upset that literary critics weren't reviewing his book of poetry. According to one account (they vary), Morris was complaining to fellow poet Oscar Wilde, "It is a conspiracy of silence against me, I tell you. A conspiracy of silence! What should I do, Oscar?"

"Join it."

8 DAMN THE TORPEDOES! American humorist Robert Benchley (whose son Peter wrote the book *Jaws*) was walking out of a fancy hotel lobby one day when he passed a man in uniform. "My good man," said Benchley, "would you please get me a taxi?" To which the man angrily replied, "I am *not* a doorman. I happen to be a rear admiral in the United States Navy!"

"All right then," said Benchley, "get me a battleship."

9 REAR VIEWS. During a radio interview, rail-thin socialite Paris Hilton dissed full-figured socialite Kim Kardashian: "Kim's butt reminds me of cottage cheese inside a big trash bag."

Kardashian's response: "At least I have a butt."

3 KINDS OF ROCKS

1 IGNEOUS ROCKS

From the same root as "ignite," *igneous* means "born of fire." Products of cooled magma (molten rock), there are more than 700 types of igneous rocks in two main groups: those that are made deep within the earth, and those made at the surface. Intrusive igneous rock forms at depths from 20 to 1,800 miles underground. They harden very slowly—over thousands or even millions of years—under immense pressure. Intrusive rocks are therefore very dense and include granite and basalt.

Extrusive igneous rocks are made at the surface from lava, which is magma that reaches the surface via volcanic activity. Lava cools relatively quickly and under little pressure, so extrusive rocks have a different makeup than those made deep underground. Examples include obsidian (a naturally made glass) and pumice, which is known for being very light—it contains air bubbles that were trapped while cooling. Pumice is so light that it actually floats on water.

2 SEDIMENTARY ROCK

Sedimentary rock is found only at the surface to a depth of several miles. As the name implies, it is made up of sediment that has been compacted into rock. It comes in three main categories based on the cause of sedimentation: Chemical sedimentary rock is formed by chemical precipitation or evaporation, such as when water evaporates from a lake and leaves behind gypsum beds; clastic sedimentary rock is formed when weathering and erosion break down large rocks into fragments, which then adhere and harden back into rock; and organic sedimentary rock forms from material left behind by living things. Limestone and chalk, for example, are made from the remains of shellfish, and coal is made from biodegraded plant material.

When several types of sedimentary rocks are tumbled in rivers and streams, they become rounded *clasts* and are fused together in a sandstone cement. These formations are called *conglomerates*. That's why it was such a big deal in 2012 when NASA's Curiosity rover found conglomerates on Mars; the discovery provided crucial evidence that water-filled streams and rivers once flowed freely on the red planet.

3 METAMORPHIC ROCK

This consists of any type of rock—including older metamorphic, igneous, or sedimentary—that has been physically and chemically changed by environmental forces, usually by the heat and/or pressure that came from being buried. For example, if limestone is subjected to high enough pressure and temperature, it becomes marble.

X XXX'S

1 **XXX:** the number 30 in Roman numerals

2 **XXX:** short for "XXXL," signifying plus-sized clothing

3 **XXX:** identifies explicit pornography

4 **XXX:** a "turkey," or three consecutive strikes in bowling

5 **XXX:** generic name for homemade "moonshine" whiskey

6 **XXX:** "Triple-X syndrome," characterized by the presence of an extra X chromosome in human females

7 **XXX:** 1999 album by ZZ Top

8 **XXX:** Filipino investigative TV show (*XXX: Exklusibong, Explosibong, Exposé*)

9 **XXX:** used to signify the official flag of Amsterdam (which has three X's on it)

10 **XXX:** "kisses" on a letter or in an e-mail

15 TOP TIPPING TIPS

1 COAT-CHECK. $1 to $3 per coat

2 HAIRSTYLIST. 20 percent (but at least 10 percent)

3 MANICURIST/MASSAGE THERAPIST. 15 to 20 percent

4 PORTER. At airport/train/bus station: $2 per bag

5 BUS DRIVER. $2 per bag

6 DRIVER. For a cab driver, limo driver, or any car service, tip 15 percent

7 TOUR GUIDE. $10 to $20 for an hours-long or all-day tour; $20 per day for more than one day

8 TRAIN ATTENDANT. $5 if they help with your bags

9 HOTEL PORTER. $1 per bag, $2 minimum

10 PARKING VALET. $2 to $5 when they bring your car

11 ROOM SERVICE. 20 percent (unless a gratuity is included in the bill)

12 BARTENDER. 15 to 20 percent

13 FOOD DELIVERY. 10 percent (more if it's lousy weather)

14 WAITER. 10 percent for lousy service, 15 to 20 percent for good service, more for great service

15 TAKEOUT. You don't have to tip! But if your food is ready and waiting when you pick it up, throw them a buck or two.

Element **117** has no official name yet. (It's unofficially called ununseptium.)

13 MEDICAL PREFIXES AND SUFFIXES DEFINED

1 **path-:** "disease"
Patho originally meant "suffering" in ancient Greek, which also gives us *pathetic* and *pathos*.

2 **-algia:** "pain"
Myalgia comes from the Greek for "muscle pain." (Another is *nostalgia*, "pain of returning home.")

3 **-emia:** "in the blood"
Leukemia is a cancer of the white blood cells. (*Leukós* is Greek for "white.")

4 **an-:** "without"
Anemia means there is insufficient blood in the body.

5 **brachy-:** "short"
People with brachydactyly have abnormally short fingers and toes.

6 **-crine:** "to secrete"
The endocrine gland secretes hormones.

7 **endo-:** "inside"
Endocrine glands secrete inside the body; exocrine glands, like sweat glands, secrete out of the body.

8 **hema/hemo-:** "blood"
A hematoma is a bruise filled with blood.

9 **-oma:** "tumor/swelling"
As in melanoma (skin tumor) and carcinoma (cancerous tumor).

10 **myo-:** "muscle"
Myopathy is any disease of the muscle tissue.

11 **xanth-:** "yellow"
Xanthoma is a fat-cell tumor that causes yellow nodules in the skin.

12 **-rrhage:** "burst forth"
A hemorrhage occurs when blood bursts forth.

13 **-rrhea:** "flow, discharge"
Diarrhea and gonorrhea occur when...other things burst forth.

5 GIFTS RICH MEN GAVE THEIR MISTRESSES

1 A CASTLE. In the 1500s, King Henry II of France was unhappily married to Queen Catherine de Médici. How unhappy? He gave his mistress, Diane de Poitiers, the castle of Chenonceau—even though it technically belonged to the crown. Diane made herself at home and added lush gardens and a bridge. She lived happily...until Henry died. Then Catherine forced Diane out and took the castle for herself. Today, Chenonceau is the second most visited castle in France, after Versailles.

2 A FILM CAREER. Actress Marion Davies was working on Broadway in 1917 when married newspaper baron William Randolph Hearst took a liking to her. His plan: turn her into a movie star. Hearst bankrolled a production company for Marion alone and made deals with MGM to premiere her films. By the end of her career, Marion had made 46 movies. She returned Hearst's generosity in the 1930s with a gift of $1 million, which saved his company from bankruptcy.

3 A QUEEN'S FUNERAL. Gabrielle d'Estrées considered herself the queen of France in the 1590s, despite the fact that King Henry IV was married to Queen Margaret. Gabrielle convinced Henry to convert to Catholicism, hoping that the pope would annul his marriage to Margaret. But before that could happen, Gabrielle died. Although she wasn't royalty, Henry gave Gabrielle "the funeral of a princess of the blood," with four days of lying in state, followed by a six-mile funeral procession.

4 A CASH PRIZE. In 1779 George, Prince of Wales, became so infatuated with actress Mary Robinson that he promised her £20,000 if she would become his mistress—that's over

$1 million in today's money. (By comparison, in 1790 only 400 people in all of England earned an average of £10,000 per year.) But George moved on to another mistress and never paid Mary, so she threatened to publish his love letters, including the one where he promised her the money. She accepted £5,000 to keep quiet.

5 **A FANCY TITLE.** Lola Montez presented herself as a "Spanish dancer" even though she was born Marie Gilbert in Ireland. But King Ludwig I of Bavaria didn't care. Her saw Montez perform in Munich in 1846 and was smitten. According to legend, he did not believe her "ample bosom" was real and accused her of padding it. So Montez tore off her dress to prove the king wrong. Impressed, he took her back to his castle and dubbed her "the Countess of Lansfeld and Baroness Rosenthal." Along with the title, Montez got her own castle and an income equivalent to $25,000 in today's money. But Ludwig's subjects did not approve of the king's extramarital affair and revolted. In 1848 he was forced to abdicate the throne, and Montez was stripped of her title and fled to England. She lived out her later days in the U.S. as an author, lecturer, and advocate for human rights.

8 BEASTLY BANDS THAT CAN'T SPELL

1 The Byrds

2 The Beatles

3 The Monkees

4 Gorillaz

5 Phish

6 Ratt

7 The Black Crowes

8 Def Leppard

9 WITCHY LISTS: WHICH WITCH IS WHICH?

6 BOOK-TO-MOVIE WITCHES

1 **Hermione Granger** (*Harry Potter and the Sorcerer's Stone*, J. K. Rowling)
2 **Glinda the Good Witch** (*The Wizard of Oz*, L. Frank Baum)
3 **The Wicked Witch of the West** (*The Wizard of Oz*)
4 **The Grand High Witch** (*Witches*, Roald Dahl)
5 **Alexandra, Jane, Suki** (*The Witches of Eastwick*, John Updike)
6 **The White Witch** (*The Lion, the Witch, and the Wardrobe*, C. S. Lewis)

6 TV WITCHES

1 **Samantha** (*Bewitched*)
2 **Endora** (*Bewitched*)
3 **Sabrina** (*Sabrina the Teenage Witch*)
4 **Willow** (*Buffy the Vampire Slayer*)
5 **Fiona** (*American Horror Story: Coven*)
6 **Hazel** (*Looney Toons*)

7 CLASSICAL WITCHES

1 **The Witch of Endor** (*The Old Testament*)
2 **Circe** (*The Odyssey*)
3 **Weird Sisters** (*Macbeth*)
4 **Tituba** (*The Crucible*)
5 **Baba Yaga** (Russian folklore)
6 **Hecate** (Greek mythology)
7 **Morgan Le Fay** (Arthurian legend)

6 WITCHES IN PICTURE BOOKS

1 **Meg** (*Meg & Mog*, Helen Nicoll)
2 **Dorrie** (*Dorrie and the Blue Witch*, Patricia Coombs)
3 **Gromelda** (*The Witch Has an Itch*, Donna Guthrie)
4 **Wendy** (*The Witch Who Was Afraid of Witches*, Alice Low)
5 **Winnie** (*Winnie the Witch*, Valerie Thomas)
6 **Miss Thornapple** (*Which Way to Witch School*, Scott Santoro)

6 DISNEY WITCHES

1 **Maleficent**
(*Sleeping Beauty*)
2 **Madame Mim** (*The Sword in the Stone*)
3 **Ursula** (*The Little Mermaid*)
4 **The Queen** (*Snow White*)
5 **Queen Narissa** (*Enchanted*)
6 **The Witch** (*Brave*)

5 ROCK SONGS ABOUT WITCHES

1 **"Rhiannon"**
(Fleetwood Mac)
2 **"Witchy Woman"**
(Eagles)
3 **"Season of the Witch"**
(Donovan)
4 **"The Witch's Promise"**
(Jethro Tull)
5 **"Black Magic Woman"**
(Santana)

1st WOMAN HANGED AS A WITCH IN THE NEW WORLD

1 **Alse Young** (Windsor, Connecticut, 1647)

8 LAST WOMEN HANGED AS WITCHES IN THE NEW WORLD

1 Martha Cory
2 Margaret Scott
3 Mary Easty
4 Alice Parker
5 Ann Pudeator
6 Willmott Redd
7 Samuel Wardwel
8 Mary Parker
(Salem, Massachusetts, 1692)

21 WITCHES' BREW INGREDIENTS (According to Shakespeare)

1 Fenny snake's fillet
2 Newt's eye
3 Frog's toe
4 Bat's wool
5 Adder's fork
6 Blind-worm's sting
7 Lizard's leg
8 Owlet's wing
9 Dragon's scale
10 Wolf's tooth
11 Witches' mummified flesh
12 Salt-sea shark's gullet and stomach
13 Hemlock root
14 Blaspheming Jew's liver
15 Goat's gall
16 Baboon's blood
17 Turk's nose
18 Tartar's lips
19 Birth-strangled baby's finger
20 Tiger's entrails
21 Yew

4 CRIMES INSPIRED BY VIDEO GAMES

1 **MARRIED TO THE MOB.** A law clerk named Bettysue Higgins was hooked on the Facebook games *Mafia Wars* and *YoVille*, but the in-game purchases kept piling up. So between 2006 and 2010, she embezzled $166,000 from her job at the Maine Trial Lawyers Association. Her jig was up when the bank told the firm's director that a check he'd "written" for $5,500 had bounced. Higgins was sentenced to three years in prison.

2 **LET'S PLAY REAL-LIFE *GTA*!** In 2008 six teenage boys on Long Island, New York, "decided they were going to commit robberies and emulate lead character Nico Belic in the violent video game *Grand Theft Auto*," said detective Raymond Cote. The teens beat and robbed a man, and tried to carjack a BMW and a van before the cops caught and arrested them.

3 **MORE *GTA* MADNESS.** In 2013 Auburn University student Zachary Burgess jumped into a parked truck with the engine running and drove off. One problem: There was a woman in the passenger seat. Burgess ignored her pleas to stop and played demolition derby in the parking lot. He was caught and charged with grand theft, kidnapping, and nine counts of hit-and-run. His excuse: "I wanted to play real-life *Grand Theft Auto*."

4 **TRAILER OF WARCRAFT.** Between 2010 and 2013, Lester Louis Huffmire and his wife Petra of Anaheim, California, kept their two young daughters locked inside their "filthy mobile home" while the crazed couple played *World of Warcraft* all day, every day. When police finally rescued the girls, they were "dirty, malnourished, and had rotten teeth." The Huffmires lost their girls and went to prison.

4 TYPES OF IRONY

1 DRAMATIC IRONY. This is a storytelling device in which the audience knows something that the characters do not.
Example: In 1997's *Con Air*, Steve Buscemi plays a serial killer who has tea with a little girl. Viewers have been informed that he once "wore a girl's head as a hat through three states," thus dramatically increasing the tension. (Buscemi lets her live.)

2 VERBAL IRONY. What you say has a different meaning than what you mean. The most biting type: sarcasm.
Example: Bart Simpson remarks that a rare drawing of Itchy is valuable. Comic Book Guy says, "Ooh, your powers of deduction are exceptional. I can't allow you to waste them here when there are so many crimes going unsolved at this very moment!"

3 COSMIC IRONY. When it almost seems as if a higher power is having a laugh at humanity's expense.
Example: In 2014 a tree planted to honor deceased former Beatle George Harrison died from an infestation of...beetles.

4 SITUATIONAL IRONY. An intended action has the opposite effect, creating an outcome contrary to what was expected.
Example: While studying the effects of climate change on a fragile underwater coral reef, the Greenpeace ship *Rainbow Warrior II* ran into the reef and caused it significant damage.

***Bonus term:* "Hipster irony."** When a bearded 20-something wearing a fedora and skinny jeans listens to Bon Iver on an iPhone hooked up to an old Victrola record player, he's ironic because he thinks he's cool, but everyone else knows better.

11 FAMOUS FARTERS

1 QUEEN VICTORIA

The queen who ruled England from 1837 to 1901 became a gassy windbag in her later years. (One reason may have been that she ate her food really fast while drinking whiskey.) But Victoria, being a queen and all, was squeamish about her squeaking: In 1897 she had an Australian journalist named John Norton tried for libel after he wrote the she was "fat, flabby, and flatulent." (Victoria lost the lawsuit.)

2 SIR HENRY LUDLOW

In 1607, during a heated debate in Parliament over Scottish naturalization, the English politician farted so loudly that it reverberated throughout the chambers. So legendary was Ludlow's fart that it inspired history's most famous (and maybe only) poem about a gassy public servant. Written over the next few years by several politicians (no one man took credit), the tongue-in-cheeky poem is called "The Censure of the Parliament Fart." An excerpt: "The Motion was good; but for the stincking / Well quoth Sir Henry Poole, 'It was a bold tricke / To Fart in the nose of the bodie politique.'"

3 WHOOPI GOLDBERG

In the 1980s, a young comedian named Caryn Johnson had such a bad farting habit that her friends said she sounded like a whoopee cushion. That's how Whoopi Goldberg got her stage name. And she's still at it: During a 2014 interview with the singer Ashanti on *The View*, Goldberg let out a massive fart that sent the other women at the table scrambling for safety. "I feel so much better now!" exclaimed Goldberg.

4 KATY PERRY

"I'm a little gassy. I don't care," admits the proud fartress—who regularly farts on stage, in interviews, and especially at home. Her ex-husband, comedian Russell Brand, once described her as a "flatulence factory," explaining, "The pop hits that she fires out of her mouth are nothing compared to what comes out the other end." Perry's defense: At least her farts aren't toxic: "Russell sleeps on the couch all the time because he lights up the sheets with his stanky arse." The couple divorced soon after.

5 BRITNEY SPEARS

Speaking of toxic, in 2010 Spears was hit with a harassment lawsuit filed by her bodyguard, Fernando Flores. The former cop accused the pop princess of parading around her house naked and routinely "beckoning him into her bedroom." Flores always declined, he said, noting that Spears was "unkempt" and "one big farting machine." Flores's lawyer added, "My client has seen cops overcome with the smell from flatulence, and he felt that he was assaulted every day by Spears and her farts." Spears's defense: She has a "potentially deadly" (for whom?) condition called *flatulencia explotatta*. "She can't help it," said the "Toxic" singer's lawyer. "She's been to the best doctors in the world. It's a disease." (Shortly after the bad press leaked, Spears settled out of court for an undisclosed sum.)

6 WOLFGANG AMADEUS MOZART

Mozart was a dirty, dirty man who appreciated farts so much that he wrote poems about the best ones he encountered. The composer composed this masterpiece in a letter to his mother: "Yesterday, though, we heard the king of farts / It smelled as sweet as honey tarts / While it wasn't in the strongest of voice / It still came on as a powerful noise."

Bonus fact: The Urban Dictionary describes a "Mozart fart" thusly: "To cut the cheese in a particularly tuneful way."

7 MARTIN LUTHER

You may know that in 1517 Luther's "95 Theses" instigated the Protestant Reformation. But did you know that the German friar was fond of using farts to make his points? He once called the head of the Roman Catholic Church "Pope Fart-ass." His go-to weapon for fighting the devil: "It is with a fart that I chase him away." And our favorite Martin Luther quote: "A happy fart never comes from a miserable ass."

8 NANCY GRACE

A foul controversy wafted over *Dancing with the Stars* in 2010 after a loud fart that sounded like someone zipping up a winter coat interrupted contestant Nancy Grace's interview with Brooke Burke. (Fittingly, Grace had just danced a waltz to "Moon River.") Grace, a bombastic former prosecutor who acts as both judge and jury on television, denied that she farted. But the video footage reveals that, just as the fart was being released, Grace closed her eyes and placed her hand on her stomach. Then her dancing partner Tristan McManus looked away awkwardly. A few days later, after denying the fart had even happened, Grace finally verified its existence...but laid the blame solely on the Dublin-born McManus, claiming that the fart "had an Irish accent."

Update: Grace never did cop to the toot, but a fetish website called "Fart Fanatics" attempted to license the farting footage from ABC, to no avail.

9 LARRY KING

Apparently, CNN's "King of Talk" used more than his mouth to communicate. Several of King's interviewees claimed that his butt often butted in. Rumor had it that King kept a fan underneath his desk that blew his emissions in the opposite direction of his guests. According to an anonymous source who sat next to King at a banquet: "He leaned left and beefed right...directly on me. He didn't even say, 'Excuse me.'"

10 GEORGE W. BUSH

Another alleged leaner is the 43rd president of the United States. Five years after Bush left office, video footage shows him sitting next to fellow former president Bill Clinton at the 2014 NCAA basketball finals. At one point, Bush shifts in his seat and appears to hold one buttock slightly higher than the other...and then smiles as he launches an unprovoked fart attack at Clinton, who doesn't seem to notice. (One of Bush's favorite gags while serving in the White House: secretly placing a "remote control whoopee cushion" in Deputy Chief of Staff Carl Rove's chair.)

11 LE PETOMANE

History's most famous farter was Frenchman Joseph Pujol (pronounced "pu-zhol" and not "poo-hole"). When he was a teenager in the late 1800s, he was taking a swim and inhaled a deep breath before submerging...and inadvertently sucked a bunch of water up his anus. When he exhaled, the water squirted back out. Pujol soon realized that he could do the same trick with air, and with a few precise twitches of his gluteal muscles, he could make musical notes. His destiny was set: When Pujol grew up, he became known as Le Petomane ("The Fartiste"), one of the most popular entertainers in Paris. Packed rectal halls—err, recital halls—would applaud wildly as the "elastic anus" farted out hit after hit, in perfect pitch. He could even imitate animal noises, thunder, and cannons. No audio recordings of Le Petomane's performances exist, and no farter since has been able to match his talent.

---

8 ALLITERATIVE NICKNAMES FOR A MUSTACHE

1 Grass grin	5 Bristle batons
2 Nose neighbor	6 Mouth mirken
3 Face furniture	7 Soup strainer
4 Lip luggage	8 Snot mop

---

20 OLD-TIMEY AMERICAN SONG TITLES

1 "I Never Knew I Had a Wonderful Wife Until the Town Went Dry" (1919)

2 "If He Can Fight Like He Can Love, Good Night Germany!" (1918)

3 "Old Abe Has Gone and Did It, Boys" (1862)

4 "When I Go Automobiling" (1907)

5 "Women's Rights: A Right Good Ballad Illustrating Women's Rights" (1853)

6 "The Band Played 'Nearer My God to Thee' as the Ship Went Down (In Memory of the Heroes of the Ill-fated *Titanic*)" (1912)

7 "Secession Quick Step" (1860s)

8 "I Think We've Got Another Washington, and Wilson Is His Name" (1915)

9 "The Ocean Telegraph March" (1858)

10 "Shiloh Victory Polka" (1862)

11 "Just Like Washington Crossed the Delaware, General Pershing Will Cross the Rhine" (1918)

12 "Pickett's Charge March" (1863)

13 "What'll We Do on a Saturday Night (When the Town Goes Dry)?" (1919)

14 "We'll Put Garfield in the Chair" (1880)

15 "Stonewall Jackson's Way!" (1862)

16 "Roosevelt, the Peace Victor" (1905)

17 "Out of the Flames! An Incident of the Late Chicago Fire" (1872)

18 "McKinley, Our Hero, Now at Rest" (1901)

19 "Rest, Noble Chieftain: Song on the Death of President Lincoln" (1865)

20 "Washington Artillery Polka" (1860)

5 CONCEPTS YOU'VE NEVER HEARD OF, NAMED FOR PEOPLE YOU'VE NEVER HEARD OF...

...that will change the way you view the world.

1 DUNBAR'S NUMBER

Do you have 1,000 Facebook friends? If so, Dunbar's Number says you're fooling yourself. Robin Dunbar is an evolutionary anthropologist and an expert on social networks. In 1992 his research revealed that we can only maintain meaningful relationships with about 150 people at a time. Our brains just aren't big enough to handle more true connections than that. So what about your thousands of Facebook friends? Sorry, but Dunbar is sticking with his number; the rest are casual acquaintances.

2 DUNNING-KRUGER EFFECT

Ever notice how some people who are terrible at something often have no clue how terrible they are (like most politicians)? That's the Dunning-Kruger Effect at work. In 1999 psychology professors Dr. David Dunning and Dr. Robert Kruger discovered that people who are lousy at tasks tend to think they do really well, while people who perform well underrate their performance. Why? Because if you're lousy at something, you don't really have the skills to evaluate how lousy you are, and if you're good enough to understand the task, you tend to be more critical. The good news: With constructive feedback, you can overcome the Dunning-Kruger Effect and learn to be realistic about your performance.

3 BAYES' THEOREM

Thomas Bayes studied probability—how likely it is that something will happen—in 18th-century England. His theorem calculates *conditional probability*. Probability in a coin toss means you have a 50/50 chance to get heads or tails. Conditional probability means that you have a 50/50 chance as long as your cheating brother-in-law didn't replace it with a fake two-headed coin. Another example: You know that if you buy zero lottery tickets, you have zero chance of winning. The more you buy, the more the odds increase, so your chance of winning is conditional on how many tickets you have. Whether or not you do the math of Bayes' Theorem, you use it in spirit every time you consider the likelihood of something happening given a set of circumstances.

4 THE OVERTON WINDOW

Joseph P. Overton was the vice president of the Mackinac Center for Public Policy. His claim to fame: the "Overton Window of Political Possibilities." Conceived in the mid-1990s, it states that at any given time, there's a narrow range for what the public considers politically acceptable. For example, in 1920 anti-alcohol groups were very popular in the U.S., so the idea of making the sale of alcohol illegal was "inside the Overton Window," and Prohibition was passed. Today, alcohol is deeply entrenched in our culture, so attempting to outlaw it is currently "outside the Overton Window."

5 THE MAILLARD REACTION

Why is toast so much tastier than bread? In 1912 French chemist Louis-Camille Maillard noted that a chemical reaction occurs between sugars and amino acids when certain foods are browned by heating. The process creates a complex mixture of toasty flavors consisting of hundreds of compounds that change into other flavors as they break down in your mouth. So your enjoyment of seared meat, dark roast coffee, and toasted marshmallows comes from the Maillard Reaction.

Iodine-131 is a radioactive isotope used to treat thyroid disorders.

13 GREAT PRODUCTS BROUGHT TO YOU BY THE CINCO FAMILY CORPORATION

Check out these great ways to enrich your life from Cinco!*

(*Disclaimer: Uncle John claims no responsibility for any bodily harm or embarrassment you may incur after using Cinco products. They have not been safety-tested—as they are purely fictional creations advertised on the late-night Adult Swim program Tim and Eric Awesome Show, Great Job! (2007–10) starring comedians Tim Heidecker and Eric Wareheim. Originally conceived by Bob "Better Call Saul" Odenkirk, the Cinco family of products is for entertainment purposes only, and some of them are really, really disgusting. Seriously, if gross things gross you out, may we suggest a list of the 20 most pleasing aromas on page 248.)

1 MY NEW PEP-PEP. From the Cinco Chemicals and Toy Division, this life-sized grandfather doll stares into the nothingness through empty plastic unblinking eyes and makes a great playmate for kids! His best feature: He smells like a real grandpa! "Just load the flavor packs into the rear of My New Pep-Pep and wait for the scent!" He also dispenses hard candy from a hole in his wrist.

2 THOCKS. "Combines the sexual allure of a woman's thong with the comfort and reliability of the gentleman business sock."

3 SLEEPWATCHING CHAIR. Endorsed by Michael "the dad from Family Ties" Gross, just place the Sleepwatching Chair in your good friend's room, have a seat, bid him good night, and then settle in for an all-night show. The chair comes standard with a zoom-lens "so you don't miss a single detail of the action." Also included: a toilet hole and an electroshock system that will give you a painful jolt if you start to fall asleep yourself. Also includes a Dreamer's Book, "perfect for recording what you think your friend is dreaming about."

4 MANCIERGE. A mobile phone that only dials Fred Willard.

5 MY EGGS. Are your breakfast bills piling up? Try this fun new product from Cinco Dairy! One pill contains real chicken embryos that incubate in your intestinal tract. Just take a pill, and three days later you'll be ready to lay a dozen tasty eggs. My Eggs comes with a paper shredder that you can use to turn its box into "straw for your toilet nest." (Warning: Egg yolks will be neon-colored.)

6 CANDY TAILS. "Now sucking on your hair is sweeter than ever!" Genuine horse-tail hair-braid extensions come with three liquid flavor pouches—"Caramel, Strawed-berry, and Chocolate"—along with a small plastic trough for dipping. After soaking the Candy Tails in the flavor juice for a few minutes, just attach to your head and then you're ready to suck. "You can barely taste the horse!"

7 CIGARETTE JUICE. When you can't smoke—or you don't even smoke but want a pick-me-up—just pop open this high-powered energy drink made from pulverized tar and nicotine.

8 T'IRD. If playtime is cutting into your work time, try T'ird. Instead of throwing your "flight wheel" back and forth all day—and getting nothing accomplished—you can harness the power of T'ird, which utilizes "the feathers of a bird and the crawling of a turtle" so you only need to throw T'ird once, and then it flies for up to half a mile before landing (that's the bird part). Then four small legs pop out (that's the turtle part), and "While T'ird sluggishly returns to your house, you can spend your day paying bills, register yourself online, plan tomorrow's work, sort some coins, repay old bills, call your brother, stare, moisten your fence wood, reposition your doorknob, dig a hole to bury a box, and T'ird is still crawling!"

9 PASTA BEAR. A teddy bear stuffed with pasta.

10 WAIT-MATE. This wonder drug is endorsed by Jeff "the nerd from *Independence Day* and *Jurassic Park*" Goldblum, who says in his signature style, "Let's say you have to attend a Lifetime Achievement Award show on Friday, but it's only Tuesday, and you just...can't...wait. Well, just take your Wait-mate, and you're off to a deep, deep sleep [two pills = two days], and when you wake up, ahh, you're there! And you haven't had to wait!"

11 CINCO NAPPLE. Another sleep aid, this one is endorsed by "Dr." Alan "the dad from *Growing Pains*" Thicke. He explains that short periods of sleep every day—i.e., "naps"—can help reduce illness, and this breakthrough fruit will make you fall fast asleep and then wake you up again in 15 minutes. How? "First, the apples are injected with a mild bowel irritant, then the apples are dipped in a sleeping gel and set in the sun to dry." After you take a few bites, you become unconscious until the active ingredient starts to irritate your bowels, waking you right back up. Thicke recommends that, to avoid any unnecessary messiness, make sure you're wearing your D-Pants. D-Pants? What are those?

12 D-PANTS. Invented by a doddering British man named Diah Riha-Jones, D-Pants are "protective plastic pants you wear underneath your trousers to capture and contain uncontrollable diarrhea." Careful, though, because although the "diarrhea almost never runs away beneath the tight elastic around the ankles," it sometimes does. But all you need to do is hose off your messy D-Pants in the backyard and you're good to go again. (Not made for "solid loafs.")

13 IT'S NOT JACKIE CHAN! This fun board game challenges players to name people, places, and things that are not action superstar Jackie Chan. If you accidentally answer "Jackie Chan" to any of the trivia questions, another player must press a really annoying buzzer for a really long time.

---

20 COLLECTIVE NOUNS

From the Book of St. Albans *(1486), purportedly written by Dame Juliana Barnes, the prioress of the Sopwell nunnery. This list comes from a section of the book entitled "Compaynys of Beestys and Fowlys." There are no explanations as to how Barnes came up with these names, but they're so fun we thought they needed reviving.*

1 A rascal of boys
2 A state of princes
3 A melody of harpers
4 A rage of maidens
5 A fighting of beggars
6 An execution of officers
7 A discretion of priests
8 A glorifying of liars
9 A blast of hunters
10 A worship of writers
11 An eloquence of lawyers
12 A holiness of nuns
13 A hastiness of cooks
14 A doctrine of doctors
15 A rout of knights
16 A gaggle of women
17 A lying of pardoners
18 A drunkenness of cobblers
19 A charge of curates
20 An abominable sight of monks

Amphicoelias fragillimus, the heaviest known dinosaur, weighed **135** tons.

11 RANDOM "TYPES OF" LISTS

10 LESSER-KNOWN TYPES OF MARRIAGE

1 **Adelphogamy:** marriage between siblings

2 **Coenogamy:** a group marriage between at least two men and at least two women

3 **Deuterogamy:** a second marriage after a spouse dies

4 **Digamy:** a second marriage after a divorce

5 **Hypergamy:** marriage into a higher social group

6 **Matrilocal:** a married couple living close to the wife's parents

7 **Patrilocal:** a married couple living close to the husband's parents

8 **Morganatic:** a marriage between a spouse of high social rank and one of low rank in which the lower-ranking spouse and offspring bear no claim to rank or property

9 **Opsigamy:** a marriage that occurs late in life

10 **Trigamy:** having three spouses at the same time

6 SPECIAL TYPES OF CLOUDS

1 **Mammatus:** low bulges that hang from thunderclouds

2 **Lenticular:** flying saucers, caused by mountain winds

3 **Fractus:** cotton candy–like fragments that break off from larger clouds

4 **Fog:** a cloud on the ground

5 **Green clouds:** found in hail and tornado-producing storms; no one knows why they're green

6 RIVER CLASSES

For canoers, rafters, and kayakers.

1 **Class I:** smooth waters with few or no obstructions

2 **Class II:** some easy rapids, maneuvering required

3 **Class III:** rapids, complex maneuvering required

4 **Class IV:** turbulent, scouting from shore required

5 **Class V:** violent, Eskimo roll required

6 **Class VI:** Stay out of the water, seriously.

5 TYPES OF ENGLISH SURNAMES

1 **Places:** Hamilton, Burton, London
2 **Professions:** Carpenter, Taylor, Weaver
3 **Descriptions:** Little, Swift, Long
4 **Geographical Features:** Brooks, Bush, Hill
5 **'Son of':** Benson, Thompson, Richardson

6 TYPES OF HANDS

According to palm readers.

1 **Elementary:** stupidity
2 **Square:** orderliness
3 **Conical:** inspirational
4 **Spatulate:** energetic
5 **Pointed:** idealistic
6 **Mixed:** adaptable

6 TYPES OF HAND GRENADES

1 **Fragmentation:** explodes into high-velocity fragments
2 **Illuminating:** used to provide light over terrain
3 **Chemical:** for light, signals, crowd control, or fire starts
4 **Offensive:** for blast effect
5 **Training:** to teach how to safely handle and throw
6 **Nonlethal:** used for diversionary purposes

7 TYPES OF POO

According to English gastroenterologist Dr. Ken Heaton's "Bristol Stool Scale" (1990s).

1 **Type 1:** separate hard lumps, like nuts (hard to pass)
2 **Type 2:** sausage-shaped, but lumpy
3 **Type 3:** like a sausage but with cracks on its surface
4 **Type 4:** like a sausage or snake, smooth and soft
5 **Type 5:** soft blobs with clear-cut edges (passed easily)
6 **Type 6:** fluffy pieces with ragged edges, a mushy stool
7 **Type 7:** watery, no solid pieces; entirely liquid

10 TYPES OF GERMAN SAUSAGE

1 **Knockwurst:** finely ground pork and beef with garlic
2 **Bratwurst:** finely ground pork and beef
3 **Weisswurst:** veal with a little pork
4 **Bockwurst:** ground veal and pork, cream and eggs
5 **Landjäger:** pork and beef mixture, dried like salami
6 **Leberwurst:** pork and pork liver (liverwurst)
7 **Wollwurst:** veal and pork, no casing

8 **Cervelat:** beef, bacon, and pork rinds (originally made with pork brains)

9 **Frankfurter:** ground pork and beef (the basis for the American hot dog)

10 **Blutwurst:** congealed pig's blood and pork

5 TYPES OF TWINS

1 **Mirror Image:** Identical twins who have the same characteristics on opposite sides of their bodies (one is right-handed, the other is left-handed; one has a birthmark on the right shoulder, the other on the left shoulder).

2 **Half Identical:** These twins have the same genes from the mother but genes from two different sperm from the father.

3 **Chimerism:** Two separate eggs are fertilized by two separate sperm, fuse into one egg, and then separate into twins.

4 **Superfecundation:** Twins who have the same mother but two different fathers.

5 **Superfetation:** The mother releases more than one egg at different times, sometimes as much as 24 days apart.

4 TYPES OF EAR PIERCINGS

1 **Helix:** a piercing in the upper ear's outer rim

2 **Tragus:** a piercing in the thick cartilage closest to the ear hole on the cheek side

3 **Anti-tragus:** a piercing in the ridge of cartilage across from the tragus

4 **Daith:** a piercing in the inner cartilage closest to the ear hole

9 TYPES OF SNOW

1 **New Snow:** fell recently, the snow's ice crystals can be seen

2 **Firn:** dense snowpack that's older than one year

3 **Névé:** young snow that's been semi-melted, refrozen, and compacted

4 **Old Snow:** snow that's been around so long that the snow crystals can't be seen

5 **Seasonal Snow:** only lasts for one season, then melts

6 **Perennial Snow:** remains on the ground year after year

7 **Powder:** dry, loose new snow—prized by skiers

8 **Snirt:** snow and dirt

9 **Yellow Snow:** Don't eat the yellow snow.

The diameter of the halo on Seattle's Space Needle is 138 feet.

10 CELEB MARRIAGES THAT DIDN'T OUTLAST MILK

A carton of milk lasts, on average, about three weeks...a month if you're brave. So a few of these famous couples might have been able to buy a second carton. Good for them!

1 6 HOURS: Rudolph Valentino and Jean Acker (1919)
These two silent film stars—an Italian heartthrob and an American starlet—married quickly, but Acker realized her mistake just as quickly and locked him out of their honeymoon hotel suite. Permanently.

2 1 DAY: Zsa Zsa Gabor and Felipe De Alba (1983)
It's wise to finalize your divorce before you remarry. Gabor failed to do that, so her marriage to the Mexican lawyer/actor was annulled the day they wed. The pair never remarried.

3 55 HOURS: Britney Spears and Jason Alexander (2004)
Not the Jason Alexander who played George on *Seinfeld*, but Jason Alexander, a childhood friend of Spears. After the ceremony, the pop princess decided that her spur-of-the-moment Vegas wedding to a "friend with benefits" wasn't the best foundation for a marriage and had it annulled. So why did the two get marred in the first place? According to Spears's record label, "They took a joke too far."

4 8 DAYS: Dennis Hopper and Michelle Phillips (1970)
"Seven of those days were pretty good. The eighth day was the bad one," said Hopper years after the split. He and the Mamas and the Papas singer were married on Halloween in 1970 and spent a tumultuous week together. (The rumor mill has it that a pair of handcuffs were involved.)

5 9 DAYS: Cher and Gregg Allman (1975)

The two singers at the height of their fame hopped a plane to Vegas three days after Cher's divorce from Sonny Bono, but Allman's alcohol and heroin addiction was too much for Cher to bear, and she filed for divorce nine days later. "I believe it's best to admit one's mistakes as quickly as possible," she said.

6 9 DAYS: Robert Evans and Catherine Oxenberg (1998)

The famous movie producer wedded the *Dynasty* actress, who was more than 30 years younger than him, but their marriage was quickly annulled. Oxenberg was Evans's fourth wife... out of seven.

7 14 DAYS: Eddie Murphy and Tracey Edmonds (2008)

Having a ceremony in Bora Bora is romantic, but it's also not recognized in the U.S. Two weeks later, the actor and the businesswoman decided to simply "remain friends."

8 16 DAYS: Sinead O'Connor and Barry Herridge (2011)

Another impulsive Vegas wedding, another quick divorce. The Irish singer blamed "certain people" in his life for their breakup.

9 30 DAYS: Drew Barrymore and Jeremy Thomas (1994)

After dating for six weeks, the actress married the bar owner at 5:00 am in his bar. (A minister/psychic/private detective performed the ceremony.) They made it a month before filing for divorce.

10 32 DAYS: Ernest Borgnine and Ethel Merman (1964)

The 50 white doves and 38 violinists at the ceremony couldn't make the marriage between the actor and the Broadway star last. Merman complained about Borgnine's temper, and he told her she could "lump it" if she didn't like it. A few weeks later, she did.

5 GREAT ATHLETES WHO BECAME GREAT BUSINESSMEN

1 DAVE BING (NBA guard, 1966–78)

"The mistake most of us make is that we think we're going to play forever," said the former Detroit Piston, who in 1996 was named one of the NBA's 50 greatest players. "Very few guys, I think, prepare for a second career." Not wanting to make that same mistake himself, Bing spent his off-seasons working as a bank management trainee. When he retired in 1978, Paragon Steel wanted to hire him as a spokesman, but Bing insisted on a two-year training program instead. In 1980 he took out a loan and founded Big Steel, a steel-processing mill. At its peak, Big Steel was the 10th-largest African American–owned company in the U.S., with profits of $61 million. Bing also owned Superb Manufacturing, which made $28 million per year.

2 GARY FENCIK (NFL Safety, 1976–87)

After graduating from Yale University, Fencik signed with the Chicago Bears and spent his entire career there, setting the team's all-time record for interceptions. In 1985, as the Bears' season was heading toward the Super Bowl, Fencik was also working his way toward his MBA by spending two nights a week at finance school (possibly making him the only athlete ever to have earned a Super Bowl ring and an MBA in the same year). "One of the benefits of going to Yale is I had roommates, classmates, even teammates who were going to med school, law school, business school," said Fencik, "so I never stopped thinking about what I was gonna do after football." He retired in 1987, and in 1992 Wells Fargo hired him to run their Chicago investment office. By 2000 Fencik was heading up global business development for Adams Street Partners, a $25 billion private equity company, where today he's also a full partner.

3 ULYSSES "JUNIOR" BRIDGEMAN (NBA shooting guard, 1975–87)

One day, the former Milwaukee Buck heard a woman on a call-in radio talk show complain, "I was at Wendy's, and I saw Junior Bridgeman working behind the counter. If that's the best these ex-athletes can do..." What the lady didn't realize was that Bridgeman was there learning his new trade from the ground up. During his time with the Bucks, he scored 11,517 points and held the franchise record for most games played consecutively. When he wasn't on the court, he worked as an insurance salesman and at the front desk of a hotel. After retiring in 1987, he bought five Wendy's hamburger franchises and learned every aspect of his business, including spending time behind the counter. Today, Bridgeman owns 195 Wendy's restaurants, making him the second-largest franchise owner in the United States. He also owns 125 Chili's restaurants and 45 Fannie May chocolate stores. Forbes lists him at #24 on their list of wealthiest black Americans and estimates his net worth at $200 million.

4 ROGER STAUBACH (NFL quarterback, 1969–79)

"It takes a lot of unspectacular preparation to have spectacular results in both business and football," says Staubach, who's done both. He led the Dallas Cowboys to two Super Bowl wins and led the NFL in passing four times. But he still found time to moonlight as a real estate broker. In 1977 he opened his own firm called the Staubach Company and worked there full-time when he retired from football in 1979. By 2008 his company had 50 offices in the United States and was bought out by Jones Lang LaSalle real estate for $640 million. Staubach was named executive chairman and now takes home a reported $12 million a year.

5 TONY HAWK (professional skateboarder, 1982–99)

Hawk was an entrepreneur before he was a household name. In 1992 he took out a second mortgage to cofound the Bird-House skateboard company. Seven years later, he solidified his reputation as one of the world's greatest skateboarders at the 1999 X Games when he landed the thought-to-be-impossible "900" (two and a half rotations in midair). Capitalizing on his fame, Hawk moved into a new arena of business: video games. "I was shopping this game idea, weighing my options when I went to Activision, but when I saw what they were working on, I said, 'This is exactly what I'd love to be involved with,' and following that gut reaction was hugely successful." How successful? The Tony Hawk video game series has made more than $1.6 billion, and his personal net worth is estimated at $120 million.

Plus One Who Crashed and Burned...

1 CURT SCHILLING (MLB pitcher, 1988–2007)

Schilling helped the Arizona Diamondbacks win one World Series and the Boston Red Sox win two. He made history in the 2004 American League Championship Series by pitching with an injury so severe that blood started leaking through his sock. That gritty determination helped inspire the Red Sox to win their first World Series in 86 years. But Schilling's prowess on the mound didn't equate to success in business. A big fan of "massive multiplayer online" games, after he retired from baseball in 2007, he decided to create his own game company, 38 Studios, with $50 million of his own money...along with a $75 million loan from the State of Rhode Island. But Schilling had no experience in either business or game design. Result: His company was grossly mismanaged and went bankrupt. Schilling had aspired to be "Bill Gates rich" but lost his—and the taxpayers of Rhode Island's—money instead. He was subsequently sued by the state. Today, Schilling has found a second career as a TV baseball analyst. He still enjoys playing video games.

5 OF LEONARDO da VINCI'S GENIUS LISTS

Historians have translated thousands of pages of notebooks that Leonardo da Vinci filled up in the early 1500s. From them, here are some lists that the original Renaissance man made when he wasn't painting, sculpting, inventing, doing math, designing buildings, collecting fossils, classifying animal species...

12 RULES FOR GOOD HEALTH

1 Do not eat when you have no appetite, and dine lightly.

2 Chew well, and whatever you take in should be well-cooked and of simple ingredients.

3 He who takes medicine is ill-advised.

4 Beware anger and avoid stuffy air.

5 Stay standing a while when you get up from a meal.

6 Make sure you do not sleep at midday.

7 Let your wine be mixed with water, take little at a time. Not between meals, nor on an empty stomach.

8 Neither delay nor prolong your visit to the toilet.

9 If you take exercise, let it not be too strenuous.

10 Do not lie with your stomach upward and your head downward.

11 Be well covered at night, and rest your head and keep your mind cheerful.

12 Avoid wantonness and keep to this diet.

DA VINCI'S GROCERY LIST

1 good beef

2 eggs

3 wine

4 mulberries

5 mushrooms

6 grapes

7 salad

8 flour

9 bran

10 herbs

11 buttermilk

12 melon

DA VINCI'S ONGOING TO-DO LIST

1 Measurement of Milan.

2 A book that treats of Milan and its churches, which is to be had at the stationer's on the way to Cordusio.

3 The measurement of the Corte Vecchio.

4 The measurement of the Castello.

5 Get the Master of Arithmetic to show you how to square a triangle.

6 Get Messea Fazio to show you about proportion.

7 Get the Brera Friar to show you *De Ponderibus* [a book].

8 Talk to Giannino, the Bombardier, re. the means of which the Tower of Ferrara is walled without loopholes.

9 Ask Benedetto Portinari by what means they go on ice in Flanders.

10 Draw Milan.

11 Ask Maestro Antonio how mortars are positioned on bastions by day or night.

12 Examine the crossbow of Maestro Gianetto.

13 Find a master of hydraulics and get him to tell you how to repair a lock, canal, and mill in the Lombard Mannersun.

14 The measurement of the sun, promised me by Maestro Giovanni Francese.

15 Try to get Vitolone, in the library at Pavia, which deals with the mathematics.

DA VINCI'S PACKING LIST FOR A TRIP TO THE UNIVERSITY OF PAVIA IN 1510

1 Spectacles with case, fork, firestick, bistoury, charcoal, boards, sheets of paper, chalk, white wax, forceps, pane of glass, fine-tooth bone saw, scalpel, inkhorn, penknife, nutmeg, boots, stockings, comb, towel, shirts, shoelaces, penknife, pens, a skin for the chest, gloves, wrapping paper, charcoal

2 Get hold of a skull.

5 THINGS TO DO IN PAVIA

1 Observe the holes in the substance of the brain.

2 Describe the tongue of a woodpecker and jaw of a crocodile.

3 Give measurement of the dead using finger as a unit.

4 Get anatomy books bound.

5 Break the jaw from the side so that you can see the uvula in its position.

10 DISTINCTIONS: ANIMALS EDITION

1 ALLIGATOR VS. CROCODILE. One sees you later, the other in a while. Another difference: Alligators have wide U-shaped snouts, and crocodiles tend to have more pointed V-shaped snouts. Alligators' upper jaws are wider than their lower jaws, so when their mouths are closed, the teeth in the upper jaws are visible, while the teeth in the lower jaws are not. Conversely, crocodiles' upper and lower jaws are about the same width, so when the mouth is closed, several lower teeth are visible. There are only two existing alligator species, the American alligator, native to the southeastern United States, and the endangered Chinese alligator, native only to the Yangtze River. There are 23 existing species of crocodile, and they're found in tropical waters in Africa, Asia, the Americas, and Australia.

2 CENTIPEDE VS. MILLIPEDE. It has nothing to do with the number of legs they have. *Centipede* means "100 feet" in Latin—and different centipede species have from 28 to 358 legs. *Millipede* means "1,000 feet"—and they have from 22 to 750 legs. The real differences: Centipedes have one pair of legs per body segment; millipedes have two. Centipedes are venomous and are almost exclusively carnivores, eating insects; millipedes are almost exclusively detritivores, meaning they eat detritus—decomposed organic matter.

3 HORNS VS. ANTLERS. The horns of antelopes and the antlers of deer, although comparable in function, differ considerably in structure. Horns, usually possessed by both sexes, are permanent features that continue to grow throughout the animal's life. They are bony projections from the skull, covered with keratin, which is tougher than bone. Antlers, by contrast, are pure bone and are formed and shed every year. They are normally grown only by male deer, but female reindeer and caribou have them as well.

4 STRAY vs. FERAL. A stray is technically a domesticated animal that once had a home, but it was abandoned or ran away, forcing it to survive in the wild. A feral animal was born in the wild, but its domesticated ancestors had homes.

5 FROG vs. TOAD. All toads are frogs, but not all frogs are toads. Both are species of amphibians. Frogs spend their lives close to water, but toads are able to venture farther onto dry land. Toads are often brown and have dry, bumpy skin. Frogs are mainly green and are wetter and smoother to the touch. Frogs have teeth, toads don't.

6 MOTH vs. BUTTERFLY. Moths have plump bodies and feathery antennae, whereas butterflies have skinny bodies and long, slender antennae. Butterflies prefer sunshine—they actually can't fly unless their wings are warm enough. That's why you only see butterflies on nice days (which they make even nicer). Moths are mostly nocturnal, but they also like light, which is why you mostly see them dive-bombing your porch light.

7 CHRYSALIS vs. COCOON. Think they're the same? That's a moth-conception! (Sorry.) When a moth caterpillar is ready to enter the pupa stage, it spins silk into a cocoon for protection until it can emerge as a winged, adult moth. A butterfly caterpillar doesn't spin a cocoon but becomes a type of pupa called a chrysalis. Instead of spinning a silk outer covering, the chrysalis itself forms into a hardened protein for protection.

8 RABBIT vs. HARE. Both are small mammals with long ears in the family Leporidae. The main difference: Rabbits (with the exception of cottontails) dig burrows and bear their young underground, and all rabbits' young are born blind and hairless. Hares, on the other hand, build nests on the ground. Their young are born fully furred with open eyes and are therefore much more able than newborn rabbits to fend for themselves. Also, hares are generally larger and have longer ears.

9 COUGAR vs. MOUNTAIN LION vs. PUMA vs. PANTHER. They're the same animal. In fact, no other single animal has more names in the dictionary. Why? Because *Puma concolor* has such a wide range—from South America all the way north to the Yukon—the wild cats go by many names. In the western U.S., some call them pumas, others call them cougars, and still others call them mountain lions. East of the Mississippi they're known as panthers, painters, and catamounts.

10 POISONOUS vs. VENOMOUS. A poisonous animal spreads its poison by touch, such as a frog with poisonous skin. It's basically a defense mechanism. A venomous animal uses its toxin primarily for predation, which it delivers via teeth or stingers. So if your friend is yelling, "Help, a poisonous snake is trying to get me!" make sure you correct his misnomer before helping him.

THE 7 DAYS AND WHAT INSPIRED EACH OF THEIR NAMES

1 **Sunday:** The Sun

2 **Monday:** The Moon

3 **Tuesday:** Tyr, Norse god of war

4 **Wednesday:** Wodin (or Odin), chief Norse god

5 **Thursday:** Thor, Norse god of thunder

6 **Friday:** Frey, Norse goddess of love

7 **Saturday:** Saturn, Roman god of harvest

---

11 McDONALD'S McMEALS AROUND THE McWORLD

1 McAloo Tikki Burger (India). A potato-and-peas patty that's deep-fried and coated with bread crumbs, then served on a Big Mac bun with all the toppings.

2 McToast (Croatia). Two pieces of cheese served between two toasted buns that are inverted so the flat sides face out.

3 Big New York (Israel). This American-style burger is a half-pound patty made of prime rib and *entrecôte* (rib steak) with all the toppings (minus cheese and bacon, which aren't kosher).

4 Tabasco McWrap (Panama). A chicken-and-bacon wrap with "Tabasco mayonnaise."

5 McSpaghetti (The Philippines). A plate of spaghetti.

6 Samurai Pork Burger (Thailand). A pork patty covered in teriyaki and pickles served on a sesame seed bun.

7 Vegemite McMuffin (Australia). An Egg McMuffin smothered in the popular paste made from leftover brewers' yeast extract.

8 McCurryWurst (Germany). Bratwurst chunks in a spicy tomato sauce topped with curry powder.

9 EBI Filet-O (Japan). A breaded shrimp burger served on a Big Mac bun.

10 McLobster (Canada). Atlantic lobster meat with celery, green onions, mayo, and a lot of lettuce served in a hot dog bun.

11 Nacho Jr. (Finland). A burger topped with tortilla chips, salsa, and sour cream...in Finland.

To protest a bad call, a soccer team in Madagascar allowed **149** goals. (They lost.)

21 "WE ARE THE WORLD" SINGERS

After the 1985 American Music Awards, dozens of major pop stars gathered in a recording studio to record "We Are the World," a song to raise relief money for the Ethiopian famine. It was a landmark cultural event of the 1980s and raised millions of dollars. All of the stars sang backup, but a few soloists each sang a line or two (Michael Jackson, who cowrote the song with Lionel Richie, got to sing more). The soloists were, in order:

1 Lionel Richie
2 Stevie Wonder
3 Paul Simon
4 Kenny Rogers
5 James Ingram
6 Tina Turner
7 Billy Joel

8 Michael Jackson
9 Diana Ross
10 Dionne Warwick
11 Willie Nelson
12 Al Jarreau
13 Bruce Springsteen
14 Kenny Loggins

15 Steve Perry
16 Daryl Hall
17 Huey Lewis
18 Cyndi Lauper
19 Kim Carnes
20 Bob Dylan
21 Ray Charles

11 "WATW" SINGERS WHO DIDN'T GET SOLOS

1 Dan Aykroyd (as part of the Blues Brothers, he's technically a musician)
2 Harry Belafonte
3 Lindsey Buckingham
4 Sheila E.
5 Bob Geldof

6 John Oates
7 Smokey Robinson
8 Bette Midler
9 Jeffrey Osborne
10 The Pointer Sisters
11 Jackie, Marlon, Randy, Tito, and La Toya Jackson

38 "WE ARE THE WORLD 25 FOR HAITI" ARTISTS

A sequel to the song was produced by Lionel Richie and Haitian-American musician Wyclef Jean in 2010 after the Caribbean island nation of Haiti was heavily damaged by an earthquake. Several of the original singers returned (including a posthumous Michael Jackson), along with a batch of new stars.

1 Justin Bieber

2 Nicole Scherzinger

3 Jennifer Hudson

4 Jennifer Nettles

5 Josh Groban

6 Tony Bennett

7 Mary J. Blige

8 Toni Braxton

9 Michael Jackson (stock footage)

10 Janet Jackson

11 Barbra Streisand

12 Miley Cyrus

13 Enrique Iglesias

14 Jamie Foxx

15 Wyclef Jean

16 Adam Levine

17 Pink

18 BeBe Winans

19 Usher

20 Celine Dion

21 Orianthi (on guitar)

22 Fergie

23 Nick Jonas

24 Mary Mary

25 Isaac Slade

26 Carlos Santana (on guitar)

27 Lil Wayne

28 Akon

29 T-Pain

30 LL Cool J

31 will.i.am

32 Snoop Dogg

33 Nipsey Hussle

34 Busta Rhymes

35 Swizz Beatz

36 Kid Cudi

37 Mann

38 Kanye West

151 **is a "palindromic prime": a prime number that's the same in both directions.**

10 CLEVER HOUSEHOLD TRICKS

1 **Lemon or orange Kool-Aid** can clean your toilet. Add the powder, scrub it around the bowl with a toilet brush, and let sit overnight.

2 **Tang, lemonade, Jell-O**, or any citric powdered mix can be used to clean the dishwasher. Just pour in one cup, run the dishwasher, and the acids will dissolve any mineral buildup. (Only do this when the dishwasher is empty!)

3 **Wrap a diaper** around a leaky pipe; it will absorb the water long enough for the plumber to arrive. If it's a big leak, it may need to be "changed."

4 **Use coffee filters** instead of paper towels to clean your windows. Why? No lint!

5 **A pillowcase** can clean ceiling fan blades without spreading dust everywhere.

Simply place the pillowcase over the blade, grip it well on both sides, and slide it off. (Make sure the fan is off before attempting this.)

6 **WD-40** will remove crayon from nearly every surface. Do a spot test first.

7 **Rub car wax** on your home's air vents to keep them from collecting dust.

8 **Apply ketchup** to a cloth, rub on tarnished copper, rinse, and dry. It's clean!

9 **Put a wide rubber band** on top of a stripped screw, then you can unscrew it with a screwdriver. Push hard.

10 **Use a dryer sheet** to clean dust from lamp-shades; it will hold onto the dust and make the shade smell nice and fresh.

The Crayola Ultimate Crayon Case has 152 colors.

7 THINGS PEOPLE HAVE HIT EACH OTHER WITH

1 A CRUCIFIX. Two priests in Florham Park, New Jersey, got into a heated argument over the use of a car. According to the police report, Father Frank Hreno threatened to kill Father Emeka Okwuosa and then "came after him with a four-foot-long crucifix which he swung through a glass door." Okwuosa's arm was injured, and Hreno was arrested and charged with "terroristic threats."

2 A TEA KETTLE. When a Massachusetts man asked his room-mate, Naresh Bhandari, to quiet down one night in 2014, Bhandari reportedly went ballistic. First, he tried to hit the victim with a wine bottle, and then a corkscrew, but neither landed. Then he grabbed a tea kettle from the stove and bonked the victim's head with it, causing severe bleeding. Bhandari was arrested for assault. The police kept the dented kettle as evidence.

3 A DEER HEAD. Pennsylvanians Stacy Varner and Glenda Snyder argued, and it escalated. According to state troopers, the two women tried to hit each other with a taxidermied deer head. Snyder suffered minor injuries after being struck with an antler.

4 A SAUSAGE. In a bizarre home invasion in Fresno, California, a man snuck into a house late one night and stole some cash. Then he got some spices and an eight-inch sausage from the kitchen, tiptoed to the bedrooms, rubbed the spices on one man who was sleeping, and then hit another sleeping man in the face with the sausage. The attacker fled the scene but left his wallet behind. The stolen money was returned, but the sausage was a complete loss. According to police lieutenant Ian Burrimond, "The dog ate the weapon."

5 A BOTTLE OF TABASCO SAUCE. Steven Connor of Frenchtown, Montana, and his brother were drinking one night in 2014 when Connor accused his brother (not named in press reports) of stealing some of his tools. When his brother tried to leave, Connor picked up the closest "weapon" he could find—a bottle of Tabasco sauce—and hit his brother over the head several times until the bottle shattered, "leaving blood and Tabasco sauce all over the victim's clothing," according to press reports. The injured brother needed 15 staples to close the head wound, and Connor went to jail.

6 A PALM FROND. Gelando Olivieri Jr., 34, walked into a Florida convenience store and demanded $50 from the clerk. His robbery weapon? A Spanish bayonet palm frond, which has very pointy leaves. The employee refused to give Olivieri any money, and another customer picked up a bar stool and chased the would-be robber from the store. Olivieri ran into a small wooded area nearby, where police found and arrested him. "Hey, at least he was recycling," Sgt. John Anderson joked. "Think green."

7 A GARBAGE CAN. In Evansville, Indiana, in 2007, a woman named Connie Deweese had been dating a man named Alejandro Valencio off and on for eight months, but she wanted nothing more to do with him—and told him so in no uncertain terms. So late one night in a drunken stupor, Valencio tried to reconcile, but Deweese locked the door. Valencio climbed onto her roof and attempted to get in through the chimney, but it was sealed and he got stuck. Someone (it's unclear who) called the fire department. When they arrived, Deweese blocked their access to the fireplace while shouting, "Leave him in there and let him die!" So the firefighters had to call the police, who came and restrained Deweese (who was later cited for disorderly conduct) as firefighters demolished the living room wall to free Valencio, who was injured and covered in soot. The next day, a local news team happened to be at Deweese's house with cameras rolling when Valencio—freshly desooted—came to apologize. Deweese hollered at him, picked up a garbage can off the porch, and hit him in the head. He still wouldn't leave, so she threw a beer bottle at his head. That did the trick. "I've dated a lot of psychos in my life," Deweese told reporters, "but nobody like that."

34 VANITY LICENSE PLATES REJECTED BY THE DMV

1 IH8DMV	18 OMG GO
2 AWCRAP	19 FBICAR
3 URADORK	20 GR8NBED
4 IMNEWD	21 PMPWGN
5 DUDU	22 BADSOB
6 EVIL666	23 ILYKPIE
7 ISHOOTU	24 SUKS2BU
8 NOFARTIN	25 AXMRDR
9 OHHLLNO	26 PUZYCAT
10 BYBYCOP	27 DBLE DS
11 INEED2P	28 EFNCOOL
12 BOOG3RS	29 WANKER
13 ADULTRY	30 BEERPLZ
14 FART HED	31 PISSTOPH
15 FARTMAN	32 DAMSXY
16 A55MAN	33 UPURAZZ
17 IHURL	34 MOONME

6 ELEMENTAL LISTS FROM THE PERIODIC TABLE

Invented In 1868 by Russian chemist Dmitri Mendeleev, the periodic table of elements is a tabular arrangement of all known chemical elements and their properties. The first entry lists elements discovered in ancient times, which explains why some chemical symbols look nothing like their English names; it's because their Latin names were used for their abbreviations, like Au for aurum (gold). Now for the rest of your chemistry lesson.

8 ELEMENTS DISCOVERED BY THE ANCIENT GREEKS AND ROMANS

1 Antimony
2 Copper
3 Gold
4 Lead
5 Mercury
6 Silver
7 Sulfur
8 Tin

18 ELEMENTS ON THE TABLE THAT ARE ALSO INSIDE YOU

1 Oxygen
2 Carbon
3 Hydrogen
4 Nitrogen
5 Calcium
6 Phosphorus
7 Potassium
8 Sulfur
9 Chlorine
10 Sodium
11 Magnesium
12 Iron
13 Cobalt
14 Copper
15 Zinc
16 Iodine
17 Selenium
18 Fluorine

10 OF THE LIGHTEST ELEMENTS

1 Hydrogen
2 Helium
3 Lithium
4 Neon
5 Argon
6 Sodium
7 Nitrogen

8 Oxygen
9 Calcium
10 Rubidium

11 OF THE DENSEST ELEMENTS

1 Osmium
2 Francium
3 Astatine
4 Iridium
5 Platinum
6 Rhenium
7 Uranium
8 Tungsten
9 Gold
10 Tantalum
11 Thorium

11 ELEMENTS THAT BECOME GAS AT ROOM TEMPERATURE

1 Helium
2 Hydrogen
3 Neon
4 Nitrogen
5 Fluorine
6 Argon
7 Oxygen
8 Krypton
9 Xenon
10 Radon
11 Chlorine

7 OF THE RAREST ELEMENTS

1 **Astatine.** A radioactive element that decays so quickly that only a few grams of it exist in the Earth's crust at any one time.

2 **Actinium.** About 10 million times as rare as gold; it's so rare that one ton of uranium contains only 0.02 mg of actinium.

3 **Polonium.** Nearly as rare as actinium, which is a good thing, since it's 250,000 times more potent than cyanide. Less than a microgram will kill an adult.

4 **Francium.** Less than an ounce is thought to exist at any time because it decays so fast.

5 **Protactinium.** There are only two to three protactinium atoms out of every trillion atoms on Earth.

6 **Rhenium.** It's 10 times as rare as gold.

7 **Gold.** It's 10 million times as rare as iron.

7 "STAPLE FOOD" FACTS

1 WHAT'S A STAPLE FOOD? A food that's eaten regularly and in large enough amounts that it supplies the majority of a region's nutritional needs.

2 COMMON STAPLES AROUND THE WORLD. Rice, wheat, corn (maize), millet, sorghum, potatoes, cassava, yams, taro, and animal products (meat, milk, eggs, cheese, and fish).

3 THE THREE MOST POPULAR. Corn, rice, and wheat make up 60% of what everyone eats. The most popular: rice. More than 1.6 billion people around the world call it their staple food.

4 CLIMATE-CONTROLLED. People in Africa, Asia, and India use beans, lentils, and chickpeas as staple foods, while those in the tropics rely on starchy fruits like breadfruit and plantains.

5 CHANGING TIMES. In the past, staples were used because they grew best in that environment, but increased ease of transportation, storage, and importing have made some changes. For example, taro was a staple of the South Pacific until around 1970, when its consumption started to fall. Instead, use of imported, nonnative cereal grains rose 40 percent.

6 LIMITED MENU. There are more than 50,000 edible plants on Earth, but only 15 of them make up 90% of people's diets.

7 BRANCH OUT. It's best to eat a variety of foods. Staples alone can't supply all nutritional needs. Plus, they're really pointy and can hurt your throat (oops, wrong kind of staple).

7 SETS OF UNLIKELY ANIMAL BUDDIES

1 BONEDIGGER, MILO, BULLET, AND ANGEL. At the Garold Wayne Zoo in Oklahoma, a 500-pound lion and three 11-pound Dachshunds have struck up an odd (and very cute) friendship. Bonedigger met the little dogs when he was a four-week-old cub; they've been inseparable ever since. And the lion aims to keep it that way: "You do not ever try to take Bonedigger's dogs out of his yard," warns their handler, Joe Exotic. "It makes him very mad."

2 SHERE KHAN, LEO, AND BALOO. During a drug raid in Atlanta, Georgia, in 2001, police discovered three cubs—a lion, a tiger, and a bear—living in a drug dealer's basement (no word on what the drug dealer planned on doing with them when they got big). Noah's Ark Animal Sanctuary offered to take the wild cubs and placed them in separate enclosures. But the animals got depressed and stopped eating. So the "BLT" was put in one big enclosure. Now all grown up, Baloo the bear, Leo the lion, and Shere Khan the tiger have been BFFs ever since.

3 WOLF AND DONKEY. In 2007 villagers in Patok, Albania, captured a wolf from the mountains and put it in a cage. When the time came to feed it, a villager put a donkey in the cage and let nature take its course. But instead of devouring the donkey, the wolf befriended it, and the two sworn enemies lived happily together for months. After the story made international news, the Albanian government ordered the villagers to return the wolf to the mountains. Amazingly, he shows up in Patok from time to time to play with his donkey friend.

4 PIPER AND GP. Julie and Nathan Free raise all kinds of animals on their Oklahoma property. One day, a newborn baby goat wasn't moving, so Julie brought it into her house. One of her dogs, a pit bull mix named Piper, sniffed the kid and then gave it a lick. The goat woke up and imprinted on its new "mother." The Frees named the goat GP ("Goat Puppy"), and Piper raised him as her own. He follows her everywhere, even over agility jumps. A leg injury has since slowed GP down, but their bond is as strong as ever. "They just absolutely adore each other," says Julie.

5 BUBBLES AND BELLA. Bubbles the elephant lives at the Myrtle Beach Safari preserve in South Carolina. In 2007 a contractor was building a swimming pool for Bubbles and left a Labrador retriever puppy behind. The elephant and the dog bonded over their mutual love of water, and now the best friends go for walks, play, and swim together.

6 TINNI AND SNIFFER. A Norwegian photographer and his German Shepherd Tinni were walking in the woods in 2013 when a fox cub approached the dog. "He was a puppy and probably his mother had died, so he sought help and company, and food," said the dog's owner, who dubbed the fox Sniffer. Sniffer now shows up whenever Tinni goes out for a walk, and the two frolic for hours.

7 SWAN AND FISH. This weird feeding habit has been witnessed at a few places around the globe. Here's an eyewitness account from a safari park in Shenzhen City, China: "A black swan feeds its fish friends every day to the amazement of passersby at the park. Every time I come to feed the swan, all the fish follow him to the bank with their mouths open, and he takes the food and puts some into each of the hungry mouths. When everyone has eaten enough, the swan goes back onto the water and plays with his fish friends again."

8 GAAAAAAPING PLOT HOLES

These movies, books, and shows are classics, but the key to enjoying them is to not think too hard about logic. Because when it comes to sloppy storytelling, not even Mr. Spock is logical.

1 *CITIZEN KANE* (1941)

Plot: Publishing tycoon Charles Foster Kane dies right as he says the word "Rosebud"—and the entire movie revolves around journalists trying to figure out what "Rosebud" means.

Hole: Kane died alone, so there's no way that anyone could have known what his last word was.

2 *THE TERMINATOR* (1984) AND *TERMINATOR 2: JUDGMENT DAY* (1991)

Plot: In the first movie, the Terminator goes back in time to kill Sarah Connor, whose son John Connor will grow up to lead the fight against the evil machines. The good guys from the future send back Kyle Reese to protect her. Then Kyle and Sarah fall in love and make a baby that turns out to be John.

Hole: John would never have been born had he not sent his father back to father him, but John spends *Terminator 2* trying to stop "Judgment Day." In the end, the good guys win: The Terminator is melted and the secrets of his futuristic design die with him. By that logic, John should have "poofed" out of existence, *Back to the Future* style.

3 *TOY STORY* (1995)

Plot: Woody the cowboy toy is jealous when his boy Andy is given a Buzz Lightyear toy for his birthday.

Hole: It's established that the toys come to life when Andy is out of the room, and they "play dead" when he's around. But

Buzz seems to follow a different set of rules. In the beginning, he thinks he's a real spaceman...so why does he play dead with the other toys? Why doesn't he just talk to Andy?

4 STAR WARS: EPISODE III (2005) AND EPISODE IV (1977)

Plot: In *Episode III*, Anakin Skywalker turns to the Dark Side and becomes Darth Vader, so Obi-Wan Kenobi must hide Anakin's twin babies Luke and Leia from their evil dad.

Hole: Obi-Wan does a good job hiding Leia; she's adopted by foster parents and raised on a distant planet. But for some reason, Obi-Wan sends Luke to live on his evil father's home planet with his relatives. Luke even keeps the name Skywalker. And instead of training young Luke to be a Jedi so he can grow up and defeat his father, Obi-Wan hides in a cave in the desert until Luke, as a young man, finally finds *him*. Yoda later says of Luke, "He is too old to begin the training." (No wonder Darth Vader had such an easy time cutting off Luke's hand.)

5 THE WALKING DEAD (2010–)

Plot: It's been more than a year since the undead have risen and society has crumbled. Towns are abandoned, there's no government, no power grid—nothing but marauding bands of frightened humans and bloodthirsty "walkers."

Hole: All the hedges are trimmed and the lawns are mowed in these "abandoned" towns. You can even see the mow lines.

6 STAR TREK II: THE WRATH OF KHAN (1982)

Plot: In the film's climax, the *Enterprise*'s warp drive has been damaged and an explosion is imminent.

Hole: None of the engineers—the people whose job it is to keep the engines running—can figure out how to fix it. The ship is saved by Mr. Spock, part of the bridge command crew, who leaves his post without telling anyone, goes down to engineering, enters a room flooded with radiation, unscrews a thingy from another thingy, and—voilà!—the ship is saved. Then Spock dies. (Sort of, but that's another plot hole.) But did Spock have to die? Earlier scenes show engineering personnel wearing protective suits. Why couldn't Spock have put one on? And it had previously been established on *Star Trek* that radiation poisoning is easy to cure in the 23rd century. Yet no one even tries to save Spock, even though he lived long enough to have a sappy conversation through glass with Admiral Kirk.

7 THE MATRIX (1999)

Plot: A computer hacker is recruited by a group of rebels who reveal that his life is actually a simulation, and he's just a prisoner serving the computers' needs. Whoa.

Hole: If the computers are the ones creating the virtual world, why do they create one where computer hackers can learn to access the Matrix? Why not place all the humans into a time period before computers existed, like 1920? And if, as the movie explains, the computers use the humans as "batteries" to power their world (because the computers blocked out the sun), why not use something like cows, which would provide more power and not try to defeat their captors?

8 THE LORD OF THE RINGS SERIES

Plot: Frodo the hobbit embarks on a quest to the evil land of Mordor so he can destroy the Ring of Power in the fires of Mt. Doom. After walking hundreds of miles through orc-infested lands, Frodo finally destroys the ring, but he's about to be killed by a volcanic eruption...when the wizard Gandalf sends giant eagles to rescue him.

Hole: Why didn't Gandalf simply have the eagles fly Frodo there in the first place? It's been argued that they had to wait until Mordor fell to fly within its boundaries—or else they would have been attacked by the Nazgul (those dead kings on flying dragons). That still doesn't explain why Frodo had to spend several months walking to Mordor. Couldn't the eagles have at least gotten him as far as the border? It was only the fate of all of Middle-earth that was at stake.

8 FAMOUS WHITE PEOPLE WITH BLACK ANCESTRY

Not everyone with African ancestry has dark skin, so some have tried to hide their heritage—for fear of discrimination—while others simply didn't know their roots. And some just don't care.

1 ALESSANDRO DE MEDICI

From 1530 to 1537, Medici governed Florence, making him the first black ruler in Italy—though few people knew of his African heritage. But his mother was a black servant, and (scandal alert) his father was 17-year-old Giulio de Medici, who would later become Pope Clement VII.

2 RASHIDA JONES

The light-complected star of TV's *Parks and Recreation* and *The Office* is the daughter of Grammy Award–winning African American music producer Quincy Jones, who has roots in Cameroon. Her mom is white actress Peggy Lipton (*The Mod Squad, Twin Peaks*).

3 MALCOLM GLADWELL

Named one of *Time* magazine's 100 Most Influential People, Canadian journalist Gladwell is an acclaimed writer for the *New Yorker* who opines on race and social issues. Growing up in predominately white rural Ontario, he was assumed to be white, but his mother is Jamaican.

4 ALEXANDRE DUMAS

The French writer's father was General Thomas-Alexandre Dumas, born to a white aristocratic father and a Haitian slave mother. The general was a French Revolution war hero who was imprisoned in a fortress by Napoleon Bonaparte's supporters. Sound familiar? His son Alexandre based *The Count of Monte Cristo* on him (and also wrote *The Three Musketeers*).

5 ALEXANDER PUSHKIN

Pushkin (1799–1837) is considered the father of Russian literature. His unfinished historical novel *Peter the Great's Negro* was based on Pushkin's real-life great-grandfather Abram Gannibal, the black servant of Peter the Great. Gannibal was treated just like royal family; the emperor was his godfather and the queen of Poland his godmother. He fathered 11 children, including Pushkin's grandfather.

6 CAROL CHANNING

When the future Broadway star of *Gentlemen Prefer Blondes* was 16 years old, her mother divulged a family secret: Carol's light-complected father was not from Rhode Island but from Augusta, Georgia...and he was half-black. Channing didn't disclose this information publicly until she was 81.

7 WENTWORTH MILLER

Known for the *Resident Evil* movies and the TV series *Prison Break*, the British-born actor has light skin and green eyes. That's why some fans find it hard to believe that he also has a father who is predominately African American and Jamaican.

8 ALEXANDER HAMILTON

The first U.S. secretary of the treasury hailed from a British-owned island in the Caribbean. Hamilton's father was from Scotland and his mother from the West Indies. Though his mom and brother were both dark-skinned, Hamilton was lighter-complected and treated as though he were white. So he fit in with the other Founding Fathers...except for the fact that he was an abolitionist. (You can see Hamilton for yourself on the $10 bill.)

10 RULES GRAMMARIANS GOTTA CHILL OUT ON

Grammar freaks often freak out about "broken rules." But most of these examples are simply indicators of a living language that's in constant flux. Here are 10 "goofs" that are up for debate.

1 OMITTING THE COMMA AFTER *HI* OR *HELLO*

Is the first comma in "Hi, Mom," necessary or superfluous? It used to be commonplace to begin a letter home with "Dear Mother." As English became less formal in the 20th century, it became "Hello, Mom," with a comma following *hello*. Since the advent of e-mail and texts, communication has relaxed so much that people simply write "Hi Mom." So in casual greetings, you can leave it off. However, according to the *Chicago Manual of Style*, "If you're writing to a client or your boss...that means putting a comma before the direct address (Hi, Fred)."

2 STARTING A SENTENCE WITH A CONJUNCTION

This rule has been drilled into grade schoolers' heads: "Never begin a sentence with *and, but,* or *or.*" It turns out there's no rule against doing so. According to *Oxford Dictionary Myth Debunkers*, "The argument against using a preposition to introduce a sentence is that such a sentence expresses an incomplete thought (or 'fragment') and is therefore incorrect." But if it has a subject and predicate (as in "And then I went home.") it's a sentence. If it doesn't ("and then home") it's not.

3 USING *SINCE* WHEN YOU MEAN *BECAUSE*

Any good writer knows that *since* refers to time, and *because* refers to cause, right? Not quite. Although this distinction is specified in many style guides, so many people continue to misuse the word *since* that dictionaries have now expanded its definition to include *because*. So consider the two words "partially" interchangeable: Only use *since* in place of *because* if it's not ambiguous. For instance, it's unclear whether *since* refers to time or cause in this sentence: "Since I've had insomnia, I've been cranky."

4 SPLITTING AN INFINITIVE

Some call this one the "Shatner rule." Many grammarians consider Captain Kirk's statement "to boldly go where no man has gone before" incorrect because it's a "split infinitive"— wherein an adverb is inserted between *to* and the verb. This rule has no foundation, though. It was made up in the 1800s, probably by linguists who compared our language to Latin, which doesn't allow for split infinitives. But English is different— take, for example, "Uncle John decided to gradually get rid of the beer in our office that we tap into during meetings." Moving *gradually* anywhere else in the sentence changes the meaning. In this case, the split infinitive can't be avoided.

5 USING *WHILE* TO MEAN *ALTHOUGH*

According to Eric Partridge in *Usage and Abusage*, using *while* in place of *although* "is a perverted use of the correct sense of *while*, which properly means 'at the same time.'" It can also cause confusion, as in this example: "While you were still learning to tie your shoes, I was able to solve this complex math problem." Does the speaker mean *although* the person was learning to tie their shoes, or *at the same time* the person was learning to tie their shoes? So don't use *while* if it muddles the meaning of what you're trying to say, otherwise it's okay.

6 USING THE PASSIVE VOICE

Teachers and editors often insist that writers use an active voice to identify who or what is acting in every sentence. Sometimes students are assigned to craft an entire story in an active voice, with no forms of the passive *be* verb (such as *am*, *was*, or *has been*). That's sound advice, but not a set rule. It's all about what mood the writer is trying to convey. For example, ending a story about a party by writing "Everyone had a good time" (active voice) might not be as strong as ending with "A good time was had by all" (passive voice).

7 USING *OVER* WHEN YOU MEAN *MORE THAN*

Historically, *over* was reserved to mean "higher than," referring to the physical proximity of objects to one another. *More than* meant "a greater amount than." For the last century, though, people have mistakenly used *over* in the numerical sense: "She made over a million dollars." In 2014 the editors at the Associated Press finally relented: "New to the Stylebook: *over*, as well as *more than*, is acceptable to indicate greater numerical value." (Note: We sent this one to our copyeditor, who protested with "more than my dead body!")

8 USING *WHICH* FOR *THAT* AS A RELATIVE PRONOUN

The rule goes: "Only *that* should introduce a restrictive clause—a clause that isn't preceded by a comma and contains information crucial to the sentence's meaning. *Which* should introduce clauses that are set off by a comma." Both of these are correct: "Jay discovered the duck that Uncle John had stolen." and "Jay discovered the duck, which Uncle John had stolen, in the bathtub." Yet some experts, including the editors of England's *Cambridge Grammar of the English Language*, insist that the rule has no basis. In their view, it's okay to say, "Jay found the duck which Uncle John had stolen." However, most American style guides specify that *which* can be substituted for *that* only in British English. So Yanks should do it the American way.

9 USE *LIKE* IN PLACE OF *AS*

According to the *Chicago Manual of Style*, "Increasingly (but loosely) today in ordinary speech, *like* displaces *as* or *as if* as a conjunction to connect clauses. For example, in 'it happened just like I said it would happen,' *like* should read *as.*" They continue: "Although *like* as a conjunction has been considered nonstandard since the seventeenth century, today it is common in dialectal and colloquial usage." Our editors follow the advice in Jack Lynch's *Guide to Grammar and Style*, "In formal writing, avoid using *like* as a conjunction."

10 ENDING A SENTENCE WITH A PREPOSITION

Experts say: Don't end a sentence with a preposition (*on, off, with, about,* etc.), arguing that the term derives from a Latin word meaning "to place before." *Oxford Myth Debunkers* says that in Latin, "a preposition should always precede the prepositional object that it is linked with—it is never placed after it." However, this "rule" wasn't applied to English until 1672. Later, grammarian Charles Allen Lloyd called it a "groundless notion...no textbook supports it, but apparently about half of our teachers of English go out of their way to handicap their pupils by inculcating it." So is it okay for you to end a sentence with a preposition? Sure, as long as it still makes sense. Or, as (legend has it) Winston Churchill shot back to an editor who changed one of his sentences to end with a preposition, "This is the sort of nonsense up with which I will not put!"

7 CLASSIFICATIONS OF *CANIS LUPUS FAMILIARIS*

1 **Herding dogs** (Rin Tin Tin)

2 **Hounds** (Snoopy)

3 **Nonsporting dogs** (*101 Dalmatians*)

4 **Sporting dogs** (Lady, *Lady and the Tramp*)

5 **Terriers** (Toto)

6 **Toys** (the Taco Bell dog)

7 **Working dogs** (Scooby-Doo)

4 RANDOM SPORTS LISTS

8 SHOTS IN BILLIARDS

1 Break (hitting the full rack of balls)
2 Straight shot
3 Rail shot
4 Off the rail shot
5 Bank shot
6 Massé shot (hitting the cue ball near the top so it curves)
7 Jump shot (hitting the cue ball so it jumps another ball)
8 Combination shot

11 19TH-CENTURY "BASE BALL" TERMS

1 **Aces:** Runs
2 **Hands:** Outs
3 **Behind:** Catcher
4 **Club Nine:** Team
5 **Cranks:** Fans
6 **Dew drop:** Slow pitch
7 **Hurler:** Pitcher
8 **Match:** Game
9 **Muff:** Error
10 **Striker:** Batter
11 **Tally:** Score

6 LITTLE LEAGUE BASEBALL DIVISIONS

1 **Little League Tee Ball:** ages 5–6 (7–8 in some places)
2 **Minor League Baseball:** ages 7–12
3 **Little League Baseball:** ages 9–12
4 **Junior League Baseball:** ages 13–14
5 **Senior League Baseball:** ages 14–16
6 **Big League Baseball:** ages 16–18

11 CRICKET POSITIONS

1 Bowler
2 Wicketkeeper
3 First slip
4 Second slip
5 Gully
6 Third man
7 Cover-point
8 Mid-off
9 Mid-on
10 Square leg
11 Deep fine leg

6 APRIL FOOL'S JOKES THAT FOOLED A LOT OF PEOPLE

1 THE SWISS SPAGHETTI HARVEST OF 1957. Back when people actually believed TV news, few questioned the April 1, 1957, report on the BBC current affairs show *Panorama* about the year's bountiful "Swiss spaghetti harvest." The report was the brainchild of BBC cameraman Charles de Jaeger, who draped 20 pounds of cooked spaghetti in the trees around a hotel in Castiglione, Switzerland, and then filmed local girls as they "picked" it. Hundreds of people called in to the BBC asking how they could grow their own spaghetti trees. That evening the network responded with..."April Fools!"

2 TUMBLR PRO. On April 1, 2014, the blogging website Tumblr invited users to try "Tumblr Pro" for free: "Here at Tumblr, we believe the sky's the limit. We believe to achieve—all the way. Whether you're livin' it up, livin' young, or headed straight for the top, nothing says Tumblr like high times. Take the next step with us. Build it. Go one step further." Thousands of users signed up for Tumblr Pro. What did they get? A tiny virtual top hat placed atop their avatars. April Fools!

3 TACO LIBERTY BELL. Thousands of Americans complained to the National Park Service (NPS) after an ad appeared in six major newspapers on April 1, 1996, announcing that Taco Bell had purchased the Liberty Bell in Philadelphia "in an effort to help the national debt." The famous icon would still be available for public viewing, but from then on it would be known as the "Taco Liberty Bell." Frustrated NPS officials held a news conference that day denying the story. Then Taco Bell issued its own press release: "April Fools!"

4 **GOOGLE NOSE.** Were you one of the Google users lured in by the "Google Nose BETA" web page on April 1, 2013? The search engine giant announced that its engineers had developed new technology that would "temporarily align molecules to emulate a particular scent." All you do is enter a search term into Google Nose (which had a helpful instructional video and a searchable database of "scentibytes"), and then your computer would emit molecules that could mimic such scents as "dollar bill," "brownies," and "college dorm." Millions of people tried in vain to smell their screens, but all that Google gave them in return was...April Fools!

5 **LEFT-HANDED WHOPPER.** On April 1, 1998, a full-page ad ran in *USA Today* announcing Burger King's new "left-handed Whopper." The southpaw-friendly burgers were identical to normal burgers except that "all the condiments are rotated 180 degrees, thereby redistributing the weight of the sandwich so that the bulk of the condiments will skew to the left, thereby reducing the amount of lettuce and other toppings from spilling out the right side of the burger." Tens of thousands of lefties reportedly went to Burger King to "have it their way" (while others requested their own "right-handed version"), only to be told..."April Fools!"

6 **PUG DELIVERY SERVICE.** MOO, a online company that prints business cards and letterheads, announced a unique new delivery service on April 1, 2014: Pug Post. Inspired by Amazon's proposed drone delivery program, MOO would be offering a "Canine Courier" option in which pug dogs would deliver business card orders strapped to their backs. Customers were urged to tip the dogs: "We've found meat-based treats are the most positively received." The next day, MOO thanked everyone for their "overwhelming response" to the new service, but they said there would be no pug deliveries because...April Fools!

7 UNBELIEVABLE OFFICIAL TITLES

Brought to you by the One and Only King of Thrones, his Hole-yness the Great and Poo-erful Porcelain God, the Proud Progenitor of Popular Privy Publishing, the Main Man Himself, the Head Honcho, the One and Only, the Exalted Uncle John.

1 **Commonly Called:** Pope Francis
Official Title: His Holiness the Pope, Bishop of Rome and Vicar of Jesus Christ, Successor of St. Peter, Prince of the Apostles, Supreme Pontiff of the Universal Church, Patriarch of the West, Servant of the Servants of God, Primate of Italy, Archbishop and Metropolitan of the Roman Province, and Sovereign of Vatican City State

2 **Commonly Called:** Prince Charles
Official Title: His Royal Highness Prince Charles Philip Arthur George, Prince of Wales, Knight of the Garter, Knight of the Thistle, Knight Grand Cross of the Order of the Bath, Order of Merit, Knight of the Order of Australia, Companion of the Queen's Service Order, Privy Counsellor, Aide-de-Camp, Earl of Chester, Duke of Cornwall, Duke of Rothesay, Earl of Carrick, Baron of Renfrew, Lord of the Isles and Prince and Great Steward of Scotland

3 **Commonly Called:** Kim Jong-il, Supreme Leader of N. Korea
Official Title: Kim Jong II, Commander-in-chief, Glorious General Who Descended from Heaven, Guiding Star of the 21st Century, Sun of the Communist Future, Shining Star of Paektu Mountain, Bright Sun of the 21st Century, Respected Leader, Wise Leader, Brilliant Leader, Unique Leader, Beloved Father, Great Marshal, Mastermind of the Revolution

4 **Commonly Called:** President Idi Amin of Uganda
Official Title: His Excellency President for Life, Field Marshal Al Hadj Doctor Idi Amin Dada, VC, DSO, MC, Lord of All the Beasts of the Earth and Fishes of the Sea and Conqueror of the British Empire in Africa in General and Uganda in Particular

5 **Commonly Called:** Gaius Julius Octavius
Official Title: Imperator Caesar Divi Filius Augustus (Emperor Augustus Son of the Divine Caesar), Pontifex Maximus (High Priest), Princeps Civitatus (First Citizen of the State), Pater Patriae (Father of the Country)

6 **Commonly Called:** Colonel Muammar Gaddafi of Libya
Official Title: The Colonel, Guide of the First of September Great Revolution of the Arab Libyan Popular and Socialist Jamahiriya, Brotherly Leader and Guide of the Revolution, Universal Theorist, Imam of Muslims, Dean of Arab Rulers, King of Kings

7 **Commonly Called:** Franz Joseph I of Austria
Official Title: His Imperial and Apostolic Majesty, Franz Joseph I, by the Grace of God, Emperor of Austria, King of Hungary and Bohemia, King of Lombardy and Venice, of Dalmatia, Croatia, Slavonia, Lodomeria and Illyria; King of Jerusalem, Archduke of Austria; Grand Duke of Tuscany and Cracow, Duke of Lorraine, of Salzburg, Styria, Carinthia, Carniola and of the Bukovina; Grand Prince of Transylvania; Margrave of Moravia; Duke of Upper and Lower Silesia, of Modena, Parma, Piacenza and Guastalla, of Auschwitz and Zator, of Teschen, Friuli, Ragusa and Zara; Princely Count of Habsburg and Tyrol, of Kyburg, Gorizia and Gradisca; Prince of Trent and Brixen; Margrave of Upper and Lower Lusatia and in Istria; Count of Hohenems, Feldkirch, Bregenz, Sonnenberg; Lord of Trieste, of Cattaro, and in the Wendish Mark; Grand Voivode of the Voivodina of Serbia

10 "LAWS" THAT PROVE LIFE IS FUTILE

1 "Anything that can go wrong, will go wrong."
—Capt. Edward A. Murphy Jr., U.S. Air Force engineer

2 "The major difference between a thing that might go wrong and a thing that cannot possibly go wrong is that when a thing that cannot possibly go wrong goes wrong it usually turns out to be impossible to get at or repair."
—Douglas Adams

3 "A shortcut is the longest distance between two points."
—Charles Issawi

4 "If it works, they'll stop making it."
—Jane Otten

5 "What we anticipate seldom occurs; what we least expected generally happens."
—Benjamin Disraeli

6 "The longer one saves something before throwing it away, the sooner it will be needed after it is thrown away."
—James J. Caufield

7 "At the bank, post office, or supermarket, there is one universal law: The shortest line moves the slowest."
—Bill Vaughan

8 "Misquotations are the only quotations that are never misquoted."
—Hesketh Pearson

9 "Ninety percent of everything is crud."
—Theodore Sturgeon

10 "Two things are infinite: the universe and human stupidity; and I'm not sure about the universe."
—Albert Einstein

The Deutsches Currywurst Museum is one of **175** museums in Berlin.

10 MINERALS AND THEIR RELATIVE HARDNESS

Developed in 1812 by German geologist Friedrich Mohs, the Mohs scale works by determining the hardest material on the list that another material can scratch. For example, a human fingernail can scratch gypsum (#2) but can't scratch calcite (#3). Human fingernails therefore have a hardness of 2.5. Because the relative hardnesses of the minerals are not mathematically proportional, the Mohs scale is very simplistic. Gypsum is twice as hard as talc, but diamond is nearly four times as hard as corundum. Even still, the scale is still used today as a relative hardness measurement.

1 Talc. The softest mineral on Earth, used in talcum powder

2 Gypsum. Formed when seawater evaporates, used in plaster of paris. Gypsum is formed when seawater evaporates from the earth's surface.

3 Calcite. Found in limestone and animal shells.

4 Fluorite. Used to make steel and glass.

5 Apatite. Found in vertebrate bones and teeth.

6 Orthoclase. Also known as feldspar.

7 Quartz. The most common mineral in the Earth's crust.

8 Topaz. Varieties include emerald and aquamarine, used to make jewelry.

9 Corundum. Varieties include sapphire and ruby, also used in abrasives.

10 Diamond. The hardest natural substance, used for both jewelry and fine cutting instruments, earns its "forever" reputation.

5 NOT-CRAZY PEOPLE WHO SAID THEY SAW A UFO

1 Ronald Reagan. "I was in a plane, and when I looked out the window I saw this white light. It was zigzagging around, so I went up to the pilot and asked, 'Have you seen anything like that before?' The surprised pilot replied, 'Nope.' I said, 'Let's follow it!' We followed it for several minutes. It was a bright, white light. We followed it to Bakersfield, and all of a sudden, to our utter amazement, it went straight up into the heavens."

2 Sir Eric Gairy, prime minister of Grenada. "I was privileged to see what I consider a UFO very far out in the sky going at tremendous speed. I could not identify any movement within the object. It was just a tremendous light."

3 Maj. Donald "Deke" Slayton, NASA test pilot, astronaut. "I was testing a P-51 fighter in Minneapolis when I spotted this object. As I got closer it looked like a weather balloon, gray and about three feet in diameter. But as soon as I got behind the darn thing it didn't look like a balloon anymore. It looked like a saucer, a disk. About the same time, I realized that it was suddenly going away from me—and there I was, running at about 300 miles per hour. I tracked it for a little way, and then all of a sudden the thing just took off. It pulled about a 45-degree climbing turn and accelerated and just flat disappeared."

4 Victor Afanasyev, Soviet cosmonaut. "It followed us during half of our orbit. We observed it on the light side, and when we entered the shadow side, it disappeared completely. It was an engineered structure, made from some type of metal, approximately 40 meters long with inner hulls. The object was narrow here and wider here, and inside there were openings. Some places had projections like small wings. The object stayed very close to us. We photographed it, and our photos showed it to be 23 to 28 meters away."

5 Jimmy Carter. "It was the darnedest thing I've ever seen. It was big, it was very bright, it changed colors, and it was about the size of the moon. We watched it for 10 minutes, but none of us could figure out what it was. One thing's for sure, I'll never make fun of people who say they've seen unidentified objects in the sky. If I become president, I'll make every piece of information this country has about UFO sightings available to the public and the scientists." (He didn't.)

3 CELEBRITIES WHO SAW A UFO (and 1 who didn't)

1 John Lennon. "I wasn't surprised to see the UFO, as it looked just like the spaceships we've all seen on the cinema growing up, but then I realized that this thing was real, and so close that I could almost touch it!"

2 Olivia Newton-John. "I have seen one when I was very young. It was unidentified and it was flying."

3 David Bowie. "They came over so regularly we could time them. Sometimes they stood still, other times they moved so fast it was hard to keep a steady eye on them."

And 1 Who Didn't: While being interviewed for the 1970s sci-fi show *One Step Beyond*, **William Shatner** claimed that in 1969, while he was pushing his broken motorcycle through California's Mojave Desert, a UFO swooped down and guided him to safety. Forty years later, in 2014, the Shat made a shocking confession: "In all those years, I've sort of gone with the story. And then I finally confessed, 'No, I made it up.'"

17 ODD THINGS SINGERS SAID TO AUDIENCES

1 "I thank you in advance for the great round of applause I am about to get."

—Bo Diddley

2 "Please forgive me, but where are we?"

—Fiona Apple (she was in Phoenix)

3 "Flint must be an extremely wealthy town. I see that each of you bought two or three seats."

—Victor Borge, to a half-filled house in Flint, Michigan

4 "The show is an endless two-hour party."

—Lady Gaga

5 "I can't do this show until everybody stand up. Unless you got a handicap pass and you get special parking and sh*t."

—Kanye West, who refused to sing until a girl in a wheelchair stood up

6 "Did I hear, 'Come on, let's go!'? I work for me, buddy!"

—Neil Young

7 "There's a good crazy and there's a bad crazy. When you throw sh*t up here, that's an epic fail. I want to get your gifts, but I don't want you to knock my people out."

—Rihanna

8 "I just hit myself in the face with my own microphone. If that's not a humbling move, I don't know what is."

—Katy Perry

9 "This song is dedicated to Frank Zappa, River Phoenix, Fred Gwynne, who played Herman Munster, Dixie Lee Ray, Thomas P. 'Tip' O'Neil, and you, dumbass, who just threw water on me."

—Kurt Cobain

10 "The more you drink, the better I sound."
—Melissa Etheridge

11 "Let's let the little twerp express himself as best he can."
—Ray Davies of the Kinks, introducing a song sung by his younger brother Dave

12 "When I finally get this damn thing in tune, I'm gonna have it welded."
—Peter Tork of the Monkees, while tuning his banjo

13 "This is the second time we've ever played in front of people, man. We're scared sh*tless."
—Stephen Stills of CSN, to the crowd at Woodstock

14 "You paid $10, but I'm making $10,000, baby! So screw you!"
—Iggy Pop, after getting stuff thrown at him

15 "I hope you all get heart attacks."
—Jerry Lee Lewis, to a crowd that booed him

16 "Clap if we played something you came to hear."
—Bob Dylan

17 At the beginning of a Smashing Pumpkins concert, **Billy Corgan** walked onstage and asked the audience, "Are you ready to rock?" The crowd cheered wildly, to which Corgan replied, "Well, you've come to the wrong place."

MAHATMA GANDHI'S "7 BLUNDERS THAT SOCIETY COMMITS"

1 Wealth without work.

2 Pleasure without conscience.

3 Knowledge without character.

4 Commerce without morality.

5 Science without humanity.

6 Worship without sacrifice.

7 Politics without principles.

---

6 OF THE BIGGEST BLUNDERS IN BOXING HISTORY

Two brawny men step into a square ring and then try to beat each other senseless. What could possibly go wrong?

1 EARLY EXIT. In a 1946 fight, Ralph Walton lasted exactly one half of one second against his opponent Al Couture. Right after the opening bell rang, Walton was still adjusting his mouthpiece when Couture stepped up, threw a punch, and knocked him out.

2 FRIENDLY FIRE. Prior to a bout in the 1992 Golden Gloves Championship, boxer Daniel Caruso tried to psych himself up the way his hero, Marvin Hagler, often had: He punched himself in the face with his gloves on. Unaware of his strength, Caruso broke his own nose. Minutes before the bout was set to begin, the ring doctor declared him unfit to box. He had to forfeit the fight.

3 DOUBLE DOWNER. In 2009 kickboxers Tyler Bryant and Sean Parker—who were both making their professional debuts—faced each other at the 8 Seconds Saloon in Indianapolis. When the opening bell rang, the fighters came out swinging. But their offensive onslaught lacked one key ingredient: defense. Coincidentally, only eight seconds into the match, each fighter landed a punch on his opponent's face. Both men fell to the mat, and neither got up (though one did attempt to raise his arms in "victory" while lying on his back). It was the quickest double KO in boxing history.

4 LANE INFRACTION.

Referee Mills Lane may be the most famous referee not in just boxing but any sport (he even got his own TV court show), and he officiated some of the most controversial title fights from the 1970s to the 2000s. In this 1998 fight, however, Lane himself was the cause of the controversy. IBF middleweight champion Bernard Hopkins was defending his title against contender Robert Allen. In the fourth round of the closely fought match, the two fighters got tangled up with each other, and Lane stepped in to pry them apart...and somehow pushed Hopkins through the ropes and onto the floor below. Hopkins landed hard and was too injured to continue. The fight was ruled a no contest, meaning neither man was declared the winner, but thankfully for Hopkins, he still received his purse of $560,000. To reiterate, he earned more than half a million dollars for getting TKO'd by the referee.

5 WEIGHT A SECOND.

In the 1936 Summer Olympics in Berlin, Germany, South African lightweight Thomas Hamilton-Brown lost his opening match by decision. The boxer was so upset that he started eating...and eating...and eating. But wait! A few days later, the judges realized that they had made a scoring error—and Hamilton-Brown had actually won the fight! Unfortunately, his eating binge had made him too heavy for his weight class, and he was disqualified from the Olympics.

6 EAR IN MOUTH DISEASE.

If you're a sports fan, you know by the title what this story is about: In 1997 Mike Tyson and Evander Holyfield faced off for the WBA Heavyweight Championship title. In the third round of a losing battle, Tyson got tangled up with his opponent, and then—for some inexplicable reason—he bit off a chunk of Holyfield's earlobe. Tyson was disqualified. After the match, he defended his bizarre bite with this bizarre statement: "I got kids to feed!" (Apparently they were fond of regurgitated ear?)

5 MORE RANDOM LISTS OF 7s

7 SISTERS OF GREEK MYTHOLOGY

1 Halcyone
2 Asterope
3 Celaeno
4 Electra
5 Maia
6 Merope
7 Taygete

7 INDENTATIONS

1 **Punt:** The indentation at the bottom of a wine bottle, originally a byproduct of the glass-making process

2 **Calyx basin:** The dent at the bottom of an apple

3 **Philtrum:** The dent between your nose and lip

4 **Dimple:** A cheek dent

5 **Cleft chin:** A chin dent

6 **Natal cleft:** The scientific name for your butt crack

7 **Dimples of Venus:** Dents on the lower back, just above the natal cleft. (If you pierce your back dimples, it's a called a Venus piercing.)

7 HARRY POTTER BOOKS

1 *The Sorcerer's Stone*
2 *The Chamber of Secrets*
3 *The Prisoner of Azkaban*
4 *The Goblet of Fire*
5 *The Order of the Phoenix*
6 *The Half-Blood Prince*
7 *The Deathly Hallows*

7 SAMURAI

1 Shimada Kambei
2 Kikuchiyo
3 Okamoto Katsushiro
4 Katayama Gorobei
5 Hayashida Heihachi
6 Shichiroji
7 Kyuzo

7 TAXONOMIC CLASSIFICATIONS OF HUMAN BEINGS

1 Kingdom: *Animalia*
2 Phylum: *Chordata*
3 Class: *Mammalia*
4 Order: *Primates*
5 Family: *Hominidae*
6 Genus: *Homo*
7 Species: *Sapiens*

10 HOTELS THAT AREN'T BORING

1 DASPARKHOTEL (Linz, Austria)
"Our unique hotel is constructed from repurposed, incredibly robust drain pipes. The simultaneously functional and comfortable concrete sleep-pipes offer the chance to experience a place in a totally new way."

2 JULES' UNDERSEA LODGE (Key Largo, Florida)
"Just to enter the Lodge, one must actually scuba dive 21 feet beneath the surface of the sea. Entering through an opening in the bottom of the habitat, the feeling is much like discovering a secret underwater clubhouse."

3 DOG BARK PARK INN (Cottonwood, Idaho)
"A bed & breakfast guesthouse inside the World's Biggest Beagle! Guests enter the body of the beagle from a private 2nd-story deck [in the rear]."

4 PALACIO DE SAL (Potosí, Bolivia)
"The Hotel Palacio is built entirely of salt: walls, floors, ceilings, and much of its implementation and decoration. Chairs, tables, beds, and sculptures are made of salt."

5 KOKOPELLI'S CAVE (Farmington, New Mexico)
"Seventy feet below the surface and 1,700 square feet, the Cave consists of a master bedroom, living area, replica Native American kiva, dining area, full kitchen, and bathroom with rock walls incorporating a waterfall shower and Jacuzzi tub."

6 ICEHOTEL (Jukkasjärvi, Sweden)

"ICEHOTEL is constructed from 1,000 tons of Torne River ice and 30,000 tons of 'snice,' a mixture of snow and ice that strengthens the structure. Open from December to April, when everything begins to slowly melt and return to the Torne River."

7 KAROSTAS CIETUMS (Liepāja, Latvia)

"Here you have a chance to spend the night in a prison cell which is considered to be even more impressive than the Alcatraz in the USA, to sleep on a prison bunk or an iron bed, and to have a prison meal. There is also a special offer to schoolchildren—an opportunity to spend a night in prison cells on bunks and mattresses."

8 THE BIRD'S NEST (Harads, Sweden)

"The treeroom's exterior is nothing but a gigantic bird's nest. The interior, on the other hand, is familiar and exclusive. The walls are clad with wood panels and the windows almost disappear in the exterior's network of branches."

9 JUMBO STAY (Arlanda, Sweden)

"Spend the night onboard a real jumbo jet—on the ground! The plane is a used jumbo jet model 747-212B made in 1976. We also offer a luxury suite in the converted cockpit with a panoramic view of the airport."

10 THE LIBRARY HOTEL (New York, New York)

"The Library Hotel concept is inspired by the Dewey Decimal System. Each of the 10 guest room floors honors one of the 10 categories of the Dewey Decimal System, and each of the 60 rooms is uniquely adorned with a collection of books and art exploring a distinctive topic within the category it belongs to." (Ed. note: "within the category to which it belongs.")

33 RANDOM POLL RESULTS

For nearly 30 years, we at the Bathroom Readers' Institute have sought out the results of odd surveys from around the globe. Here are the oddest.

1 1% of Americans polled say they have no friends.

2 9% of American households dress up their pet for Halloween.

3 10% of office workers say they're satisfied with their jobs.

4 10% of Brits put their underwear in the refrigerator to help stay cool.

5 10% of Canadians say they've had sex in a canoe.

6 11% of Americans have thrown out a dish just because they "didn't want to wash it."

7 12% of Americans think Joan of Arc was Noah's wife.

8 12% of American boat owners name their boat *Serenity*.

9 20% of Americans believe it would be okay to clone extinct species.

10 21% of Americans are regularly "bored out of their minds."

11 22% of Australians claim to have an ancestor who was a convict.

12 27% of Americans say broccoli is their favorite vegetable.

13 27% of all readers skip ahead to find out what will happen in a book before they finish it.

14 27% of Facebook users have checked their status on the toilet.

15 27% of female lottery winners hid their winning ticket in their bra.

16 29% of Americans admit they've stolen something from a store.

17 38% of Canadian women prefer chocolate to sex.

18 40% of nurses said they would not want to be treated at the hospital where they work.

19 49% of Americans don't know that white bread is made from wheat.

20 52% of Americans say they'd "rather spend a week in jail" than be president.

21 53% of women would dump their boyfriend if they didn't get a Valentine's Day gift.

22 57% of British kids think Germany is the most boring country in Europe.

23 58% of Americans have called in sick to work when they weren't sick.

24 62% of Americans say Monday is the worst day of the week.

25 67% of American men prefer boxers to briefs.

26 70% of Italians say they tell seven lies per day.

27 75% of college students expect to become a millionaire.

28 76% of Bathroom Readers' Institute members (go team!) prefer their TP to hang over the top.

29 82% of TV viewers think reality TV shows are scripted.

30 84% of American office workers are against unisex bathrooms.

31 87% of people said they were "likely" to go to heaven.

32 90% of Americans rode in a grocery cart when they were kids.

33 95% of people put their left sock on first.

A "187" is police code for a homicide.

3 STAGES OF A THUNDERSTORM

1 CUMULUS STAGE

The weather starts turning nasty when a cold front contacts warm, moist air. It causes the warm air—which is less dense than cool air—to rise. As it does, it cools, causing the moisture inside it to condense, forming cumulus clouds—those vertically aligned "fluffy" clouds. The process of condensation in turn causes more heat to be released, warming the air and causing an updraft to form, pulling more and more warm, moist air upward into a tower shape. That updraft is the storm's cell.

2 MATURE STAGE

The rising warm air meets a "ceiling" of even warmer air, which stops it from rising any more. This causes it to spread horizontally, forming an anvil-shaped cumulonimbus cloud. The water in the cloud freezes in droplet form, falls, and melts into rain. If the water freezes into large enough droplets, they don't have enough time to melt. Result: hail. The falling rain and/ or hail creates a downdraft, which can accentuate and interfere with the existing updraft, causing very turbulent winds and often very severe weather. Lightning occurs when static electricity builds up in a cloud, caused by the interaction of water and ice. When enough static builds up—*crack!*—it has to be released. A lightning bolt superheats the air around it and creates a pressure wave that we hear as thunder.

3 DISSIPATION STAGE

When the cool downdraft pushes away the supply of warm air fueling the updraft, the storm peters out. If you're lucky, you might see a pretty rainbow.

5 LEFTY LISTS

10 LEFT-HANDED A-LISTERS
1 Oprah Winfrey
2 Lady Gaga
3 Justin Bieber
4 Angelina Jolie
5 Brad Pitt
6 Scarlett Johansson
7 Tom Cruise
8 Jon Stewart
9 Tina Fey
10 Eminem

5 THINGS THAT ARE HARDER IF YOU'RE A LEFTY

1 **Writing in a spiral binder.** Because the coils interfere with your left hand.

2 **Writing with a ballpoint pen.** Ink gets all over your hand.

3 **Writing in grade school.** Most school desks were made for righties.

4 **Playing guitar.** You either have to learn how to play upside down (like Jimi Hendrix) or buy a special left-handed guitar (like Paul McCartney).

5 **Using scissors...**and kitchen appliances, power tools, video game controllers, etc. Most things in this world are made by righties, for righties.

8 SOUTHPAWS-IN-CHIEF
1 James Garfield
2 Herbert Hoover
3 Harry S. Truman
4 Gerald Ford
5 Ronald Reagan
6 George H. W. Bush
7 Bill Clinton
8 Barack Obama

Note: It's not entirely clear if any presidents before Garfield (1881) were lefties —it was most likely "trained" out of them at a young age (which happened to Reagan).

That leads us to...

8 WAYS LEFTIES HAVE BEEN DISCRIMINATED AGAINST
1 **In ancient Rome,** the Latin word for "left" was *sinister*.

Another meaning: "evil." The word for "right" was *dexter*. Another meaning: "skillful." The word *ambidextrous* literally means "right-handed with both hands."

2 The **tradition of throwing salt** over your left shoulder for good luck came about because the salt will go into the eyes of the devil, who lurks just behind us...to the left.

3 **Traditional Christians** believed that on judgment day, God will bless the saved with his right hand and cast sinners out of heaven with his left, which explains why nuns used to commonly hit southpaws' knuckles with a ruler. (That's also where the word "righteous" comes from.)

4 **Devout Muslims** only eat from communal bowls using their right hand. That's because the left hand is reserved for "unclean" tasks (like wiping).

5 Some **Native American tribes** strapped kids' left arms to the mother's cradleboard, which caused most infants to become right-handed.

6 Nineteenth-century Italian psychiatrist **Cesare Lombroso's** book *The Delinquent Male* asserted that left-handers were more likely to be psychological "degenerates" and prone to violence. His views were deemed "cutting-edge science."

7 In the 1940s, psychiatrist **Abram Blau** penned a controversial article called "Don't Let Your Child Be a Lefty." Blau wrote that parents who don't retrain their kids to be righties "no doubt think they are being 'modern' and 'progressive' by not trying to get their child to do something seemed to be against his nature. But how wrong such an attitude can be!"

8 Even today, **psychiatrists and psychologists** know a lot more about the brains of right-handers because left-handers aren't included in most neurological and behavior studies. Why not? Because their brains are actually *that* different.

7 SIDE EFFECTS OF BEING LEFT-HANDED

(Consult your physician if any of these conditions persist.)

1 Mental Illness. Although lefties make up only about 11 percent of the population, 20 percent of schizophrenics are left-handed. Lefties make up 15 to 30 percent of all patients in mental institutions. They're also three times more likely than righties to become alcoholics.

2 Upset Innards. Per capita, lefties have higher rates of high blood pressure and irritable bowel syndrome. They're also more prone to allergies, insomnia, migraines, and a host of other maladies.

3 Shorter Fuse. Lefties tend to get angrier faster. According to a 2010 study, this occurs because in the brains of lefties and ambidextrous people, the two hemispheres interact more, which means that lefties' emotions can interfere with logic. (An odd side effect: It's also easier to scare a lefty.)

4 Duh. Lefties are more likely to be on the extreme ends of the intelligence scale than the general population. (The good news: A higher proportion of people with IQs over 140 are lefties.)

5 SLOD Disorder. Because most power tools were designed for righties, lefties in the workshop are more likely to suffer from "Sudden Loss of Digits" disorder. (That's not a real medical term, but it should be.)

6 Dain bramage. According to *The Straight Dope*'s Cecil Adams (a lefty himself): "There's a fair amount of evidence that left-handedness is caused by minor brain damage at birth (though there seems to be a genetic component as well). Possibly as a result, lefties are clumsier if perhaps also more creative."

7 Premature Death. According to several studies, southpaws have shorter life spans than righties—which isn't surprising considering entries 1 through 6 above.

12 THINGS POLITICIANS ACTUALLY BELIEVE

Well, they may or may not believe them...but they did say them.

1 "When a physician removes a child from a woman, that is the largest organ in a body."
—Rep. Mary Sue McClurkin (R-AL)

2 "Men often do need maternity care."
—Kathleen Sebelius (D), Health and Human Services chief

3 "The earth's about 9,000 years old."
—Rep. Paul Broun (R-GA), member of the House Committee on Science, Space and Technology

4 "The Internet...has not done well, just like when Google started doing all their things, it didn't work out well."
—Sen. Harry Reid (D-NV), defending the botched rollout of the Obamacare website

5 "Presidents Washington, Lincoln, and Roosevelt have all authorized electronic surveillance on a far broader scale."
—Attorney General Alberto Gonzalez (R)

6 "Every month that we do not have an economic recovery package, 500 million Americans lose their jobs."
—Rep. Nancy Pelosi (D-CA), Speaker of the House

7 "The temperature on Mars is exactly as it is here. Nobody will dispute that."
—State Sen. Brandon Smith (R-KY)

8 "My fear is that the whole island will become so overly populated that it will tip over and capsize."

—Rep. Hank Johnson (D-GA), concerned about a proposal to station 8,000 Marines on the island of Guam

9 "Just because the Supreme Court rules on something doesn't necessarily mean that that's constitutional."

—Rep. Jim Bridenstine (R-OK), forgetting the primary function of the Supreme Court

10 "We've lasted 400 years, operating under a constitution that clearly defines what is constitutional and what is not."

—Rep. Sheila Jackson Lee (D-TX), forgetting the Constitution was enacted in 1789

11 "We're the country that built the intercontinental railroad."

—President Barack Obama (D), speaking about the *transcontinental* railroad

And one statement that everyone can agree on...

12 "It is perfectly American to be wrong."

—Rep. Newt Gingrich (R), former Speaker of the House

---

6 FLAGS OVER TEXAS

Over the past 500 years, six different nations' governments have laid claim to the Lone Star State.

1 Spain (1529–1685, 1690–1821)

2 France (1685–1690)

3 Mexico (1821–1836)

4 Republic of Texas (1836–45)

5 Confederate States of America (1861–65)

6 United States of America (1845–61, 1865–present)

---

11 VINTAGE AD CLAIMS YOU WON'T SEE TODAY

Nowadays, it seems like nothing is good for you. Back in the early to mid-20th century, everything was good for you... especially the stuff considered the worst for you today.

1 **Swift's Premium Bacon:** "Authorities recommend bacon for children."

2 **Cocaine Tooth Drops:** "Instantaneous cure for toothaches!"

3 **Hires' Root Beer:** "The great health drink."

4 **Lard Information Council:** "They're happy because they eat lard!"

5 **Sugar Information Council:** "If sugar is so fattening, how come so many kids are thin? Sugar—it isn't just good flavor. It's good food."

6 **Beech-Nut Macaroni & Cheese:** "This macaroni can be eaten every day, like potatoes."

7 **Towle's Log Cabin Syrup:** "Eat Towle's Log Cabin Syrup every day of the week!"

8 **Sanitized Tape Worms:** "Eat! Eat! Eat! And always stay thin!"

9 **Camel Cigarettes:** "Grow to 100 years old! More doctors smoke Camels than any other cigarette."

10 **Blatz Beer:** "A case of Blatz Beer in the house means much to the young mother, and baby participates in its benefits. The malt in the beer supplies nourishing qualities that are essential at this time, and the hops act as an appetizing, stimulating tonic."

11 **Swifts Meat for Babies:** "As digestible as milk. A recent study shows babies fed meats have fewer colds. Here's meat they can eat at 3 weeks!"

Macallan **194** whiskey (aged 64 years) sells for $460,000 a bottle.

10 REASONS WHY LAUGHTER IS NOT "THE BEST MEDICINE"

In 2013 the British Medical Journal *reported a study in which the old axiom—laughter is the best medicine—was put to the test. Not only did the study find that laughter is* not *the best medicine (most doctors recommend taking actual medicine), but excessive or uncontrollable laughter can lead to:*

1 Asthma attacks

2 Cerebral tumors

3 Syncope (fainting)

4 Cataplexy (sudden muscle weakness)

5 Cardiac rupture

6 Abdominal hernia

7 Headache

8 Interlobular emphysema (excessive air in tissues)

9 Jaw dislocation

10 Incontinence

The researchers' conclusion: "Laughter is not purely beneficial. The harms it can cause are immediate and dose related, the risks being highest for Homeric (uncontrollable) laughter." Speaking of Homeric, that may explain this quote by Homer Simpson: "Me lose brain? Uh-oh! Ha ha ha! Why I laugh?"

So if you have a medical condition that "only hurts when you laugh," don't read this:

Bart: "I don't want a new dog! I want Santa's Little Helper!"

Homer: "Well, crying isn't gonna bring him back, boy, unless your tears smell like dog food. So you can either sit there crying and eating can after can of dog food until your tears smell enough like dog food to make your dog come back, or you can go out there and find your dog!"

Bart: [Runs away.]

Homer: "Rats, I almost had him eating dog food."

11 YELLOW THINGS AND WHY THEY'RE YELLOW

1 THE YELLOW TRAFFIC LIGHT

In 1920 roads were becoming more crowded and more dangerous, so Detroit police officer William Potts converted railroad signal lights into the first traffic light. Railroad lights were initially white, green, and red, but in the early 1900s, yellow replaced white because it was deemed more visible.

2 THE BANANA

A banana starts out green because its peel contains chlorophyll, like any other green plant. As the fruit inside ripens, a chemical reaction in the peel causes the chlorophyll to break down. As the chlorophyll level drops, the green fades, and the banana turns yellow.

3 A YELLOW RIBBON TIED TO A TREE

An early 20th-century folk tale tells of a convict returning home—if his family welcomed him, they would tie a white ribbon around an apple tree. In 1971 *New York Post* writer Pete Hamill penned a dramatic retelling—except in the version he'd heard, the ribbon was yellow and the tree was oak. That article inspired an ABC TV movie and then a song composed by Irwin Levine and L. Russell Brown called "Tie a Yellow Ribbon Round the Ole Oak Tree." It became a huge hit for Tony Orlando in 1973. The ribbon got its modern meaning—remembering the military—during the 1980 Iran Hostage Crisis when Penne Laingen, wife of the captive U.S. ambassador Bruce Laingen, told the *Washington Post* that she tied a ribbon around a tree in her yard: "One of these days, Bruce is going to come home and untie that yellow ribbon." (He did.)

4 THE YELLOW JERSEY

In the annual Tour de France bicycle race, the leader at the start of each stage wears *le maillot jaune,* or "yellow jersey." The race itself dates to the turn of the 20th century, but the yellow jersey made its first appearance in 1919 to make the leader more conspicuous. Why yellow? Because a magazine called *L'Auto* sponsored the race, and it was printed on yellow paper.

5 THE YELLOW PAGES

The business phone book owes its distinctive color to a printer in Cheyenne, Wyoming, who in 1883 ran out of white paper while printing one of the first ever phone directories (the phone had only been patented a few years earlier). So the printer finished the job on yellow paper, and it caught on.

6 THE SUN

The sun is yellow, right? Wrong. It's white. Why white? Because sunlight contains all the colors of the spectrum. But the photons that come from the sun are mostly in the green spectrum. So if the sun is white, and most of its photons are green, how do we see it as yellow? Earth's atmosphere is to blame: Red, yellow, and orange aren't scattered as easily as the rest of the spectrum, so when sunlight is filtered through the atmosphere, those are the colors that we see.

7 THE YELLOW RIVER

The *Huang He,* or "Yellow River," is the second-longest river in China (3,395 miles), and the seventh-longest in the world. It was named for the billions of tons of yellow silt that it carries.

8 A NEWBORN BABY

When your body replaces old red blood cells, it creates bilirubin, which is yellow. The liver normally removes bilirubin, but when a baby is in utero, the placenta removes it. When the baby is born, the liver doesn't always start filtering immediately. Result: The bilirubin causes a yellowing of the skin and eyes. Called *physiological jaundice*, the baby is yellowest at two to four days old. Although this type of jaundice can look alarming, it's usually harmless. (But it should be checked by a doctor.)

9 YELLOW JOURNALISM

In the 1890s, Joseph Pulitzer's *New York World* was among the first newspapers to use sensationalism and hyperbole to sell issues. One of the *World*'s comic strips, "Hogan's Alley" by Richard F. Outcault, featured a popular character called the Yellow Kid. When William Randolph Hearst launched the rival *New York Journal*, he hired Outcault away from the *World*. Pulitzer vowed revenge: He hired a new cartoonist to create a second Yellow Kid, and as the two newspapers traded barbs back and forth, their style of over-the-top reporting came to be known as "yellow journalism."

10 THE YELLOW TAXICAB

In 1915 Chicago businessman John Hertz founded the Yellow Cab Company. He commissioned a university study to "scientifically ascertain which color would stand out strongest at a distance." The winner, of course, was yellow. But Hertz wasn't the first: In 1909 Albert Rockwell operated a fleet of yellow cabs in New York City. He wasn't as scientific, though—he chose yellow because it was his wife's favorite color.

11 URINE

Urochrome is a compound that forms when your body breaks down worn-out red blood cells. Because the kidneys act as waste filters, urochrome travels through them and into urine. What does that have to do with the color of pee? Urochrome is a yellow pigment. The concentration of urochrome affects the color: Drink more, the urochrome is diluted, and the pee is less yellow; drink less, there's more urochrome, and it's darker.

12 THEORIES ABOUT HIDDEN MEANINGS IN "YELLOW SUBMARINE"

We were originally going to include this as a single entry in the "11 Yellow Things and Why They're Yellow" list (see page 196), but as we scoured Beatles books and Internet message boards, we kept finding more and more outlandish theories of supposed secret meanings in this seemingly innocuous kids' song from the Beatles' 1966 album Revolver. It starts off innocently enough...

> **In the town where I was born,**
> **Lived a man who sailed to sea,**
> **And he told us of his life,**
> **In the land of submarines...**

1 THE "YELLOW SUBMARINE" IS A DRUG. This is the most common fan theory, but which drug? In the 1960s, marijuana rolling papers were yellow, hence the slang term for a "fat joint" was "yellow submarine." Another theory goes that yellow Darvon sleeping pills—popular in San Francisco at the time—were called "yellow submarines," and that's what the song is about. Another theory goes that the song was inspired by a yellow LSD pill. Stranger still: "Yellow Submarine" is about smoking yellow banana peels. Regardless of which drug inspired the song, the "man who sailed to sea" is a drug dealer. The lyric "And our friends are all aboard" means that all the Beatles' friends liked to do drugs, too.

2 THE SONG WAS INSPIRED BY AN ACID TRIP. This story goes that John Lennon, George Harrison, and Ringo Starr were tripping on LSD at Harrison's house when Lennon hallucinated that he was "under the sea." He kept saying, "It's like we're all living in a yellow submarine, man." (A variation goes that they were tripping in a car and Lennon remarked that a house they passed looked like a yellow submarine.)

3 THE SONG IS ABOUT GETTING DRUNK. The phrase "yellow sub" is Cockney rhyming slang for a pub, where the Beatles spent a lot of time with friends who were "all aboard."

4 IT WAS INSPIRED BY A REAL YELLOW SUBMARINE. Not far north of the Beatles' hometown of Liverpool, England, is the town of Barrow-in-Furness, which has a shipyard where submarines were built during the war years. Before the vessels were painted black, they were given a primer coat of yellow ocher. One of the Beatles (depending on which version you hear) visited the shipyard and later told his bandmates he saw a "yellow submarine." Another rumor goes that one of the Beatles was inspired by a yellow submarine in southern France.

5 IT WAS INSPIRED BY A WHALE IN A CHURCH. An anonymous Beatles fan wrote on an Internet message board: "While on a visit to Liverpool last week, I came across a man at Saint Peter's church, where he first met Paul and John. He showed me a picture on a wall of a whale. He said that the whale gave John the idea of a yellow submarine."

6 IT'S A METAPHOR ABOUT FAME. The color yellow is symbolic of all the "bright attention" the Beatles were receiving; the submarine is symbolic of the box that they were trapped in by all that fame. But they had their friends there—"every one of us has all we need"—so they made the best of it.

7 IT'S ABOUT FEAR. People who are afraid to share their true feelings go "beneath the waves" to hide inside a submarine that is yellow, the color of cowardice.

8 IT'S ABOUT COMMUNISM. As evidenced by the "every one of us has all we need" lyric. (So shouldn't it have been called "Red Submarine"?) The "sea of green" in this case refers to money. A related theory: Yellow refers to China—the song is a political statement about Western governments ignoring the plight of the Chinese people.

9 IT'S ABOUT A BUG FROM OUTER SPACE. One night Paul McCartney dreamed that an "alien praying mantis" (which resembles a yellow submarine) visited him and gave him the idea for the song. The (lone) Internet commenter who put forth this theory said he wrote a letter to McCartney for verification but didn't receive a reply.

10 IT'S BATHROOM HUMOR. According to yet another Internet commenter: "Sorry to be so graphic. Ever notice in the toilet after you use it, it often leaves 'submarines' that can be close to yellow on occasion? My humble understanding was that considering all the politicians, wars, etc., it can often seem as if we are living inside sh*t."

11 IT'S FURTHER PROOF THAT "PAUL IS DEAD." This bizarre rumor (spread by an American deejay) dogged the band in their later years, with fans uncovering all sorts of "evidence" that Paul McCartney had been killed in a car accident and replaced by a lookalike. In this theory, the yellow submarine represents a pine coffin, and the lyric "sky of blue and sea of green" is Paul's grave in a grassy graveyard on a sunny day. Some people claim that among all the yelling and sound effects in the background of the song, you can clearly hear Lennon say, "Paul is dead."

12 IT'S A CONSPIRACY! The Beatles were pawns of the Illuminati. The secretive cult actually wrote all of the Fab Four's tunes and scripted their interviews in an attempt to weaken Western civilization with "drugs and free love" so the Illuminati could take over the world. "Yellow Submarine" is symbolic of the "Golden Phallus" that serves as the capstone of the Ziggurat pyramid...or something along those lines. If you want to know more, you try reading through all of those conspiracy websites. We give up.

AND THE 1 REAL MEANING OF "YELLOW SUBMARINE" IS...

It's just a kids' song. According to Paul McCartney, who wrote the melody and most of the lyrics, there are no hidden meanings in "Yellow Submarine." In Barry Miles's 1997 biography *Many Years from Now*, McCartney explains how the idea popped into his head:

> I remember thinking that a children's song would be quite a good idea, and I thought of images and the color yellow came to me, and a submarine came to me, and I thought, "Well, that's kind of nice, like a toy, a very childish yellow submarine."

Here's the story: In early 1966, McCartney was living in girlfriend Jane Asher's parents' house when he got the idea for the song as he was falling asleep one night. "I was thinking of it as a song for Ringo, which it eventually turned out to be, so I wrote it as not too rangey in the vocal, then started making a story, sort of an ancient mariner, telling the young kids where he'd lived." Despite McCartney's explanation, however, the fan theories persist to this day. In a recent interview, he reiterated, "It's a happy place, that's all! And there's nothing more to be read into it than there is in the lyrics of any children's song."

Bonus fact: One of the most colorful lyrics in "Yellow Submarine" was provided by the Scottish singer Donovan. He and McCartney were friends, and one day Paul asked him for help with a song. "He said he was missing a line and would I fill it in," recalled Donovan. "I left the room and returned with this: 'Sky of blue and sea of green / In our yellow submarine.' It was nothing really, but Paul liked it and it stayed in." (But what does it *mean*?)

10 INTERNATIONAL SAYINGS TO ADD SPICE TO YOUR ENGLISH

INSTEAD OF:		TRY:
1 Money doesn't grow on trees.	⟶	The sky doesn't throw chicks. (Arabic)
2 A drop in the bucket.	⟶	Nine cows, one hair. (Chinese)
3 Nice guys finish last.	⟶	A cat in gloves catches no mice. (Spanish)
4 Don't count your chickens until they're hatched.	⟶	Don't praise the day before evening. (German)
5 Out of the frying pan, into the fire.	⟶	Fallen from the sky, stuck on a date palm. (Hindi)
6 To cost an arm and a leg.	⟶	To cost the eyes in your head. (French)
7 All talk and no action.	⟶	If he made 100 knives, none would have a handle. (Farsi)
8 To beat around the bush.	⟶	To walk like a cat around hot porridge. (Swedish)
9 The grass is always greener on the other side.	⟶	Tasty is the fish from someone else's table. (Yiddish)
10 Nothing ventured, nothing gained.	⟶	If you don't enter the tiger's cave, you won't catch its cub. (Japanese)

6 CANNED LISTS

5 ODD CANNED FOODS
1 Yoders Canned Bacon
2 Westlers Canned Hamburgers in Onion Gravy
3 B&M Canned Brown Bread
4 Westlers Canned Breakfast
5 Heinz Canned Spotted Dick

4 SOUVENIR CANS
1 "Genuine Los Angeles Smog" (1958)
2 "Canned Air from Paris" (2012)
3 "Genuine Canned Florida Sunshine" (1970s)
4 "Canned Radiation, Three Mile Island" (1979)

8 MEATS THAT COME IN CANS
1 Pork Brains
2 Fish Mouths
3 Smoked Rattlesnake
4 Cajun Style Alligator
5 Elk Au Jus
6 Kangaroo Chili
7 Reindeer Pâté
8 Whole Chicken

5 FOODS BY "THAILAND UNIQUE"
1 Canned Oven Baked Tarantula, $15.99
2 Unseasoned Canned Cicada Eggs, $8.50
3 Canned Salted Firewood Larvae, $6.80
4 Canned Asian Forest Scorpion, $8.90
5 Canned Black Ants with Salt, $6.50

4 NOVELTY VIBRATING CANS
1 "Los Angeles Earthquake"
2 "Hawaiian Hula Hips"
3 "100% American Whoop-Ass"
4 "Elvis"

3 UNCANNY CANS
1 The can-can, a dance invented in 1830s Paris
2 Can, an experimental rock group from 1960s Germany
3 *Uncle John's Canoramic Bathroom Reader* (2014), a great book with a can-do attitude!

A chessboard has 204 squares if you include all of its dimensions.

8 FUTURE STARS WHO GOT CANNED

1 HUGH JACKMAN: 7-Eleven
"I got fired because the boss said I talked too much to the customers."

2 SNOOP DOG: Supermarket
"I was better at stealing the groceries than I was at bagging them."

3 KATE WALSH: Burger King
"I had a runny nose and the assistant manager didn't like me."

4 MADONNA: Dunkin Donuts
"I was sacked for squirting a donut jelly all over the customers."

5 ROBERT REDFORD: Supermarket and Oil Man
"I was a failure at everything I tried. I worked as a box boy at a supermarket and got fired. Then my dad got me a job at Standard Oil—fired again."

6 TERRENCE HOWARD: Paperboy
"They fired me after two weeks because I didn't get up early enough."

7 WALT DISNEY: *Kansas City Star*
Disney's editor said that he "lacked imagination and had no good ideas."

8 BILL HADER: Movie theater
"One night a group of sorority girls came in and were blocking the doors. I asked them to move. They were being really rude to me. So, as I tore the tickets I said, 'By the way, the boat sinks at the end, Leo dies. It's great, you think he's sleeping, but he's frozen! Oh, and the old lady throws the jewelry in the ocean. Enjoy the movie.' My always-stoned boss came over and said, 'Did you just tell them the end of *Titanic*? I have to fire you.'"

6 MAJOR EXTINCTIONS IN EARTH'S HISTORY

The demise of the dinosaurs was the most recent of five major extinctions that have occurred in our planet's tumultuous past. Here's a bit about each one, along with some alarming evidence that the sixth mass die-off may already be upon us.

1 **The Ordovician-Silurian Extinction**, which occurred about 440 million years ago, was a result of climate change caused by sudden global cooling, particularly in the tropical oceans. There was little or no life on land at the time, but nearly 85 percent of life in the seas disappeared.

2 **The Late Devonian Extinction** occurred about 370 million years ago. Possible reasons: asteroid collisions that triggered volcanic lava floods, and environmental changes due to tectonic plate movements in the early formation of the continents. Another theory: the "Devonian Plant Hypothesis," which goes that the expansion of plant life on land killed 70 to 87 percent of animal life on land and in the oceans.

3 **The Permian-Triassic Extinction**, about 250 million years ago, was the deadliest of the five mass extinctions. Paleontologists once believed that this "Great Dying" took millions of years to occur, but many now think it took between 8,000 and 100,000 years, a mere blip on the geological timetable. The impact and explosion of a bolide (a large meteor) the size of Mount Everest might have accelerated the climate change that was already taking place as a result of greenhouse gases released by volcanic lava floods and tectonic plate shifts. An estimated 97 percent of the planet's existing species were wiped out.

4 **The End-Triassic Extinction** took place 200 to 215 million years ago, not too long after dinosaurs and mammals first evolved. It's the most mysterious of the five mass extinctions. In addition to the 22 percent of marine families that were lost, an unknown number of vertebrate-animal species on land also went extinct. In all, it's estimated that at least 76 percent of all species on Earth were wiped out. Causes may include volcanic lava floods, shifting continents, and bolide explosions.

5 **The Cretaceous-Tertiary Extinction**, the most recent and best known of the five mass extinctions, occurred about 65 million years ago. One or several bolide collisions are probably to blame, which caused lava floods that disrupted the planet's ecosystems. The extinction killed 16 percent of marine families and 50 to 80 percent of vertebrate families on land, including—most famously—the dinosaurs.

6 **The Anthropocene Extinction** is the proposed name for the sixth mass extinction, which may already be happening. Also referred to as the Holocene Extinction (the name of our current epoch), the more dire predictions warn that 50 percent of Earth's species will be gone by 2100. Unlike the other mass extinctions, this one is being caused by a single species—us. According to the National Wildlife Federation, nearly 30,000 species per year—about three per hour—go extinct, many from man-made causes such as pollution and habitat destruction.

In 2014 a study conducted by an international team of scientists concluded that we are in "what appears to be the early days of the planet's sixth mass biological extinction event." As in the other extinctions, the large animals are in the most danger because they require more room and more food, and they reproduce at a slower rate. With the larger mammals in decline, smaller mammals—especially rats—will increase dramatically, as will the diseases and famines that they spread. This could eventually lead to our own demise. That is, if a cataclysmic eruption or nuclear war doesn't wipe us out first.

57 COCA-COLA SLOGANS

1 "Drink Coca-Cola" (1886)

2 "Delicious and refreshing" (1904)

3 "Coca-Cola revives and sustains" (1905)

4 "The great national temperance beverage" (1906)

5 "Good til the last drop" (1908)

6 "Three million a day" (1917)

7 "Thirst knows no season" (1922)

8 "Enjoy life" (1923)

9 "Refresh yourself" (1924)

10 "Six million a day" (1925)

11 "It had to be good to get where it is" (1926)

12 "Pure as sunlight" (1927)

13 "Around the corner from anywhere" (1927)

14 "Coca-Cola...pure drink of natural flavors" (1928)

15 "The pause that refreshes" (1929)

16 "Ice-cold sunshine" (1932)

17 "America's favorite moment" (1937)

18 "The best friend thirst ever had" (1938)

19 "Thirst asks nothing more" (1938)

20 "Coca-Cola goes along" (1939)

21 "Coca-Cola has the taste thirst goes for" (1939)

22 "Whoever you are, whatever you do, wherever you may be, when you think of refreshment, think of ice cold Coca-Cola" (1939)

23 "Coca-Cola is Coke!" (1941)

24 "The only thing like Coca-Cola is Coca-Cola itself" (1942)

Oklahoma has 208 rigs actively drilling for oil and natural gas.

25 "How about a Coke?" (1944)

26 "Coke means Coca-Cola" (1945)

27 "Passport to refreshment" (1945)

28 "Coke knows no season" (1947)

29 "Where there's Coke there's hospitality" (1948)

30 "Coca-Cola...along the highway to anywhere" (1949)

31 "What you want is a Coke" (1952)

32 "For people on the go" (1954)

33 "Coca-Cola...makes good things taste better" (1956)

34 "The sign of good taste" (1957)

35 "The cold, crisp taste of Coke" (1958)

36 "Be really refreshed" (1959)

37 "What a refreshing new feeling" (1961)

38 "Things go better with Coke" (1963)

39 "Coke...after Coke... after Coke" (1966)

40 "Coke has the taste you never get tired of" (1967)

41 "It's the real thing" (1969)

42 "I'd like to buy the world a Coke" (1970)

43 "Look for the real things" (1974)

44 "Coke adds life" (1976)

45 "Have a Coke and a smile" (1979)

46 "Coke is it!" (1981)

47 "Red White & You" (1986)

48 "Catch the wave" (for New Coke) (1986)

49 "Can't beat the real thing" (for Coca-Cola Classic) (1991)

50 "Always Coca-Cola" (1993)

51 "Enjoy" (1990s)

52 "Life tastes good" (2001)

53 "Make it real" (2005)

54 "Live on the Coke side of life" (2007)

55 "Open happiness" (2009)

56 "Twist the cap to refreshment" (2010)

57 "Life begins here" (2011)

6 SCIENCE FACTS THAT SOUND LIKE SCIENCE FICTION

On page 67, we told you about some weird science-"fact"ion stuff like real death rays. In this installment, we look at some bizarre experiments taking place in the animal kingdom.

1 CYBORG MOTH. In 2014 researchers at North Carolina State University implanted a chip into a moth that allows the team to direct and control where it flies. Lead scientist Dr. Alper Bozkurt hopes that their "cybermoths" will "create a flexible aerial sensor network that can identify survivors or public health hazards in the wake of a disaster."

2 EAR-RAT-IC. In 2013 a team at Boston's Massachusetts General Hospital engineered an ear from scratch. First, they took cow and sheep tissue and grew it over a frame shaped like a human ear. Then the ear was implanted onto the back of a rat whose immune system had been suppressed so its body wouldn't reject the ear. Twelve weeks later, the ear was the size of an adult human's and was just as flexible as the real thing. Human clinical trials are coming soon.

3 COW-PEOPLE. Scientists at Newcastle University in England inserted human DNA into an unfertilized egg cell from a cow and "activated" the egg with a tiny electric shock, creating a cell with 0.01% cow DNA. The scientists promise they would never implant such an egg into a cow and attempt to bring it to term. So why create the hybrid? To skirt controversial laws restricting the use of "normal" human embryos for stem-cell research. The cloned cells wouldn't be completely human.

4 **THE CHESHIRE...FROG?** Masayuki Sumida, a professor at the Institute for Amphibian Biology at Japan's Hiroshima University, engineered transparent frogs in 2007. His goal: create a "cruelty-free" teaching tool. "You can watch organs of the same frog over its entire life," he said. "That way you don't have to dissect it!" He created the see-through amphibian by breeding frogs that have recessive pale genes over and over until a transparent offspring was produced. It's the first transparent animal to be created by scientists.

5 **I SQUEAK, THEREFORE I AM.** In 2013 researchers at the University of Rochester New York and UCLA grafted human brain cells into baby mice, resulting in rodents that could remember more and learn new tasks faster than nonmodified mice. The experiment's success amazed even the scientists: "This is a profoundly surprising and unexpected finding," said UCLA professor Alcino Silva. The experiment, he says, was not conducted to make smart mice but to better understand how humans learn and remember things. The ultimate goal: to cure brain disorders such as Huntington's disease and Alzheimer's.

6 **SPIDER GOAT.** Spider silk is stronger than steel; in large quantities, it could be used to build bridges and airplanes. But you can't farm spiders—they're territorial and have the annoying habit of eating each other. Goat milk glands, it turns out, are similar in composition to spider silk glands. Scientists at the University of Utah have successfully placed the genes that create spider silk into goat embryos. The resulting "spider goats" look and act like ordinary goats, but their milk contains a protein that is filtered out to yield spider silk. By 2012 the University of Utah had a herd of around 30 spider goats. Their goal: a legion of spider goats that will yield large quantities of industrial-quality spider silk at a fraction of the cost it takes to manufacture steel. (Of course, once the spider goats realize they can spin incredibly strong webs, they'll probably team up with the genius mice and the cyborg moths and take us over.)

10 TIPS FROM GREAT SCREENWRITERS

1 "Grab 'em by the throat and never let 'em go."
—Billy Wilder
(Some Like It Hot)

2 "If it can be written or thought, it can be filmed."
—Stanley Kubrick
(The Shining)

3 "Secure writers don't sell first drafts. They patiently rewrite until the script is as director-ready, as actor-ready as possible. Unfinished work invites tampering, while polished, mature work seals its integrity."
—Robert McKee (*Abraham*)

4 "A good film script should be able to do completely without dialogue."
—David Mamet
(The Untouchables)

5 "Technique is of less interest than character and story."
—William Friedkin
(To Live and Die in L.A.)

6 "Screenwriting is like ironing. You move forward a little and go back and smooth things out."
—Paul Thomas Anderson
(There Will Be Blood)

7 "I was excited about going to jail; I learned some great dialogue."
—Quentin Tarantino
(Pulp Fiction)

8 "There's no story if there isn't some conflict. The memorable things are not how pulled together everybody is."
—Wes Anderson
(The Royal Tenenbaums)

9 "Do not be told something is impossible. There is always a way."
—Robert Rodriguez (*Once Upon a Time in Mexico*)

10 "Write it. Shoot it. Publish it. Crochet it. Sauté it, whatever. MAKE."
—Joss Whedon
(The Avengers)

World's fastest typist: Barbara Blackburn's 212 wpm is 5 times faster than average.

8 FALSE SCARES IN SCARY MOVIES

Like a skilled magician, a skilled horror filmmaker will use misdirection to fool the audience into complacency before letting loose with the real scares. In poorly made movies, these false scares only cause us to roll our eyes. But when handled by the true masters of horror, they add to the tension and make the real scares even scarier.

1 JUST THE CAT

The heroine (usually a teenager) is afraid that someone is in the house, so she slowly creeps along the hallway as a closet door creaks open and...MEOW! But it's just the cat. (This false scare is sometimes called the "spring-loaded cat" because the feline somehow manages to pop out at chest height.)

2 RATS! OR BATS! OR A DOG!

A variation on Just the Cat, nearly any noise in an abandoned warehouse (or sewer, old house, etc.) will be a rat (the first time, anyway). The protagonist might exclaim, "EWWWW," but he or she will relax because it's "only" a rat (this time). Bats might also be used in this fake-out. And if a character is walking along a chain-link fence at night, expect a vicious dog to attack the fence and scare the hell out of the audience.

3 THE INANIMATE MONSTER

Most often used in movies featuring kids with messy bedrooms: Little Bobby sees a monster in his dark room and screams for help. Mom rushes in, flips on the light, and the "monster" is revealed to be a pile of monster-shaped clothes (or a toy clown, which should be illegal). A variation: A menacing figure looming in a dark foyer is almost always a coat rack.

4 THE PRACTICAL JOKER

The practical joker thinks it's hilarious to sneak up behind the heroine and grab her, but neither the heroine nor the audience finds it funny. Of course, in a slasher film, the practical joker has doomed himself to be the next one to die.

5 THE SUDDEN APPEARANCE

There's someone behind you! Never mind...it's just a random neighbor, or a friend, or a harmless jogger, and so on. The star breathes a sigh of relief; while we're wondering just why the neighbor was hiding in the bushes, the real killer appears.

6 IT'S ONLY ME

Our hero (usually a cop) turns a corner, sees the villain, and fires his weapon! Then a mirror shatters—it was only a reflection all along. When no guns are involved, the hero jumps and freezes in terror until he realizes it's just his reflection, and then he chuckles ruefully at having scared himself. The next time something frightens him, he won't be so lucky.

7 THE BLIND BUMP

As the two teens flee in terror, one goes in one direction while the other goes in another. They manage to end up at opposite sides of a corridor, so they turn around and start walking backward. (Doesn't everyone?) When the two teens inevitably back into each other, they scream and enjoy a moment of comic relief that only lasts until the killer crashes through the wall and attempts to dismember them.

8 THE RANDOM NOISE

Whether it's a car speeding by or a door slamming shut, it's the sound that scares you more than the visual element. The only reason sudden noises like this exist in horror movies is to keep you from getting too comfortable in your seat.

10 LAST WORDS OF DEATH ROW INMATES

1 "How's this for a headline? French fries."
—**James D. French (1966)**

2 "Somebody needs to kill my trial attorney."
—**George Harris (2000)**

3 "Where's a stunt double when you need one?"
—**Vincent Gutierrez (2007)**

4 "Well folks, soon you'll see a baked Appel."
—**George Appel (1928)**

5 "Viva Italia! Goodbye to all poor peoples everywhere! Pusha da button!"
—**Giuseppe Zangara (1933)**

6 "Gents, this is an educational project. You are about to witness the damaging effect electricity has on Wood."
—**Frederick Charles Wood (1951)**

7 "Please tell the media, I did not get my Spaghetti-Os, I got spaghetti. I want the press to know."
—**Thomas Grasso (1995)**

8 "Yeah, I think I'd rather be fishing."
—**Jimmy Glass (1987)**

9 "You are about to witness the execution of a wrongly convicted and innocent man. The state broke its own law in destroying DNA evidence in my case so I could not prove my innocence. To my wife and family, I want to say I love you all. And that's it."
—**Robert Waterhouse (2012)**

10 "Now, my statement to the world: I am in the midst of truth. I am good, I am straight, don't trip. To all my partners, tell them I said, like Arnold Schwarzenegger, I'll be back."
—**Carroll Joe Parr (2013)**

7 RANDOM ACTS OF KINDNESS

1 BROKEN DOWN ON THE SIDE OF THE ROAD

In Need of Help: Jenni Fontanez, a 23-year-old single mom from Lancaster, Pennsylvania, was eight months pregnant with her fourth child when she lost her job as a nursing aide because of complications from her pregnancy. Then she got evicted for not paying rent, and she had no family or friends in the area. With no one to turn to, the now-homeless mom sat on the side of the road with her baby on her lap...and started crying.

The Kindness of Strangers: That's when Cherish Doutrich, a 26-year-old teacher of autistic children, drove past Fontanez. She stopped and asked if she needed help. Fontanez told her story. "It just broke my heart," Doutrich later said. "She works so hard and just couldn't catch a break." So Doutrich and her husband Andrew took Fontanez to the store and bought her some formula and diapers. When she wasn't looking, Andrew slipped $500 into her bag so she could find a place to live. Fontanez tried to give it back, but they insisted she keep it.

Update: Not only did Fontanez find a place and return to nursing school, she's since started a campaign to help other homeless mothers: "We need people to motivate each other."

2 HOARDED AND BURGLED

In Need of Help: Linda Tims, 65, a recently widowed grandma from Phoenix, Arizona, couldn't even live in her own house—it was overrun by mounds of trash and junk that had once belonged to her parents. Making matters worse: Tims's drug-addicted son broke in and stole her valuables, appliances, and even the copper pipes leading into the house, which caused damaging floods. Out of money and options, Tims had to abandon her home and stay with one of her daughters.

The Kindness of Strangers: Phoenix police officer Glenn Branham responded to one of the burglary calls and realized that he was in a unique position to help Tims. He has a background in construction and a few connections, so he wrangled up some volunteers to clean the house and make repairs. The cop didn't want any publicity, but his boss alerted the local news. Once the story got out there, the donations started flooding in. The news station arranged for Tims to receive a $1,500 gift certificate for furniture. Then several other local companies and charities stepped in to help. Now back at her clean, furnished home, Tims calls Officer Branham her "guardian angel."

3 NAVY MEN

In Need of Help: Mary Morphet of Yucca Valley, California, is another widow who was having trouble making ends meet. After her husband died, she left the master bedroom untouched for several months...and then decided she was ready to sleep in there again. But the bathroom sink didn't work, so she called a plumber to look at it. He said it would cost "hundreds of dollars to repair, perhaps more depending on the damage." Morphet decided to get a second opinion.

The Kindness of Strangers: She called another plumber named Mike Reynolds. While he was looking at the sink, Morphet told him that her late husband was a World War II veteran who served on a submarine the Pacific. "I know of another World War II submarine vet," Reynolds said, "and he told me some amazing stories, so there's a special place in my heart for submarines and Navy men." After hearing the story, he fixed Morphet's sink and charged her $20. (His minimum fee is usually $80.) Said Morphet, "I was just so flabbergasted at this wonderful, gorgeous man's generosity!"

4 A CUT ABOVE THE REST

In Need of Help: In 2014 John McCormick, 65, was mowing his lawn in Baytown, Texas. When he was about halfway finished, he suffered a heart attack and collapsed on the grass.

The Kindness of Strangers: Members of the Baytown Fire Department arrived, preformed CPR until they got a pulse, and then rushed McCormick to the hospital. But that's their job— it's what happened next that made headlines. On their way back to the station, the firefighters stopped at McCormick's house and, feeling bad for his wife, finished mowing the lawn. The good deed would have gone unnoticed had a neighbor not snapped some photos, which went viral on the Internet and then got picked up by media outlets. "They say honor is doing the right thing when nobody's looking," said McCormick's son-in-law. "The firefighters were very honorable."

5 SIGNED, SEALED, DELIVERED

In Need of Help: One of the most difficult things about being a public school English teacher: Most of the reading material is not supplied by the school district, forcing the students and (most often) teachers to pay for books.

The Kindness of Strangers: That's why 10th-grade teacher Sally White from Chattanooga, Tennessee, was so grateful for an envelope that appeared on her classroom desk. Inside it was a note typed on an old-fashioned typewriter and signed with an Atticus Finch stamp, a character from *To Kill a Mockingbird.* (That's Black's favorite book, so the anonymous benefactor obviously knows her.) Along with the note were eight $100 gift certificates for a used bookstore. "I can't imagine what would possess someone to do this," said the grateful teacher, who shared the gift with the rest of the English department.

Update: After the story made headlines, an art teacher at the same school said she received a similar note and gift certificates. The mysterious benefactor is still unknown.

6 WARDROBE MALFUNCTION

In Need of Help: In Conroe, Texas, a fifth-grade boy's clothes were stolen, and his destitute family didn't have the money to buy new ones.

The Kindness of Strangers: Two police officers, Wes McCord and Andy Riley, responded to the call and felt bad for the boy. "All he had were the clothes on his back," said Riley. They knew that it would be difficult to find the culprit, but they felt compelled to help. So the two cops went to Walmart. They asked a shopper named Samantha Gregory where the boys' clothing section was. While she took them to it, they told her the story. Sensing the officers were out of their element, Gregory asked them the boy's size and then helped them pick out some pants and some sneakers—the ones the kid had stolen were a size too small. Officers McCord and Riley thanked Gregory for her help and then took the new clothes to the boy's family. "It was like a kid on Christmas morning, just happy," Riley told reporters (after Gregory alerted the local news about the officers' good deed).

7 ALL DRESSED UP

In Need of Help: There are millions of impoverished children all over the world. One of the many things they lack are clothes. It's even worse for little girls in developing nations. They often have to wear rags or ill-fitting hand-me-downs.

The Kindness of Strangers: A 99-year-old woman named Lillian Weber learned about the little girls' plight in 2011 while watching a documentary about a Christian outreach group called "Little Dresses for Africa" that sends clothes to impoverished children all over the world. So now Weber passes the time at her senior living community in Davenport, Iowa, by sewing dresses for little girls who she will never even meet. As of 2014, she's made nearly 900 of them. All of the dresses are made from a unique pattern, and Weber tries to personalize each one with decorative ruffles and bows. Seeing photographs of the smiling girls in their new dresses is the only reward she requires. Weber told the local news that she plans on making dress #1,000 by the time she turns 100: "When I get to that thousand, if I'm able to, I won't quit. I'll go at it again."

5 PEOPLE WHO NEVER DO STUFF

1 JOAN PICK NEVER GASSES UP. Joan Pick of London, England, stopped driving a car in 1973 and has only ridden in a gas-powered car twice since then. She also cut off the gas supply to her English home, which means no power for cooking and no heat, so she eats raw foods and wears heavy clothes to keep warm. Why no gas? "I adopt a lifestyle that is consistent with the sustainable management of the world's resources. Everyone knows we have to have very severe cutbacks to meet that standard."

2 PAUL KERN NEVER SLEPT. In 1915, during World War I, a Hungarian soldier named Paul Kern was shot in the head. For the next 20 years, Kern claimed that he couldn't fall asleep, not even for an hour. According to a newspaper account from 1938, "Doctors, brain specialists, nerve specialists and hypnotists have all tried to cure Kern of his mysterious disease, but all have failed." The lack of sleep didn't bother Kern, though, who said he felt fine.

3 JILL PRICE NEVER FORGETS. Jill Price of Los Angeles remembers every single thing that has ever happened to her...*everything*. Medical tests have revealed that certain parts of her brain are three times larger than normal, which may explain her gift. Although, to Rice, sometimes it feels more like a curse: "I still feel bad about stuff that happened 30 years ago, and I really live it and feel it like it just happened."

4 AMOU HAJI NEVER WASHES. How happy would you be if you hadn't had a shower for 60 years, your diet consisted of rotten porcupine and water from a rusty oil can, and you smoked a pipe full of animal dung? Probably not as happy as Amou Haji, an Iranian man who believes that if he cleans himself and eats clean food, he'll become sick. The 80-year-old Iranian hermit (who looks like someone who hasn't bathed in 60 years) is reportedly very healthy...and very happy.

5 NGUYEN VAN CHIEN NEVER CUTS HIS HAIR. The Vietnamese man always loved his long, flowing hair, but his schoolteachers forced him to cut it, which Chien did not like. "So I dropped out of school when I was 17 and have kept growing my hair ever since." That was more than 70 years ago. Today, he keeps his 13+ feet of matted locks rolled up in a ball that's tucked into a really big hat.

10 OF THE MOST EXPENSIVE PLACES ON EARTH TO TAKE A VACATION

1 **Zephyr Palace** (Costa Rica); $9,300/night

2 **Casa El Destino** (Punta Mita, Mexico); $15,000/night

3 **Deerfield Estate** (Heber City, Utah); $17,000/night

4 **Hugh Hefner Sky Villa**, Palms Casino (Las Vegas, Nevada); $34,000/night

5 **Musha Cay** (Bahamas); $37,500/day

6 **Nygard Cay** (Bahamas); $42,000/day

7 **Royal Villa at Grand Resort Lagonissi** (Athens, Greece); $50,000/night

8 **Necker Island** (British Virgin Islands); $51,000/day

9 **Royal Penthouse Suite**, Hotel President Wilson (Geneva, Switzerland); $52,000/night

10 **Isla de sa Ferradura** (Spain); $230,000/week

12 DISTINCTIONS: OUTSIDE EDITION

1 CANYON VS. GORGE. Both are deep ravines with a stream or a river cutting through the bottom—but canyons have wider, sloping walls, whereas gorges are much narrower and steeper. But don't go by the geographic names of these features. For example, the Columbia River Gorge in Oregon and Washington is actually a canyon.

2 LAKE VS. POND. The descriptions vary, and many small "lakes" could just as easily be called a pond, and the famed Walden Pond in Concord, Massachusetts, is actually a lake. The main distinction: A pond is shallow enough that light penetrates all the way to the bottom. Although there is no set size for either, most geographers agree that when a body of fresh water is over 12 acres, it's a lake. Smaller than that, it's a pond.

3 STALACTITES VS. STALAGMITES. Formed by water and minerals, a stalac*tite* hangs "tight" from a cave ceiling. (It has a "c" for ceiling; a stalagmite has a "g" for ground.)

4 BUTTE VS. MESA VS. PLATEAU. A plateau is the largest of the three; it's a flat-topped hill or mountain. A mesa is medium-sized. When it erodes away into a smaller formation, it becomes a butte.

5 SWAMP VS. BOG VS. MARSH. All three are types of wetlands. But a bog is on high ground, so water drains away from it and is replenished only by rainfall. Bogs are covered in peat moss, which makes it difficult for aquatic animals to breathe or survive there. Swamps are low, flat areas where slow-moving water from rivers collects; they're usually muddy and are home to trees and fish. A marsh borders a lake, ocean, or other large body of water; it's got grasses and reeds (but not trees or peat) and lots of underwater life and birds.

6 HURRICANE VS. CYCLONE VS. TYPHOON.

All three describe the same kind of oceanic storm with sustained winds reaching higher than 74 mph—the difference is in their location. If it strikes North America from the Atlantic Ocean, it's a hurricane (named for Hurikan, the Mayan god of evil). If it strikes China or Japan, it's called a typhoon (from the Greek *tuphõn*, "whirlwind"); to Filipinos and other Southeast Asians, they are called *baguios*. And in the Indian Ocean, it's called a cyclone—coined in 1848 by English scientist Captain H. Piddington, who derived the name from the Greek *kyklon*, "to move in a circle." Today, any storm that has a circular motion—but isn't strong enough to be a hurricane or typhoon—is referred to as a cyclone.

7 ELEVATION VS. ALTITUDE.

If you're hiking up a mountain and brag on Facebook that you're "at an altitude of 6,000 feet!"—first, put away your device and enjoy the outdoors. Second, altitude is used to describe a point above sea level *in the air,* which is why pilots say *altitude.* Elevation is a point above sea level on land.

8 HAIL VS. SLEET.

Both are irregularly shaped ice chunks that fall from clouds, but hail most commonly occurs in the warmer months. Why is hail larger? Because it forms in large thunderheads—the winds push the lump of ice high into the atmosphere, sometimes several times, making it grow larger and larger until it's heavy enough to fall. Sleet isn't associated with these massive updrafts, so it doesn't take as much ice forming around a water droplet before gravity kicks in and makes it ruin your morning commute.

9 WEATHER vs. CLIMATE. Weather—a combination of atmospheric events that determine temperature, precipitation, and humidity—can be tracked daily. Weather is specific from region to region. Climate, on the other hand, is a much more wide-ranging system that is tracked over long periods of time. In other words, climate is a long-term trend, and weather is the variation around this trend.

10 CITY vs. TOWN vs. VILLAGE. A city is an incorporated human settlement, which means it's governed by a single entity (a mayor and city council) that is enclosed in a larger entity (county, state, country). A town is smaller than a city, but like a city it can also have a mayor. But unlike a city, a town's municipal services (utilities, transportation) are handled by the county. A village has no central governing body and can be part of a town or city.

11 ISLAND vs. CONTINENT. Continents are big, and islands are small, right? Well, yes, but there's an even bigger difference. A continent is a landmass composed of low-density rock that "floats" on top of the earth's mantle—it is bordered by tectonic plates and has mountain ranges and a plethora of cultures. Oceanic islands are landmasses composed of heavier rock that have risen partially above sea level. That's why Greenland is the world's largest island, not Australia, which is technically a continent.

12 TWILIGHT vs. DUSK. Dusk happens once a day, after sunset. It's the darkest stage of twilight, which occurs when the sun is below the horizon but still showers the landscape in indirect light. Twilight happens twice every day— before sunrise and then again after sunset (but vampires only sparkle during twilight).

40 NAUGHTIEST PLACE NAMES IN THE UK

1	Scratchy Bottom	21	Moisty Lane
2	Crackpot	22	Fanny Street
3	Sandy Balls	23	Wetwang
4	The Glory Hole	24	The Hoe
5	Back Passage	25	Bladda
6	North Piddle	26	Hooker Road
7	Pratts Bottom	27	Slutshole Lane
8	Butt of Lewis	28	Juggs Close
9	The Knob	29	Bitchfield
10	Ugley	30	Fanny Burn
11	Twatt	31	Groan
12	Broken Wind	32	Slag Lane
13	Upper Bleeding	33	Butt Hole Road
14	Prickwillow	34	Golden Balls
15	Shitterton	35	Backside
16	Cock-A-Dobby	36	Upper Thong
17	Titty Ho	37	Bonks Hill
18	Crapstone	38	Turkey Cock Lane
19	Crotch Crescent	39	Busty View
20	Pennycomequick	40	Happy Bottom

England has a stockpile of 225 nuclear warheads.

5 CRAZY BURGERS YOU HAVE TO TRY ONCE

1 666 BURGER
Found at: The Wiener and Still Champion in Evanston, Illinois
Pile it on: Feel like sinning? This cheeseburger is topped with six slices of bacon, six slices of cheese, and six cheese sticks.

2 LASAGNA-BUN BURGER
Found at: PYT in Philadelphia, Pennsylvania
Pile it on: Several slices of deep-fried lasagna serve as the bun, which surrounds a beef patty smothered in provolone and marinara sauce.

3 THE KING
Found at: Boston Burger Company in Boston, Mass.
Pile it on: If Elvis Presley should ever return from the dead, he'd probably order this burger inspired by his favorite snacks: It's a beef patty smothered in peanut butter, bacon, and fried bananas rolled in cinnamon sugar. (Then he'd die again.)

4 ABSOLUTELY RIDICULOUS BURGER
Found at: Mallie's Sports Grill in Southgate, Michigan
Pile it on: This monster contains 120 pounds of ground beef, 40 pounds of bun, and 30 pounds of toppings. Cost: $1,999

5 HOT FUDGE BURGER
Found at: McGuire's Irish Pub in Pensacola, Florida
Pile it on: And for dessert, feast on this beef patty topped with vanilla ice cream and hot fudge.

---

9 KILLER NATURAL DISASTERS

1 SOUTHERN CHINA FLOODS (China, 1931)
Southern China's rivers were already swollen from heavy spring precipitation, so when torrential rains fell for most of the summer, there was nowhere for all that water to go but over the rice fields that banked the Yangtze and Yellow Rivers. The floods wiped out the crops, and the standing water became contaminated. That deadly combination led to starvation and outbreaks of typhoid and dysentery. Final death toll: 3.7 million.

2 HUANG HE FLOODS (China, 1887)
The river called "China's Sorrow" earned its name in 1887 when it flooded 500,000 miles of the surrounding lands. The river filled 11 cities and hundreds of villages with water, leaving 2 million people homeless. Final death toll: 900,000.

3 SHAANXI EARTHQUAKE (China, 1556)
An 8.0-magnitude earthquake shook Shaanxi, China, on the evening of January 23. In the city of Huaxian, every single building collapsed, and similar devastation occurred in several other cities. Final death toll: 830,000.

4 TANGSHAN EARTHQUAKE (China, 1976)
Eighty-five percent of buildings were destroyed in the city of Tangshan when an earthquake measuring 7.8 on the Richter scale hit early in the morning on July 28. More than half of the city's 1 million people were injured. Final death toll: 240,000.

5 THE GREAT BHOLA CYCLONE (Bangladesh, 1970)
This destructive cyclone (what we call a hurricane) hit

Bangladesh on November 11. With little warning, 140-mph winds and a 20-foot storm surge laid waste to the small country in the Bay of Bengal. One district lost 45 percent of its population. Final death toll: from 300,000 to 500,000.

6 THE HOOGHLY RIVER CYCLONE (India, 1737)

It might seem that a river would be safe from a hurricane, but the Hooghly River Cyclone proved otherwise. The storm hit the Ganges River Delta on October 11 and blew waves 30 to 40 feet high. Add to that the 15 inches of rain that fell in only six hours, and it's the perfect recipe for disaster. The storm traveled 200 miles inland and destroyed 20,000 boats and countless buildings. Final death toll: from 300,000 to 350,000.

7 HAIYUAN EARTHQUAKE (China, 1920)

The largest Chinese earthquake of the 20th century—7.8 magnitude—killed half the population of Haiyuan County and caused extensive damage to the region. Final death toll: 230,000.

8 INDIAN OCEAN TSUNAMI (11 countries in the Indian Ocean, 2004)

On the day after Christmas, a 9.0-magnitude earthquake struck off the coast of Sumatra. Because it occurred deep underwater, the quake disrupted the seafloor with the equivalent of 23,000 atomic bombs, which caused massive tsunami waves up to 50 feet high on the coasts of 11 countries. Final death toll: 226,000.

9 HAITI EARTHQUAKE (Haiti, 2010)

On January 12, a 7.0-magnitude earthquake hit 10 miles from the island nation's capital. More than 1.5 million people lost their homes. (Many are still living in "temporary" refugee camps.) Final death toll: 200,000 from the quake, and thousands more from the cholera epidemic that broke out afterward.

6 CONSPIRACY THEORIES TO GO WITH YOUR TINFOIL HAT

Here at the BRI, we've been reporting odd conspiracy theories since the late 1980s, but when mysterious black helicopters started hovering over our office, we cooled it for a while...until now.

1 A-LIST CELEBRITIES ARE MEMBERS OF THE ILLUMINATI...

The Illuminati, a secret organization that controls everything, counts many of our favorite stars among its ranks. Want proof? Look no further than the name of Jay-Z and Beyoncé's child—Blue Ivy—which allegedly stands for "Born Living Under Evil Illuminati's Very Youngest." Still not convinced? Just watch Katy Perry's "Satanic" performance of her song "Dark Horse" at the 2014 Grammy Awards. The conspiracy website Infowars says it's "essentially an Illuminati-themed occult ritual."

2 ...EXCEPT THE BRAIN-WASHED STARS WHO ARE ILLUMINATI SLAVES

Miley Cyrus didn't twerk her heart out for fame at the 2013 Video Music Awards. She did it because her overlords ordered her to. At the time, there was a crisis brewing in Syria, and the Illuminati needed a distraction, which turned out to be Cyrus. (Similarly, Britney Spears's 2007 meltdown was staged to draw attention away from the Bush administration.) So the next time you see a starlet act out, she's probably being mind-controlled.

3 THE *TITANIC* WASN'T THE *TITANIC*

At the turn of the 20th century, American business magnate J. P. Morgan financed the luxury liners *Titanic*, *Olympic*, and *Britannic*, but the *Olympic* was damaged in a collision and had to be repaired. Instead, Morgan ordered the ships' identities to be swapped—making the *Olympic* look like the *Titanic*—and then ordered the captain of the not-*Titanic* to ram it into an iceberg in the North Atlantic. Reason: to collect the insurance money. So even though Morgan was worth $1.2 billion in today's money, conspiracy theorists claim he condemned more than 1,500 people to death just to avoid repairing the *Olympic*.

4 THE FEDS HAVE A STOCKPILE OF GUILLOTINES

The U.S. government owns 30,000 guillotines and is storing half in Montana and half in Georgia. Why? To execute political dissenters once martial law is established (which should be happening any day now). Why guillotines? It's a method of execution that won't damage the organs; that way the dissenters' corpses can be harvested and sold to the Chinese.

5 STEVIE WONDER ISN'T BLIND

Steveland Hardaway Morris was born in 1950 with detached retinas that left him blind. But some conspiracy theorists claim that Wonder has been pretending to be blind since he was a kid. The ruse helped make him famous, so he stuck with it. The proof? A video clip of Wonder catching a microphone stand that Paul McCartney knocked over at the White House. Another piece of supposed evidence: Boy George was at a party one night when Wonder walked up and playfully strangled him. "How could he know where I was," remarked George, "if he's completely blind?" The truth: Stevie Wonder is blind. *Or is he?*

6 THE SHADOW PEOPLE ARE PREPARING FOR...SOMETHING

Ever caught what you thought was a shadow out of the corner of your eye, only to turn and see nothing? Has that shadow been a little more substantial lately? Is one of them ... watching ... you ... right ... now? Recent reports have shown a disturbing uptick in these shadowy figure sightings. There's no consensus on what or who these things are. The conspiracy theories range from ghosts to demons to aliens to time travelers to interdimensional beings preparing to take over our dimension. Be afraid. Be very afraid.

7 SECRET AGENCIES

This list will self-destruct in 3...2...1...RUN!

1 KGB (*Komitet Gosudarstvennoy Bezopasnosti*)

Formed in 1954, the "Federal Security Service" was the notorious Soviet Cold War-era spy agency. It gathered intelligence, spied on citizens, quashed political dissent, monitored the military, and once tried and failed to assassinate John Wayne. After trying and failing to depose President Mikhail Gorbachev in 1991, the KGB was dissolved, as was the Soviet Union.

2 STASI (*Staatssicherheit*)

The East German Stasi agents, mostly former Nazis, worked with the KGB to spread Communism starting in 1950. The "Ministry of State Security" worked its way into every level of society, and by the late 1980s, 2 percent of all East Germans either worked for the agency or were unpaid informants. The Stasi kept an estimated 25 million pages of records on people, including "smell samples," pieces of clothing sealed in glass bottles that could be given to tracking dogs.

3 MOSSAD (*HaMossad leModi in uleTafkidim Meyu adim*)

Formed in 1951, Israel's "Institute for Intelligence and Special Tasks" collects intelligence and combats terrorism, focusing especially on Arab nations. Prime Minister David Ben Gurion said, "For our state, which since its creation has been under siege by its enemies, intelligence constitutes the first line of defense...we must learn well how to recognize what is going on around us." One of Mossad's greatest successes was the location and capture of Nazi war criminal Adolf Eichmann, who was living under an assumed name in Argentina in 1960.

4 SMERSH (*Spetsyalnye Metody Razoblacheniya Shpyonov*)

Best known as James Bond's Soviet nemesis, SMERSH's real-life duties included spying on the Germans and preventing Nazi infiltration of the Red Army during World War II. The "Special Methods of Spy Detection's" motto, said to have been written by Joseph Stalin, was *Smert Shpionam*, or "Death to Spies." SMERSH was later absorbed into the KGB.

5 SAVAK (*Sazeman-i Ettelaat va Amniyat-i Keshvar*)

Formed in 1957, Iran's "National Organization for Intelligence and Security" was tasked with protecting the Shah. SAVAK spies monitored political opponents and imprisoned dissidents in the agency's own prison for as long as they wanted to. SAVAK was responsible for killing up to 15,000 people during demonstrations against the Shah in 1978. When the Shah fled Iran, SAVAK was disbanded and its leaders executed.

6 BND (*Bundesnachrichtendienst*)

Created in 1956, Germany's "Federal Intelligence Service" gathers intelligence and provides counterintelligence. In 1962 the BND warned the U.S. that the Soviets were planning to deploy missiles to Cuba. Follow-up by American intelligence confirmed it, leading to the Cuban Missile Crisis.

7 NSA (National Security Agency)

This U.S. intelligence agency was founded in 1954 to continue codebreaking activities begun during World War II. According to its website, the NSA "gathers information that America's adversaries wish to keep secret" and is responsible for the security of America's information systems. In 2013 the NSA's own secrets became front-page news after low-level government contractor Edward Snowden leaked classified documents that revealed the agency's massive scope of surveillance, both domestic and foreign—proving that it's a lot harder than ever before for a secret agency to keep its secrets.

15 CLEVER CELEBRITY AUTOBIOGRAPHY TITLES

Uncle John is thinking about calling his autobiography I'm Getting Too Old for This Sit. *Here are some more apt titles.*

1 **Leading with My Chin,** by Jay Leno (former *Tonight Show* host with a big chin)

2 **They Made a Monkee Out of Me,** by Davy Jones of the Monkees

3 **Out of Sync,** by Lance Bass of the boy band NSYNC

4 **Landing on My Feet,** by Kerri Strug (Olympic gymnast)

5 **Winking at Life,** by Wink Martindale (game show host)

6 **Losing My Virginity,** by Richard Branson (CEO of Virgin)

7 **Kiss and Make-Up,** by Gene Simmons of KISS

8 **Nerd Do Well,** by Simon Pegg (British actor famous for playing nerds)

9 **My Word Is My Bond,** by Roger Moore (who played James Bond)

10 **Underneath It All,** by Traci Lords (adult film star)

11 **It's Not Easy Bein' Me: A Lifetime of No Respect but Plenty of Sex and Drugs,** by Rodney Dangerfield

12 **Tall, Dark and Gruesome,** by Christopher Lee (famous for playing bad guys)

13 **Pryor Convictions,** by Richard Pryor (comedian who had several run-ins with the law)

14 **Life and Def,** by Russell Simmons (head of Def Jam Records)

15 **The Hardest (Working) Man in Showbiz,** by Ron Jeremy (adult film star)

7 KIDS' PRODUCTS AND THE SCIENCE BEHIND THEM

1 SILLY STRING

It's not really the "string" that makes Silly String work; it's the ingredient that gets it out of the can that makes it all happen. The strands are created from an acrylic resin—plastic—and a surface-acting agent—foam. But it's the propellant that's crucial to the process: Not only does it push the string out of the can when sprayed, it also causes the reaction between the resin and the surface-acting agent to form the sticky strands.

2 ELMER'S GLUE-ALL

Although many glues were traditionally manufactured from the collagen in animal hooves, horns, and bones, Elmer's never has been. The first glue factory that Gail Borden bought in 1929 used a milk by-product to make its glue, and Borden Inc. expanded into resin-based glues in the 1930s. Elmer's Glue-All was introduced in 1947 and was made from a synthetic resin, which is still in their product today. So kids can play happily in the knowledge that no horses were harmed in the making of their Elmer's.

3 SLIME

Toy slime—sold by Mattel from the 1970s to the 1990s—is what's called a non-Newtonian fluid. That means it changes density depending on how much pressure is applied. Use a light touch, and a non-Newtonian fluid feels as thin as water. Press hard, and it feels thick. In slime, it's the ratio of polymer to gelling agent that makes it a non-Newtonian fluid. Usually, that's a 5-to-1 ratio of polyvinyl alcohol (the polymer) to Borax (the gelling agent); the rest is water, fragrance, and coloring.

4 PLAY-DOH

Although Hasbro won't reveal its exact recipe, Play-Doh is essentially wheat starch and warm water with some lubricants and preservatives. The water makes the wheat starch swell and become supple, giving the Play-Doh its moldable quality. (That's why it gets hard and crumbly if left out: The water evaporates, and the wheat starch shrinks and loses its flexibility.)

5 MAGNA DOODLE

What lets you draw on a Magna Doodle time and time again? There's a layer of honeycombed plastic under the top screen, and each honeycomb cell contains thickened water and magnetic particles. When the magnet on the pen is drawn over the screen, it pulls the particles to the surface, and the water solution is thick enough that they can't float back down. (The solution is also colored white so that the particles are more visible.) When the picture is erased, a magnetic bar along the bottom pulls all the particles back down; the water's thickness keeps them from floating up until the pen is used again.

6 SUPER BALL

Polybutadiene is a synthetic rubber that's brittle when cold and goo when hot, neither of which is useful in a ball. But add sulfur, cook the rubber at 285 to 340°F while adding 500 to 3,000 pounds of pressure, and it becomes super-bouncy. Size matters: The Super Ball must be molded to about two inches in diameter, or the heat and pressure process won't work.

7 LEGO BRICKS

Giant hoses suck different-colored plastic granules from trucks into three-story-high metal silos. They're fed into molding machines, heated to 450°F, then fed into hollow LEGO brick molds. The machine applies hundreds of tons of pressure to make sure each brick has the perfect shape. Then the bricks are cooled and ejected. But you have to put them together.

14 ALARMING STATISTICS THAT WILL MAKE YOU WORRY ABOUT AMERICA

Here are the results of some various polls conducted in recent years. We don't know who's answering these polls, but clearly some of them got dropped on their heads a few times too many.

1 25% of Americans polled don't know that Earth revolves around the Sun.

2 32% don't know that "GOP" refers to the Republican Party.

3 11% think "HTML" is a sexually transmitted disease.

4 25% don't know that the U.S. gained independence from England (many said France or China).

5 35% don't recognize the donkey as a symbol of the Democratic Party.

6 80% support "mandatory labels on food containing DNA" (all food has DNA).

7 80% don't know there are 100 U.S. senators.

8 35% couldn't name one of the three branches of the federal government (see page 34).

9 16% don't know that Bill Clinton is a Democrat.

10 44% don't realize that Common Core refers to school curriculum standards.

11 58% think astrology is a science (like astronomy or chemistry).

12 6% couldn't circle U.S. Independence Day on a calendar.

13 29% think that "cloud computing" involves an actual cloud.

14 8% of Americans believe Congress is doing an "excellent" job.

Dr. Seuss used 236 different words in *The Cat in the Hat*.

6 LISTS ABOUT DRAGONS THROUGH THE AGES

10 BEANIE BABY STUFFED DRAGONS

1 Legend
2 Stuffy
3 Dewi Y Ddraig
4 Dwynwen
5 Y Ddraig Goch
6 Bali
7 Loong
8 Slayer
9 Scorch
10 Magic

10 DRAGONS FROM CHINESE MYTHOLOGY

1 **Ao Guang.** The most powerful of the Four Dragon Kings and ruler of the Eastern seas.
2 **Ao Chin.** Ruler of the Southern Sea and one of the Four Dragon Kings.
3 **Ao Jun.** One of the Four Dragon Kings and ruler of the Western Seas.
4 **Ao Shun.** Ruler of the Northern Seas and a Dragon King.
5 **Bai Long.** The White Dragon, caused a thunderstorm right before the White Dragon Festival.
6 **Pulao.** Craftsmen put the sea dragon's form on top of alarm bells because he bellows loudly when attacked by an enemy.
7 **Qing Long.** The Blue Dragon.
8 **Fei Lian.** The god of the wind who sometimes appears in dragon form.
9 **Qing Long Pa Jiang Jun.** Green Dragon General, guards the hall of the Jade Emperor.
10 **Chu Lung.** Torch Dragon, brings light to the Northern lands by opening his eyes.

10 DRAGONS FROM GEORGE R. R. MARTIN'S *A SONG OF ICE AND FIRE* SERIES

1 Drogon
2 Rhaegal
3 Viserion
4 Balerion

5 Meraxes

6 Vhagar

7 Sunfyre

8 Vermithrax

9 Ghiscar

10 Valryon

10 DRAGONS FROM JAPANESE MYTHOLOGY

1 **Yamata-no-Orochi.** This monstrous serpent has eight heads and eight tails, long enough to cover eight valleys.

2 **Ryujin.** The Dragon King; his palace is at the bottom of the sea. One day in the Dragon Palace equals 100 human years.

3 **Otohime.** Dragon Princess of the Sea and one of the Dragon King's daughters.

4 **Mizuchi.** A river god.

5 **Kiyohime.** When her lover abandoned her, the woman Kiyohime was so angry she changed into a dragon.

6 **Nureonna.** Dragonlike ghosts, often found near rivers.

7 **Kuniyoshi.** Another of the Dragon King's daughters.

8 **Watatsumi.** God of the sea (and an alternate name of Ryujin).

9 **Tamayori.** Another daughter of the Dragon King.

10 **Zennyo Ryuo.** A blue dragon that could bring rain if prayed to and given offerings.

10 DRAGONS FROM *HOW TO TRAIN YOUR DRAGON*

1 Toothless

2 Cloudjumper

3 Changewing

4 Flightmare

5 Gruff

6 Grump

7 Hookfang

8 Meatlug

9 Red Death

10 Scauldron

6 METAPHORS FROM OUR FAVORITE DRAGON

"My armor is like tenfold shields, my teeth are swords, my claws spears, the shock of my tail a thunderbolt, my wings a hurricane, and my breath death!"

—Smaug, from J. R. R. Tolkien's *The Hobbit*

8 DUMB CROOKS WHO LED THE COPS RIGHT TO THEM

1 A FINE METH

"Yep, those are meth-making components," remarked Franklin County, Missouri, detective Jason Grellner while watching a video that Jennifer Harrington posted on her Facebook page; it clearly showed her and some friends manufacturing meth. The video led to several arrests for drug offenses.

2 SMILE!

Leslie Paul Ash wore a mask to conceal his identity while he stole computers from a recycling center in Highbridge, England. Unfortunately (for him), he waited until he was standing in front of a surveillance camera before putting the mask on.

3 NICE TO MEAT YOU

Brice Edward Bennett Jr., 52, from York County, Pennsylvania, appealed a July 2013 conviction for shoplifting, claiming there was a "lack of evidence" in his original case. So the appeals court judge took a look at the evidence: 1) Several supermarket employees saw Bennett, with overloaded pockets, run out of the store; 2) A police officer testified that he "saw hot dogs fly out of Bennett's pocket as he tried to run away"; and 3) When the cop caught Bennett, there was "a pork loin and a shrimp wheel stuffed inside his jacket." The conviction stood.

4 FROM WINNER TO LOSER

After eluding North Carolina police for nine months in 2014 on felony burglary charges, Bradley Hardison, 24, entered a doughnut-eating contest. Good news: He wolfed down eight glazed doughnuts in two minutes for the win! Bad news: The contest was part of the "Elizabeth City Police Department's National Night Out Against Crime" event. When a local newspaper printed Hardison's picture the next day, police had their man. "I did congratulate him," said the deputy who arrested Hardison. "Good for him. He can eat a lot of doughnuts."

5 NOT HER BEST SIDE

As part of their Facebook "Warrant Wednesday" program, Columbus, Ohio, police posted a mug shot of Monica Hargrove. Unhappy with how she looked in the photo, Hargrove called and said, "I want my picture down." The detective told her, "Come on in and we'll talk about it." So Hargrove did...and was immediately arrested on the outstanding warrant that put her on the department's Facebook page in the first place.

6 AT LEAST HE MADE THE MEETING?

Gary Harding carjacked a Honda CRV in New Haven, Connecticut, and later used it in a bank robbery, where he didn't wear a mask. His probation officer recognized Harding from surveillance photos, so he called him and asked if he'd come to a meeting. Harding did...in the stolen car. He was arrested.

7 ARMED BURGLARY

After a Frederick, Maryland, tattoo shop was burglarized, the shop's owner looked at the surveillance video and saw that the burglars had covered their faces. But one of them—Max Goransson—forgot to cover up his arms, one of which had a large tattoo that was recently inked at the shop he burgled.

8 A LITTLE HELP HERE

In 2014 police in the Netherlands received a call from a crying drunk man who said he was trapped inside a building. He told them (through sobs) that he'd broken a window and tried to steal several items, but then he couldn't find his way out. So the police came and freed—and then jailed—him.

9 LITTLE-KNOWN CELEBRITY FLINGS

1 LIAM NEESON & JULIA ROBERTS, 1987
She was 19, he was 35. The future A-listers fell for each other while filming the girl-rocker movie *Satisfaction*. They even got an apartment together in Venice Beach but split up soon after.

2 SUSAN SARANDON & DAVID BOWIE, 1983
Sarandon and Bowie had a brief fling on the set of the 1983 British horror film *The Hunger*. "Bowie's just a really interesting person," gushed Sarandon. "He's a talent, and a painter, and... he's great!" (Bowie has yet to comment on the affair.)

3 JANET JACKSON & MATTHEW McCONAUGHEY, 2002
The singer and the actor may or may not have gone on a date after they met at the 2002 Grammy Awards. McConaughey claimed at the time, "She's a sweetheart, but we're not dating, we're just friends." Or were they? Years later, Jackson referred to their time together as a "brief affair."

4 JAY LENO & SHARON OSBOURNE, 1979
Before Sharon met Ozzy and became Mrs. Prince of Darkness, she and Leno dated briefly. "The fling was more fling for me," said Osbourne, "and not fling enough for Jay. Because a couple of months in, he brought around the *real* love of his life [Leno's future wife Mavis] for me to meet, and she was lovely."

5 CHER & TOM CRUISE, early 1980s
In 2013 Cher publicly divulged her secret affair with Cruise, who was 16 years younger: "It was pretty hot and heavy for a

little minute. The person that I knew was a great and lovable guy." Cher blamed their incompatible filming schedules for ending the fling, or else it could've been "a great big romance."

6 ANDRE AGASSI & BARBRA STREISAND, 1992

Although not talked about much any more, the Streisand–Agassi affair was the juiciest gossip to hit the tennis world since Chris Evert dated Burt Reynolds in the 1970s (also not talked about any more). Streisand was smitten: "He's very intelligent, very sensitive, very evolved; more than his linear years." How far did the relationship go? Agassi refused to kiss and tell: "She's a real good friend, more than that I cannot say."

7 GLENN CLOSE & WOODY HARRELSON, 1991

Although the *Fatal Attraction* star was 15 years older than the *Cheers* star, they hit it off during the play *Brooklyn Laundry*. According to Jackie Swanson, who played Harrelson's girlfriend on *Cheers*, "Woody always had a new girl visiting the set. I remember seeing at different times Moon Zappa, Ally Sheedy, and Glenn Close. I also had a crush on him. Who didn't?"

8 BILLY CORGAN & TILA TEQUILA, 2009

He's 6'3", she's 4'11". He's the lead singer of the Smashing Pumpkins, she made a sex tape and got a reality show. As far as anyone can tell, their fling only lasted long enough for them to be photographed together at an awards show. Corgan is also rumored to have dated Jessica Simpson, who said of him, "Billy braids my prayers," whatever that means.

9 CHRISTIAN BALE & DREW BARRYMORE, 1987

Five years after starring in 1982's *E.T.: The Extra-Terrestrial*, Barrymore, 12, visited director Steven Spielberg on the set of *Empire of the Sun*, which featured the 15-year-old future *Batman* star. He later said, "We went to see some bloody awful horror film, and that was the end of it. She never called again."

10 PLAGUES OF EGYPT AND THEIR "NATURAL" CAUSES

Was it divine intervention...or something more earthly?

BACKGROUND: In the Hebrew Bible book of Exodus, Moses and Aaron try to convince Pharaoh that there is only one God, but Pharaoh counters that there are many gods...and he refuses to release his Israelite slaves. Bad idea: The one true God proves his power by smiting Egypt with ten plagues.

But did God have help? Biblical scholar Ziony Zevit of American Jewish University posits, "The most sophisticated attempt to relate the Egyptian plagues to natural phenomena does so in terms of Egypt's ecosystem. This ecological explanation of the plagues does not prove that the biblical account is true, but only that it may have some basis in reality." So here is each plague, along with Zevit's theory as to how it may have occurred (other than the obvious one, that God did it).

Plague 1. All the water in Egypt—including the Nile—was turned into blood, which killed the fish.
Natural explanation? The Ethiopian highlands are made up of red clay. So it was possible that torrential rains could have started a mud-red flood that turned the Nile red and choked out the fish, which got infected with anthrax.

Plague 2. Millions of frogs invaded villages and homes and then died en masse.
Natural explanation? The frogs were trying to escape the muddy waterways. They all died because they were also infected with anthrax.

Plagues 3 and 4. Lice infected the Egyptian people's heads, and swarms of gnats and flies darkened the skies.
Natural explanation? The lice, gnats, and flies were feasting on the dead frogs.

Plague 5. Pestilence killed cattle by the thousands.
Natural explanation? The fields from which the cattle fed were turned toxic by plagues 3 and 4.

Plague 6. People's skin broke out in festering boils.
Natural explanation? The boils were symptoms of the same disease that caused the pestilence in the animals.

Plague 7. A destructive hailstorm laid waste to crops and killed thousands of animals and people.
Natural explanation? Destructive hailstorms are uncommon in northern Africa, but have been known to occur there.

Plague 8. Millions of locusts covered the landscape.
Natural explanation? Locust swarms are a common occurrence in the region, especially after heavy rainy seasons.

Plague 9. A dust storm blocked out the sun.
Natural explanation? Easterly winds blew dust from neighboring Libya over Egypt. The storm was made worse by the recent loss of crops (not unlike America's "Dust Bowl" during the Great Depression).

Plague 10. The deaths of all the firstborn sons in Egypt.
Natural explanation? The other nine plagues made conditions so harsh that the infant mortality rate skyrocketed. Of course, that doesn't explain how older firstborns were killed, but with all of that death and destruction "plaguing" the region, it sure would have seemed to the Egyptians that someone up there was angry at them.

7 SIGNS THAT FONZIE IS A GOD

Could it be true that the most powerful fictional being of all time came from the 1950s-set 1970s sitcom Happy Days? *Sure, Luke Skywalker has the Force, and Samantha from* Bewitched *has magic, but Arthur "Fonzie" Fonzarelli (Henry Winkler) has an even greater and more mysterious power: the power of Cool. It gives the Fonz...*

1 CONTROL OVER INANIMATE OBJECTS. Not only can Fonzie start up a jukebox just by hitting it, but he can also get it to play whatever song he wishes. And not just jukeboxes: One time Fonzie and Richie (Ron Howard) are standing in front of a vending machine, Fonzie kicks it, and not one but two Cokes fall out. How could it have known the Fonz wanted two Cokes? The power of Cool can also start car engines and turn lights on and off. And whenever Mr. Cunningham (Tom Bosley) can't get a stuck door to open, Fonzie "listens" to it, hits it in just the right spot—and voilà!—it's open. Ayyy.

2 CONTROL OVER THE OPPOSITE SEX. Fonzie's famous finger snap is a powerful aphrodisiac for any girl he desires. In a roomful of girls, the finger snap will instantly communicate to the specific girl that it's time to stop whatever she is doing and walk over to kiss, hug, or dance with the Fonz. Ayyy.

3 CONTROL OVER NATURE. One night Fonzie tries to fall asleep outside in the wilderness, but all of the crickets, frogs, and owls are making such a loud racket that he can't doze off. Frustrated, Fonzie sits up and yells, "Cool it!" And lo, all of the animals are quiet. Ayyy.

4 SUPERHUMAN STRENGTH. When a group of bullies threatens to beat up Richie at Arnold's Diner, Fonzie demonstrates to them why that would be a bad idea: He walks over to the restroom doors, and with barely any effort, he knocks both doors off their hinges. Upon seeing this, the bullies run awayyy.

5 PERFECT HAIR. The Fonz carries a comb in his back pocket (because he's cool, you see), but his hair is always so perfectly feathered that he never needs to comb it. Ayyy.

6 POWER OVER ALIEN LIFE-FORMS. When Mork from Ork (Robin Williams) visits Earth and threatens to kidnap Richie for one bleem (2,000 Earth years), Fonzie challenges Mork to a duel. Mork uses his magic alien finger to freeze the Fonz in his tracks, but the power of Cool contained within Fonzie's thumb is strong enough to break Mork's spell. Fonzie is unfrozen, and the battle continues. Ayyy.

7 OMNIPOTENCE. After a closely fought battle, Mork declares himself the winner. But had he known the true power of Cool, the alien would have left well enough alone. Instead, Mork decides to kidnap Fonzie and take him back to Ork.

That's when the Fonz unveils what is perhaps his greatest weapon: omnipotence. He tells Mork that if he lets him go, he will tell him the secret of the universe. Mork agrees, and Fonzie and Richie are safe! (So what is the secret of the universe? Mork later shares it with his boss, Orson: "First, tell a chick she's cool. Second, tell her she's got great zhebobnees.") Ayyy.

> "All things are possible through the Lord God Arthur Fonzarelli."
>
> **—Peter Griffin, *Family Guy***

16 SHAQADELIC QUOTES

In 1989 Shaquille O'Neal—who was 6' 10"—led his high school basketball team—average-sized white guys—to a 36-0 record and a state championship. Afterward, a reporter asked him, "What do you attribute your team's success to?" Shaq's answer: "I attribute it to me." Here are 16 more quotes from the most "quotacious" (his word) NBA star of our time.

1 "If you go 72-11 and don't win the championship, it doesn't mean anything. Actually, it does. It means you've cheated and played an extra regular-season game."

2 "Our offense is like the Pythagorean Theorem. It ain't got no answer."

3 "There is no answer to the Pythagorean theorem. Well, there is an answer, but by the time you figure it out, I got 40 points, 10 rebounds, and we're planning for the parade."

4 "I don't know how it is for you earthlings, but where I'm from, strength is mental."

5 **Interviewer:** "Let's just say that a snake bit your mom right in the chest area. Would you be willing to suck the venom out to win the title?"
Shaq: "No, but I would with your wife."

6 "I am Superman. And the only thing that can kill Superman is Kryptonite. And Kryptonite doesn't exist."

7 "I'm a freak of nature. You've never seen anyone this big—this sexy—move this way."

8 "It's just one more win. I don't give a sh*t how we do it, long as we get it done. Did I say sh*t? I'm sorry."

NGC 247, one of the closest galaxies to ours, is only 11 million light-years away.

9 "To me, basketball is ballet, hip-hop, and kung fu. The ballet is grace, the hip-hop is cool, and the kung fu is kill the opponent."

10 "I am the worst yoga student in the history of yoga."

11 "Me shooting 40 percent at the foul line is just God's way of saying that nobody's perfect. If I shot 90 percent from the line, it just wouldn't be right."

12 "He awokened a sleeping giant. I know that's not a word."

13 "Nietzsche was so intelligent and advanced. And that's how I am. I'm the black, basketball-playing Nietzsche."

14 *Our favorite Shaq tweet:* "Just got dat underwater ipod adaption device jammy so I can hear music unda water, I b aqua jammin, Waaa Waaa Shaq-mu The quilla."

15 "I'm tired of hearing about money, money, money, money! All I want to do is play basketball, drink Pepsi, and wear Reebok."

16 "I'm just a weird big guy."

---

20 AROMAS THAT HUMANS FIND THE MOST PLEASING

1 Lime	11 Fir
2 Grapefruit	12 Viridine (earthy, green)
3 Bergamot (citrus-like)	13 Lilial (Lily of the Valley)
4 Orange	14 Tarragon
5 Peach	15 Balsam
6 Peppermint	16 Fennel
7 Freesia	17 Nutmeg
8 Amyl acetate (banana-like)	18 Eucalyptus
9 Cassia (cinnamon)	19 Wintergreen
10 Mimosa	20 Castoreum (leathery)

The NSA surveilled the phone records of **248** Americans in 2013...or so they say.

5 RIGHTS THE FIRST AMENDMENT GUARANTEES ...AND 5 IT DOESN'T

5 RIGHTS THE FIRST AMENDMENT GUARANTEES

1 Freedom to practice any religion

2 Freedom of speech

3 Freedom of the press

4 Freedom to peacefully assemble

5 Freedom to petition the government to address grievances

5 RIGHTS THE FIRST AMENDMENT *DOESN'T* GUARANTEE

1 **Unlimited free speech.** Hate speech, terroristic threats, slander, libel, and "fighting words" (words intended to provoke immediate violence) aren't protected speech.

2 **Unlimited freedom of the press.** Journalists have no different or special rights than ordinary citizens. They're subject to the same limits on slander, libel, hate speech, etc.

3 **Unlimited peaceful assembly.** Local governments can pass laws that require permits and set limits on hours, noise, and blocked traffic, and a private property owner is not required to allow any demonstrations at all.

4 **Unlimited job security.** Citizens have the right to express themselves, but it's legal for business owners to discipline and fire their employees for what they say—especially if their free speech causes a "hostile work environment."

5 **Unlimited freedom of expression.** Private property owners can set limits on what can and can't be worn—so "no shirt, no shoes, no service" is not a violation of the First Amendment.

10 SORDID STUFFED-ANIMAL STORIES

1 KILL ME ELMO. *Sesame Street*'s Elmo is gentle and lovable... except when he threatens to murder you! In 2008 Florida mom Melissa Bowman changed the batteries in her son James's recordable "Elmo Knows Your Name" doll. When she turned the toy on, Elmo started saying, "Kill James." She remarked, "It's not something that really you would think would ever come out of a toy. But once I heard it, I was just kind of distraught." Fisher-Price offered to replace the doll and promised to check the sound files on other Elmos, but no other incidents were reported.

2 HIPPO-BOTTOM-GAS. You never know when a prop will become a fan favorite. Just ask Bert the Farting Hippo. After the stuffed animal appeared on the hit CBS cop drama *NCIS*, he became so popular that the network offered the farting toy for sale. In 2014 the company that made Bert, Folkmanis Inc., sued CBS, claiming the network had initially bought the farting toy from Folkmanis but later hired a Chinese toy company to make cheaper, unlicensed versions of Bert the Farting Hippo. In an official statement, a CBS spokesperson mocked the lawsuit: "We believe this to be a flatulent abuse of the legal system, and we intend to clear the air on this matter immediately." (The suit is pending.)

3 THE RETURN OF HOBBES? When a large tiger was spotted hiding in a grassy field near Hampshire, England, in 2011, the townspeople fled indoors and the police went on high alert. A helicopter carrying thermal imaging equipment flew over the field to track the beast, and police asked the nearby Marwell Zoo to send staff with tranquilizer guns. When thermal imaging failed to detect any body heat, the helicopter flew in closer and then, according to a police spokesman, "The tiger then rolled over in the downdraft and it was at that point it became obvious it was a stuffed life-size toy."

4 BAD NEWS BEARS. In 2012 youth activists in the small European country of Belarus took part in antigovernment protests by placing a dozen teddy bears of varying sizes near a bus stop in the capital city of Minsk. The stuffed animals held signs that read "Where is the freedom of the press?" and "Toys against lawlessness." An "injured" bear displayed a sign that said "Cops tore my eye out." Perturbed police promptly hauled the bears away.

5 SCOOBY DON'T. In 2007 Hit Entertainment, which owns the trademarks to kid-friendly characters like Barney the Dinosaur, contacted the Queens, New York, district attorney's office about a man named Julio Quevedo, who was allegedly counterfeiting costumes of their characters in order to sell them to adult movie producers. (Apparently, a fringe group known as "furries" enjoys having "relations" in animal costumes, and watching movies where people do that.) The DA office set up a sting: An investigator posed as a producer looking for costumes for an "erotic shoot." Quevedo gave him a choice of Scooby-Doo, the Tasmanian Devil, and others, but settled on a Bob the Builder costume for $250. Quevedo was arrested. The DA's office called the case "particularly troublesome."

6 POLLY WANTS SOME AIR. A couple entering Arizona from Mexico got stopped at the border because they had mangoes. (There are strict controls on bringing produce into the U.S.) A subsequent search of their belongings led to an even more troubling discovery: There were two bedraggled parrots inside a stuffed Elmo doll. The mangoes were destroyed, the parrots confiscated and placed in quarantine, and the couple was fined $300. No word on what happened to Elmo.

7 SICKY MOUSE. "Did that stuffed mouse really just sing 'Pedophile, Pedophile'?" asked dozens of bewildered parents in Great Britain in 2009. The mouse was supposed to sing "Jingle bells, jingle bells," but it sounded (to the parents) like the naughty word. After several people complained, the Chinese toy manufacturer explained that the worker who made the recording couldn't pronounce "jingle bells" properly, so the toymaker sped up the soundtrack to disguise it, which resulted in the accidental distortion. The mouse was recalled.

8 "JAPAN TRAVEL AGENCY FOR STUFFED ANIMALS" For only $55 (plus shipping), you can send your stuffed animal on a two-week tour of Japan. (Not you, just your stuffed animal.) Unagi Travel offers four package tours: a hot spring, a historic shrine, Tokyo, and a "mystery" tour...just for inanimate objects that can neither think or see. However, your beloved stuffed animal will post its vacation pics to your Facebook page while it's traveling, so there's that. And then there's this odd disclaimer from the travel agency's website: "We will make sure not to have your stuffed animal injured or kidnapped. However, in case of any unfortunate missing incidence, we will compensate up to US$100."

9 MY TERRORIST PONY. "It just looked like it was placed in a really suspicious place," said concerned citizen Scott Kilwein about a two-foot-tall stuffed pony that someone either deliberately placed or accidentally left in a cul-de-sac near an Orlando, Florida, elementary school in 2010. Panic nearly ensued: The school was locked down, and police arrived at the scene to investigate the pony...but then decided it might be safer if the bomb squad did it. So the bomb squad showed up and sent in a remote-controlled robot to get a closer look. But the little pony wouldn't divulge its secrets, so the bomb squad blew the toy to smithereens. Afterward, an Orange County Sheriff's spokesman declared the pony to be "nonthreatening."

10 IT'S A JUNGLE OUT THERE.

In 2014 a monkey and a zebra were buying snacks at an English supermarket when the monkey saw a man threatening a female customer in an adjacent aisle. The monkey (who was carrying a stuffed zebra toy) alerted the zebra (who was carrying a stuffed monkey toy), and the two furry beasts confronted the culprit—who became agitated and chased the female customer outside. The monkey and the zebra ran after him and tackled him in the street. They kept the man subdued until police arrived and took him away. So who were these heroic animals? Two off-duty cops—Tracy Griffin and Terri Cave—who were wearing full-body animal costumes (with matching stuffed animals) on their way to a "fancy dress party." The West Midlands police force tweeted a picture of the two women with the caption "Off duty officers dressed in Zebra & Monkey onesies arrest a violent man in the street. Keeping you safe whatever it takes."

THOMAS JEFFERSON'S "A DECALOGUE OF CANONS FOR OBSERVATION IN PRACTICAL LIFE," 1825

1 Never put off till tomorrow what you can do today.

2 Never trouble another for what you can do yourself.

3 Never spend your money before you have it.

4 Never buy what you do not want, because it is cheap; it will be dear to you.

5 Pride costs us more than hunger, thirst, and cold.

6 We never repent of having eaten too little.

7 Nothing is troublesome that we do willingly.

8 How much pain have cost us, the evils which have never happened.

9 Take things always by their smooth handle.

10 When angry, count to ten before you speak; if very angry, a hundred.

9 ORIGINS OF BUZZWORDS PEOPLE ARE SICK OF

1 AWESOMESAUCE

This slang term for "good" was first uttered by the character Strong Bad in the *Homestar Runner* web series of animated shorts, created by brothers Mike and Matt Chapman in the early 2000s. In one webisode, after Strong Bad pours ketchup all over his computer (so his e-mail replies will be funnier), he asks the Cheat, "Aren't you going to get your 409 or Awesome Sauce or whatever you're going to clean this up with?" Today, #awesomesauce is one of the most popular Twitter hashtags.

2 UNDER THE BUS

The origin of this go-to reality-show phrase, writes Paul Dickson in the book *Slang: The Topical Dictionary of American-isms*, comes from minor league baseball in the late 1970s. When it came time to leave for the next game, the call went out: "Bus leaving. Be on it or under it." The phrase first appeared in print in a 1980 *Washington Post* article, and in 1984 rocker Cyndi Lauper helped popularize it when she said, "In the rock 'n' roll business you are either on the bus or under it."

3 MEME

Evolutionary biologist Richard Dawkins coined the term *meme* in his 1976 book *The Selfish Gene*, where he used it to describe concepts and behaviors that spread from person to person in a given culture. The Internet later snapped up the term, but Dawkins doesn't mind: "The meaning is not that far away from the original. I did actually use the metaphor of a virus. So when anybody talks about something going viral on the Internet, that is exactly what a meme is."

4 MEH

Lisa Simpson is credited with bringing "meh" into wide-spread use, but where did the *Simpsons* writers pick it up? John Swartzwelder explains, "I had originally heard the word from an advertising writer named Howie Krakow back in 1970 or 1971 who insisted it was the funniest word in the world," but where Krakow learned it remains a mystery. It's most likely a Yiddish term, meaning, well, "meh."

5 BLING

As far back as the early 1990s, "bling-bling" was in use in the New Orleans rap music community. In early 1996, Tupac Shakur recorded a song called "Friendz," where he rapped "Check out my diamonds...everyone gonna blink," while "bling bling" is repeated in the background. But that song wasn't released until 2001, so rapper B.G. is credited with introducing the phrase in his 1999 song "Bling-Bling." A year later, Shaquille O'Neal popularized it when he boasted that the Lakers' championship rings would go "bling-bling." He was right: The phrase "bling bling" was carved into the sides of their official rings after they won the finals. *Bling* entered the dictionary in 2003.

6 FRENEMY

This portmanteau of "friend" and "enemy" dates back to 1953 when columnist Walter Winchell coined it in this headline: "Howz about calling the Russians our Frienemies?" Two decades later in 1977, British journalist Jessica Mitford used it in a *Daily Mail* article. Despite that, the word didn't catch on until 1998 when the pop band New Radicals used it in its hit "You Get What You Give." It was cemented as a pop-culture buzzword in a 2000 episode of *Sex and the City* titled "Frenemies."

7 HIPSTER

It's a word generally said with scorn today, but that wasn't always so. It dates back to the jazz scene of the 1930s, when singer Cab Calloway wrote in his book *Hepster's Dictionary: Language of Jive* that a *"hep cat"* was "a guy who knows all the answers, understands jive." The *hepster* in the book's title soon changed to *hipster* and became a catchphrase in the 1940s jazz scene. As the jazz counterculture faded, so did the term, until it was revived in the 1990s to describe someone who tries way too hard to be cool.

8 D-BAG

This method of cleansing a woman's genitalia—known as douching—has been around since the 1700s, but its slang use as an insult can be traced to a 1939 book called *Ninety Times Guilty*, which featured a character named Jimmy Douchebag. In 1946 the term was used in the military to refer to someone who was "a misfit," and the shortened "douche" was college slang as far back as 1968. The insult went mainstream thanks to this exchange in the 1984 movie *Revenge of the Nerds*:

> **Stan:** "What are you looking at, nerd?"
>
> **Booger:** "I thought I was looking at my mother's old douchebag, but that's in Ohio."

9 BROMANCE

This portmanteau of *brother* and *romance* describes two guys who have deep affection for each other—albeit in a totally platonic, manly way. Where the term originated is unclear, but credit is usually given to Dave Carnie, editor of the 1990s skateboarding magazine *Big Brother* (which spawned the MTV show *Jackass*). In a 2011 interview, Carnie lamented, "I'm sorry about *bromance*. I don't think that I invented that stupid word, but if I did, I'm truly sorry. I should also say that I don't mind taking credit for it, at least until the true author steps forward. Because, as you know, as a writer, to have created a word that actually comes out of people's faces, well, that's the greatest honor that could be bestowed upon me." Well said, bro.

10 DISTINCTIONS: FOOD EDITION

1 **FRUIT vs. VEGETABLE.** Botanists consider a fruit to be the plant's ovary, which is why they classify tomatoes, cucumbers, eggplants, and the like as fruits. Vegetables are the other parts of an edible plant—roots (carrots), leaves (lettuce), stems (broccoli), etc. But chefs classify tomatoes and eggplants as vegetables because of how they're used in cooking—a veggie is a savory part of a meal's main course, a fruit is a sweet snack.

2 **BAKING POWDER vs. BAKING SODA.** These carbon dioxide bubble producers may seem nearly identical...until you goof up and use baking *powder* when the recipe calls for baking *soda*. Big difference: Baking powder is simply baking soda with a dry acid (such as cream of tartar) mixed in. The acid produces two chemical reactions, the first of which takes place when you add moisture to the mixture. The acid reacts against the baking soda, producing carbon dioxide. Once you place the batter in the oven, the gas expands, and the cake rises. Baking soda is much stronger because it's pure. Recipes that use baking soda also call for some sort of acid (like lemon or buttermilk). When you mix the two together, the baking soda starts working at once. That's why you have to put batters made with baking soda into the oven immediately—so all the gas bubbles don't escape before the cake is baked.

3 **ENRICHED vs. FORTIFIED.** If nutrients that were lost during food production are added back, then the food is enriched. For example, white bread is enriched with B vitamins that were lost when the wheat was refined. When nutrients are added to a food that doesn't usually contain them (such as adding vitamin D to milk), then it's fortified.

4 **JAM vs. JELLY vs. PRESERVES vs. MARMALADE.** What they all have in common: They're fruits or vegetables in which the water has been reduced and sugar added to sweeten the taste. They all include a jelling agent such as pectin and citric acid for tartness. The differences: Jelly is smooth because it's made from strained fruit juices; jam is chunkier because it's made from crushed fruit; preserves are even chunkier because they're made from entire fruits; and marmalade has more of a punch because it's made from citrus fruit—peel and all.

5 **MUSHROOM vs. TOADSTOOL.** Scientifically speaking, they're the same. But most people refer to edible fungi as mushrooms and nonedible fungi as toadstools.

6 **DEHYDRATED vs. FREEZE DRIED.** Both remove the water from fruits to make them last longer, but each one utilizes a different process: Dehydrating is done by placing the food in the sun or a dehydrator. It removes about 75 percent of the water content and leaves the fruit chewy. It will keep for two to three years, depending on how it's stored. Freeze-dried food can last up to 20 or even 30 years because 98 percent of the water has been removed. But the process is much more difficult. As its name implies, a machine flash-freezes the fruit, and then heat is added to vaporize the water content.

7 **FOOD ALLERGY vs. FOOD INTOLERANCE.** A food allergy is an immune system response that occurs when, or directly after, eating the problem food. Even a tiny amount can trigger an attack. A food intolerance is a digestive system response due to an enzyme deficiency, and it can take longer to show symptoms. Sufferers can often get away with eating a little bit of the food, whereas allergy sufferers can't even have a taste.

8 **CAGE-FREE vs. FREE-RANGE.** There's no official government standard for cage-free foods—the claim is that egg-producing poultry are not raised in cages. But cage-free eggs can still come from birds raised entirely indoors in crowded warehouses. The free-range label is regulated by the USDA, but only for meat-producing poultry—not for pigs, cattle, or egg-producing poultry. The label promises that the chickens are "not confined," meaning they get to go outside at least once a day. But the USDA requires only five minutes of outside time to qualify for the free-range label, and there's no requirement about exactly where outside the chickens go. That means that a free-range chicken could have spent 23 hours and 55 minutes of its days in a cage, and 5 minutes on a concrete slab "outside." So if you really want to eat an egg that was laid by a happy chicken, look for eggs with the "Certified Humane Raised and Handled" label. These farms operate under strict guidelines for humane care and feeding.

9 NATURAL vs. ORGANIC. Only meat and poultry products have official USDA guidelines for natural or all-natural claims. Such meat can only undergo "minimal processing" and cannot contain "artificial colors, artificial flavors, preservatives, or other artificial ingredients." But this doesn't mean that natural meats are organic. It also doesn't require that animals be free of added hormones or antibiotics. For all other types of food, from potato chips to soups, the natural or all-natural label is only a marketing term. Organic foods have much stricter guidelines. According to the U.S. Department of Agriculture, "Before a product can be labeled organic, a government-approved certifier inspects the farm where the food is grown to make sure the farmer is following all the rules necessary to meet USDA organic standards." For a farm to be certified organic, it must go three full years without any use of commercial fertilizers or herbicides.

10 MASHED POTATOES vs. PEA SOUP. You mean you don't know the difference between mashed potatoes and pea soup? The difference is...anyone can mash potatoes.

80 REASONS BRITSPEAK BEATS AMERICA-SPEAK

BOOTS & BONNETS

1 Truck: *Lorry*

2 Trailer/RV: *Caravan*

3 Car hood: *Bonnet*

4 Car trunk: *Boot*

5 Antenna: *Aerial*

6 Overpass: *Flyover*

7 Parking lot: *Car park*

8 Gasoline: *Petrol*

9 Crosswalk: *Zebra crossing*

10 Crossing guard: *Lollypop man/lady*

11 Yellow light: *Amber light*

12 Subway: *Underground/ tube*

13 Elevator: *Lift*

KNICKERS & NAPPIES

14 Sweater: *Jumper*

15 Vest: *Waistcoat*

16 Pants: *Trousers*

17 Suspenders: *Braces*

18 Pajamas: *Jim jams*

19 Diaper: *Nappy*

20 Robe: *Dressing gown*

21 Men's undies: *Pants*

22 Women's panties: *Knickers*

BEVVIES & BANGERS

23 Sausage: *Banger*

24 Bacon: *Streaky bacon*

25 Fish stick: *Fish finger*

26 Cookie: *Biscuit*

27 Popsicle: *Ice lolly*

28 Cotton Candy: *Candyfloss*

29 Beer: *Bevvy*

30 Cheap wine: *Plonk*

MINTED & PISSED

31 Drunk: *Pissed*

32 Awesome: *Ace*

33 Poor: *Skint*

34 Rich: *Minted*

35 Attractive: *Fit*

36 Loud-mouthed: *Gobby*

Lots of reading room: The sultan of Brunei's palace has 260 bathrooms.

37 Stupid: *Daft*

38 Useless: *Duff*

39 Suspicious: *Dodgy*

40 Clueless: *Gormless*

41 Crazy: *Barmy*

NUTTERS & TOSSERS

42 Regular guy: *Bloke*

43 Idiot: *Cockwomble*

44 Dimwit: *Muppet*

45 Crazy person: *Nutter*

46 Jerk: *Tosser/wanker*

47 Mocking someone: *Taking the piss out of*

48 Pulling someone's leg: *Having a laugh*

49 That's BS!: *That's a load of bollocks!*

CHEMISTS & THEATRE

50 Pharmacist: *Chemist*

51 Doctor's office: *Surgery*

52 Operating room: *Theatre*

53 Very tired: *Knackered*

54 Sickly/pale: *Off colour*

55 Sick with the flu: *Lurgy*

56 Hemorrhoids: *Piles*

57 Vomit: *Honk*

58 Committed: *Sectioned*

FORTNIGHTS & CHIN WAGS

59 Chat: *Chin wag*

60 Costume party: *Fancy dress party*

61 Two weeks: *Fortnight*

62 Wait in line: *Queue*

63 Thrilled: *Chuffed to bits*

64 Shocked: *Gobsmacked*

KNOBS & KNOCKERS

65 Ass: *Arse*

66 Breasts: *Knockers*

67 Penis: *Knob/willy*

68 Man bits: *Twig and berries*

69 Lady part: *Fanny*

70 Kiss passionately: *Snog*

71 Fart: *Blow off*

72 Urinate: *Spend a penny*

TELLYS & LOOS

73 Eraser: *Rubber*

74 Math: *Maths*

75 Vacation: *Holiday*

76 Apartment: *Flat*

77 Bathroom: *Loo/toilet*

78 Yard: *Garden*

79 TV: *Telly*

80 Telephone booth: *Phone box (or TARDIS)*

11 FACTS ABOUT THE ENGLISH LANGUAGE

1 An estimated 25 percent of the world's population speaks English. That works out to about 1.75 billion English speakers.

2 However, "only" 375 million people speak English as their first language.

3 That means there are 750 million people on Earth who speak English as a foreign language.

4 Fifty percent of Facebook users speak English. That works out to more than half a billion people.

5 There are roughly 100,000 adjectives in the English language. The 10 we use most often are *old*, *new*, *first*, *last*, *good*, *long*, *little*, *great*, *other*, and *own*.

6 More than 55 percent of all websites are in English...as of 2014. As Asia continues to open up to the Internet, expect to see a lot more non-English websites in the near future.

7 The 10 English nouns we use most often are *hand*, *time*, *man*, *thing*, *day*, *person*, *way*, *world*, *year*, and *life*.

8 Seventy-five countries either have English as an official language or give it special status.

9 The 25 verbs English speakers use most often have only one syllable.

10 The official language of the skies: English. All of the world's pilots must have a basic understanding of the language. That rule has been in place since 1944, but it's only been strictly enforced since 2011.

11 Fifty-one percent of worldwide Tweets are in English. #NowYouKnow.

6 PEOPLE ECLIPSED BY THEIR FAMOUS SIBLINGS

1 FRANCESCO CASANOVA

When you hear the name "Casanova," you probably picture the Italian womanizer, not a successful Italian painter. Giacomo Casanova was the more famous one—in his storied life, he reportedly bedded hundreds of women. Only art history buffs know that his half-brother, Francesco Giuseppe Casanova, was a respected artist in the mid to late 1700s in both Paris and Vienna, best known for his paintings of battle scenes and landscapes. Although Casanova's art hangs in the Louvre and the Hermitage, he never achieved the fame of his randy sibling.

2 TOMMIE AARON

"I think if Tommie played with another ball club, he probably would have had a better major league career. The media was always comparing us," said Hank Aaron of his younger brother. Like Hank, Tommie Aaron played first base for the Atlanta Braves, but he had a .229 batting average to his brother's .305. Together, though, they hold the record for most home runs by brothers: 769 (756 by Hank, 13 by Tommie).

3 BILLY CARTER

One became president; the other became a punch line. When older brother Jimmy ran for the nation's highest office in 1976, Billy played the country bumpkin to the hilt: "I got a red neck, white socks, and Blue Ribbon beer!" Riding on his brother's coattails, Billy worked the talk show circuit and sold his own brand of "Billy Beer," but a drinking problem and a pro-Libya, anti-Israel rant (while his brother was in office) left him mired in scandal. Billy Carter died of pancreatic cancer in 1988.

4 JOE ESTEVEZ

Estevez describes himself as a "steady working actor," having appeared in over 100 movies (usually minor parts in low-budget films). But while he's made a living at acting, he's never achieved the name recognition of the rest of his family: His brother is Martin Sheen, and his nephews are Emilio Estevez and Charlie Sheen. But chances are, if you're a film buff, you've at least heard Joe's voice: It's almost identical to Martin's, so Joe often fills in for additional dialogue recording when his brother is too busy. For example, Joe provided most of the narration for *Apocalypse Now*. In 2012 he published an autobiography called *Wiping Off the Sheen*.

5 ELIZABETH FÖRSTER-NIETZSCHE

Friedrich Nietzsche was a respected German philosopher, social critic, and great quotation generator. (Our favorite: "That which does not kill us makes us stronger.") But in the years since his death in 1900, Nietzsche's critics have accused him of anti-Semitism. He wasn't, but his sister Elizabeth was. That's why she altered her brother's manuscripts after his death to make his writings appear anti-Semitic.

6 DOUG PITT

In most other families, Doug would be the most famous sibling. In 1991 he founded the successful tech company Service-World Computer Center and has since served on the boards of several charities—including Big Brothers Big Sisters, the Red Cross, and Easter Seals. He was honored by Bill Clinton for his work as Goodwill Ambassador for the United Republic of Tanzania. Doug is also an accomplished photographer—his work has been displayed in galleries all over the world. In 2011 he became the first American to ascend and then descend Mount Kilimanjaro on a mountain bike. To top it off, Doug has a perfect set of teeth, chiseled cheekbones, and dreamy blue eyes... just like his big brother Brad.

---

7 HORROR LISTS TO MAKE YOU SCREAM

10 *ATTACK OF THE KILLER...*

1 *Tomatoes* (1978)
2 *Lampreys* (2014)
3 *Refrigerator* (1990)
4 *Manatee* (1997)
5 *Bees* (2013)
6 *Hog* (2003)
7 *Chihuahua* (2009)
8 *Duct Tape* (2007)
9 *Trees* (2014)
10 *Shrews* (1959)

DICK SMITH'S (MAKEUP ARTIST ON *THE EXORCIST, THE GODFATHER, TAXI DRIVER*) INGREDIENTS FOR FAKE BLOOD

- 1 quart white corn syrup
- 1 level tsp. methyl paraben
- 2 oz. Ehler red food color
- 5 tsp. Ehler yellow food color
- 2 oz. water
- 2 oz. Kodak Photo-Flo *Warning: Poisonous! (Only available at photo supply stores)

10 KILLERS WHO JUST WON'T QUIT

1 **Norman Bates:** 5 films, 1 TV show (*Psycho*)
2 **Hannibal Lecter:** 5 films, 1 TV show (*The Silence of the Lambs*)
3 **Chucky the doll:** 7 films (*Child's Play*)
4 **Lubdan the leprechaun:** 7 films (*Leprechaun*)
5 **Leatherface:** 7 films (*The Texas Chainsaw Massacre*)
6 **Jigsaw:** 7 films (*Saw*)
7 **Pinhead:** 9 films (*Hellraiser*)
8 **Freddy Kruger:** 9 films (*Nightmare on Elm Street*)
9 **Michael Myers:** 10 films (*Halloween*)
10 **Jason Voorhees:** 13 films (*Friday the 13th*)

2 WORDY HORROR MOVIE TITLES

1 *The Incredibly Strange Creatures Who Stopped Living and Became Mixed-up Zombies*

The largest known star, R136a1, weighs as much as 265 of our Suns.

2 *Night of the Day of the Dawn of the Son of the Bride of the Return of the Revenge of the Terror of the Attack of the Evil, Mutant, Alien, Flesh Eating, Hellbound, Zombified Living Dead Part 2 in Shocking 2-D* (1991)

3 UNUSUAL KILLING DEVICES

1 Pogo stick (*Leprechaun*, 1983)

2 Umbrella (*Silent Night, Deadly Night 2*, 1984)

3 Leg of lamb (*Serial Mom*, 1994)

6 ACTORS YOU MAY NOT KNOW WERE IN A HORROR MOVIE

1 Clint Eastwood (*Revenge of the Creature*, 1955)

2 Harrison Ford (*The Possessed*, 1977)

3 Matthew McConaughey (*Texas Chainsaw Massacre: The Next Generation*, 1994)

4 George Clooney (*Return to Horror High*, 1987)

5 Leonardo DiCaprio (*Critters 3*, 1991)

6 Tom Hanks (*He Knows You're Alone*, 1980)

5 UNSETTLING HORROR QUOTES

1 "I feel it. I feel it breathing on me."
—Katie, *Paranormal Activity* (2007)

2 "To her, it simply is another child. To us, it is the Beast."
—Tangina, *Poltergeist* (1982)

3 "It puts the lotion on its skin. It does this whenever it's told."
—Buffalo Bob, to his victim, *Silence of the Lambs* (1991)

4 "You can choose to repeat this hour over and over again, or you can take advantage of our express checkout system."
—Voice on the phone in the evil hotel room, right before a noose appears, *1408* (2007)

5 Doctor: "You don't want to hurt anyone."
Samara: "But I do, and I'm sorry. It won't stop."
—*The Ring*, 2002

9 WEIRD CELEBRITY BABY NAMES EXPLAINED

1 ROSALIND ARUSHA ARKADINA ALTALUNE FLORENCE. Daughter of Uma Thurman and Arpad Busson. The couple couldn't agree on one name. "We call her Luna," said Thurman. "The rest, she can just name her own children all these interesting names."

2 CRICKET PEARL. Daughter of actress Busy Philipps and screenwriter Marc Silverstein. He chose the name because he pictures a girl named Cricket as "the greatest, happiest kid on the block, the coolest camp counselor, she's hot in college!"

3 SPARROW JAMES MIDNIGHT. Son of socialite Nicole Richie and Joel Madden. Said Richie: "I wanted to give him a name that he's going to have to stand up for."

4 PILOT INSPEKTOR. Son of Jason Lee, who's a big fan of the band Grandaddy. "Their song, 'He's Simple, He's Dumb, He's the Pilot,' absolutely blew my mind when I first heard it. It was from this track that my wife, Beth, came up with the name Pilot."

5 AUDIO SCIENCE. Son of actress Shannyn Sossamon and kids' book author Dallas Clayton. "We wanted a word, not a name, so Dallas read through the dictionary three or four times. We were going to call him Science, but thought it might get shortened to Sci, as in Simon."

6 BEAR BLU. Son of Alicia Silverstone and Christopher Jarecki. "We narrowed it to five names, but we couldn't decide. My husband suggested Bear or Blu, and I loved them both!"

Hurricane Irene left **267** tons of debris in Washington, D.C., in 2011.

7 AUTUMN, SONNET, OCEAN, TRUE. Children of Forest Whitaker and Keisha Nash. "We want them to kind of touch their destiny by their names: Autumn is sort of flighty, Sonnet is much more of an artist, True is very strong, and Ocean just has a big heart."

8 ROCKET AYER. Son of singer Pharrell Williams and Helen Lasichanh. "In the same way that the Indians name their children after a force or an animal or an element, we named him after a man-made machine that was meant to ascend. Metaphorically, it was because of Stevie Wonder's 'Rocket Love,' Elton John's 'Rocket Man,' and Herbie Hancock's 'Rocket.' All of my favorite musicians. And his middle name is not 'Man.' It's Ayer after [funk legend] Roy Ayers."

9 SUNDAY ROSE. Daughter of Nicole Kidman and Keith Urban. "Sunday, that's our favorite day," said Kidman. "If you're lonely, Sundays are a very lonely day. And if you're happy and you've got your family around you, then Sunday's a beautiful day. So our baby's called Sunday."

8 MORE ODD CELEBRITY BABY NAMES

1 **Royal Reign,** daughter of Lil Kim and Mr Papers

2 **Summer Rain,** daughter of Christina Aguilera and Matthew Rutler

3 **Bodhi Ransom,** son of Megan Fox and Brian Austin Green

4 **Happy,** son of Macy Gray and Tracy Hinds

5 **Keen,** son of Mark Ruffalo and Sunrise Coigney

6 **Seven Sirius,** son of Erykah Badu and Andre 3000

7 **Bronx Mowgli,** son of Ashlee Simpson and Pete Wentz

8 **Jermajesty,** son of Jermaine Jackson and Alejandra Oaziaza

8 SIMPLE RULE'S FOR USING AN APOSTROPHE

Rule #1: Don't put an apostrophe where it doesn't belong (like the one in the plural noun "rules" in the title).

1 Own something? Use 's to show it: *John's toilet*. If the name ends in s: Add another 's after it: *Chris's plunger*. Inanimate objects can also "own" something, so instead of tweeting, "Yesterdays rainbow," tweet: *Yesterday's rainbow*.

2 A group owns something? Put ' after the s: *The BRI members' toilets.*

3 The group doesn't end in s? Add 's: *Children's potties*

4 More than one owns the same thing? Add 's to the second one: *John and Gordon's toothbrush*

5 Something not usually plural? Add 's to make it plural: *Cross your t's*

6 Taking out letters? Replace with 's. Here is = here's. If it's a curved "smart quote" (not "straight quotes" like this), then the apostrophe must face in the direction of the missing text. It's not "I told 'em I had a BM back in '09." It's "I told 'em I had a BM back in '09."

7 Is it *it's* or *its*? Use it's when you could say "it is": *It's my toilet* = *It is my toilet*. Use its for belonging to: *The cheeky monkey pooped its pants*. (The pants belong to the monkey; you wouldn't say, "The cheeky monkey pooped it is pants.")

8 Is it *you're* or *your*? Use you're when you could say "you are": *You're wrong* = *You are wrong*. Use your for "belonging to": *I can see your underwear*. The underwear is yours, so it's not "I can see you are underwear." (Unless, of course, you actually are underwear.)

11 QUOTES THAT MAKE YOU GO

It wouldn't be a true Uncle John's book if we didn't include at least one list of bathroom quotes.

1 "Men who consistently leave the toilet seat up secretly want women to get up to go the bathroom in the middle of the night and fall in."

—Rita Rudner

2 "That game was dedicated to Rick Adelman. I'm at home, in the bathroom, trying to take a dump, flipping through the channels and he's complaining about how I'm stepping over the line [shooting free throws]. I can't even do a No. 2 in peace."

—Shaquille O'Neal, after the opposing coach had complained about Shaq making 12 free throws in a game

3 **Mrs. Weasly:** "Now, you two—this year, you behave yourselves. If I get one more owl telling me you've blown up a toilet or—"

Fred: "Blown up a toilet? We've never blown up a toilet."

George: "Great idea though, thanks, Mum."

—J. K. Rowling, *Harry Potter and the Sorcerer's Stone*

4 "Ignoring fame was my rebellion, in a funny way. I was insistent on being normal and doing normal things. It probably wasn't advisable to go to college in America and room with a complete stranger. And it probably wasn't wise to share a bathroom with eight other people in a coed dorm. Looking back, that was crazy."

—Emma Watson, on attending Brown University after wrapping up the Harry Potter movie series

5 "As Robert flushed, an unexpected realization hit him. This is the Pope's toilet, he thought. *I just took a leak in the Pope's toilet.* He had to chuckle. The Holy Throne."

—Dan Brown, *Angels & Demons*

6 "I'm shy. I can go on a trip for days and not go because I won't sit on a toilet seat on a plane. I'm certainly not going to go on someone's lawn. Could you imagine, in a cocktail dress?"

—Farrah Fawcett

7 "You know, I've been to some superstars' houses, and I've been really disgusted when I see their platinum discs hanging in the toilet. They're just there on the walls glaring at you when you're trying to be occupied with other things."

—John Lydon of the Sex Pistols

8 "Every time someone uses a bathroom and they flush, all the bacteria is shot into the air."

—Megan Fox

9 "Poop humor is fun. If you do the toilet scenes well and commit to them, they can be really, really powerful."

—Sandra Bullock

10 "Today, the degradation of the inner life is symbolized by the fact that the only place sacred from interruption is the private toilet."

—Lewis Mumford

11 "I have finally come to the conclusion that a good reliable set of bowels is worth more to a man than any quantity of brains."

—Josh Billings

10 PROCESSED FOODS AND HOW THEY'RE PROCESSED

1 CHEWING GUM

Gum's main ingredient: latex—as in latex rubber. It originally came from the sap of rubber trees, but most gums today contain only 10 to 20 percent natural rubber. The rest are synthetic, with tasty names like butadiene-styrene rubber, polyethylene, and polyvinyl acetate. To make gum, the latex is ground, dried, and melted into a syrup. Then it's filtered, and flavorings and softeners are added. The mixture is kneaded for several hours before it's rolled out, cut into strips, and packaged.

2 GELATIN

Used as a thickener in foods like Jell-O and marshmallows, gelatin is essentially collagen, the protein found in connective tissue. But it's not made from horns and hooves, as is often thought (although what it comes from isn't much better). Pig and cow bones and skin are broken down in hot water or acid and then dried, refined, and purified into gelatin. For use as a thickener, the gelatin is ground into granules or powder.

3 IMITATION CRABMEAT

Fake crabmeat is fish...mostly. The fish part is usually Alaska pollock or walleye pollock. After the fish is cleaned, it's minced and mixed with starch, salt, a bit of real crabmeat, egg white, and flavoring. Then the mixture is ground into a paste, which is pressed into sheets and cooked. To give it that crabby look, the sheets are cut into thin strands, and it's colored. The "crabmeat" is cooked one more time and vacuum packed.

4 RICE CAKES

Moistened rice is placed in a mold that gets heated and then pressurized in a vacuum. After 8 to 10 seconds, the rice explodes like popcorn. Once it's popped, flavors are sprayed on and dried before the cakes are packaged. (Ever have a rice cake with an unappetizing texture? It either had too much air, not enough rice, or too much moisture when it was popped.)

5 BOLOGNA

Supermarket bologna really earns its "mystery meat" reputation. The process begins with unused bits of beef, pork, and sometimes poultry. Which bits? That's the mystery. Whatever it is, it gets ground up and liquefied into a paste, and a blend of spices (also a secret) is added. The pasty concoction is extruded into a casing, then boiled or smoked, sliced, and packaged.

6 EVAPORATED AND CONDENSED MILK

To extend its shelf life, milk is "evaporated": pasteurized, put at a pressure lower than atmospheric pressure, and then boiled. This vacuum evaporation process concentrates the milk to 30 to 40 percent solids, which delays spoiling. Then it's homogenized (to keep cream from separating to the top), and a stabilizing salt and vitamin D are added before it's sealed in cans. The difference between evaporated and condensed: Condensed milk is evaporated milk with lots of sugar added.

7 PRINGLES

Why do Pringles say "potato crisps" and not "potato chips"? Because to achieve the uniform, stackable shape, Pringles are made from pressed dough rather than sliced potatoes. Dried potato flakes, corn and rice flour, wheat starch, and oils are mixed together to make the dough, and then it's rolled out, cut, cooked in oil, and dried. The 42-percent potato crisps are then sprayed with flavoring and packed into the iconic tubes.

8 JAWBREAKERS

The main ingredient: granulated sugar. It's poured into a round kettle that rotates over heat. The second ingredient: liquid sugar. A worker called a "panner" pours it into the kettle; it sticks to the granulated sugar, and balls start to form. The panner continues to add liquid sugar off and on for 14 to 19 days, pouring as many as 100 coats into the rotating kettle. When the jawbreakers are nearly full size, color and flavor are added. Finally, the sugar balls are spun in a polishing pan with a food-grade wax, separated into batches, and bagged.

9 CHEESE SLICES

The next time you buy plastic-wrapped cheese slices, check to see if the label says "pasteurized process cheese" (which contains 80 to 85 percent natural cheese) or "pasteurized process cheese food" (as low as 51 percent cheese). Processed cheese is a blend of natural cheese like cheddar or Colby, oils, and milk fat. The cheese is heated to its melting point and then mixed with oil and emulsifiers, an additive that makes the slice melt evenly on a burger. Then the mixture is re-formed into blocks and cooled, cut into slices, and packaged.

10 SPAM

Once short for "SPiced hAM," today only 10 percent of Spam is actually ham (along with sugar, potato starch, and spices). The other 90 percent: pork shoulder meat. Hormel, which has made Spam since the 1930s, says it's short for "Shoulder of Pork and hAM." (The pink color comes from the preservative sodium nitrite.) The meat is ground, then dropped below freezing before the other ingredients are added. It's mixed in a machine with an airtight seal to keep the amount of water released during the process low; too much water leads to a lot of gelatin. The uncooked mixture is plopped into cans, which are sealed, and then the entire can is cooked in hot water. Over 122 million cans of Spam are sold every year.

15 LISTS THAT CHANGED THE WORLD

*As this list proves, without lists, we'd be a lot less civilized.
Long live the list!*

1 THE CODE OF UR-NAMMU (21st century BC)

Why It's Important: Thanks to this list—the oldest known set of laws that codified both criminal and civil rules—what we call "modern society" began to take shape. Though it was written 300 years before the brutal Code of Hammurabi, its penalties are much less severe. Why? Because Mesopotamia's King Ur-Nammu believed his people inherently knew how they should behave, so a monetary fine was enough to set them straight.

2 CODE OF HAMMURABI (18th century BC)

Why It's Important: Another list that helped modernize society, it's the most complete set of ancient laws we have. In contrast to Ur-Nammu, Babylonian King Hammurabi's penalty for most transgressions was death. His list gave us the phrase "an eye for an eye, a tooth for a tooth." (Or, in the words of the Code, "If a man put out the eye of another man, his eye shall be put out. If a man knock out the teeth of his equal, his teeth shall be knocked out.") Along with that gem, the 282 codes governed everything from doctor fees to divorce decrees.

3 TANG CODE (6th century BC)

Why It's Important: The earliest complete Chinese code of law went on to influence the penal codes of Korea, Vietnam, and Japan. It was divided into two sections: general principles of law and specific crimes and punishments. The latter section included the "Ten Abominations": the ten most serious crimes anyone could commit. Number one? Plotting rebellion.

4 12 TABLES OF LAW (5th century BC)

Why It's Important: One of the earliest surviving pieces of Roman literature, the 12 Tables established an empire-wide written legal code and laid the foundation for all later Roman law. Written by a commission of 10 scholars, it established laws and rights for both the rich and the common man.

5 ARISTOTLE'S *POETICS* (335 BC)

Why It's Important: Writers from Shakespeare to Tarantino have dutifully followed the *Poetics*, the list that set the standard for the structure of classic drama. The three main tenets—"unity of action, unity of place, unity of time"—established the characteristics of plot. Aristotle's list also defined the six parts of tragedy and the qualities of the hero.

6 MANU-SMRITI (1st century BC)

Why It's Important: This list's 2,694 verses and 12 chapters govern every aspect of Hindu life, both religious and secular. Although its harsh attitude toward women and the lower castes of Indian society is no longer considered acceptable, it's still considered one of the fundamental books of the Hindu canon.

7 THE TEN COMMANDMENTS (1st century BC)

Why It's Important: For more than 2,000 years, this list from the Old Testament has been the primary behavioral code of Western religions, and the commandments are still at the forefront of both Judaism and Christianity.

8 SHARI'AH (AD 8th–9th century)

Why It's Important: First laid out in the Qur'an, this list of rules, teachings, and behavior has governed all aspects of Muslim life for 1,100 years. Unlike the Western separation of church and state, religious beliefs and law are interwoven in Shari'ah, which means "the path leading to the watering place."

9 THE MAGNA CARTA (1215)

Why It's Important: Before the "Great Charter," kings and queens could do whatever dastardly things they wanted to without fear of repercussion. That abuse of power came to a head under King John, which led the English nobility to revolt: They forced him to sign this document that not only restricted the power of royalty but also guaranteed citizens certain rights. (Civil war broke out in spite of the king's signing, and the Magna Carta was revised and reissued in 1216, 1217, and 1255.)

10 NINETY-FIVE THESES (1517)

Why It's Important: This list of grievances sparked the Protestant Reformation and helped usher in an era of religious freedom that still exists today. Fed up with the abuses of the Catholic Church, a friar named Martin Luther nailed this list of questions that debated Catholic doctrine to the door of the Castle Church in Wittenberg, Germany. The pope threatened to excommunicate Luther, and the Holy Roman Emperor ordered his work to be burned, but Luther refused to recant, and his theses forever changed Western society.

11 NEWTON'S THREE LAWS OF MOTION (1666)

Why It's Important: Isaac Newton's seemingly simple list gave birth to modern physics. The laws: "1. An object will remain in a state of inertia unless acted upon by force. 2. The relationship between acceleration and applied force is F=ma. 3. For every action there is an equal and opposite reaction." With those revelations, Newton was able to figure out how gravity works. Before then, people believed that different sets of rules governed the heavens and the Earth. Result: For the first time in human history, traveling to space was within reach.

12 DECLARATION ON THE RIGHTS OF MAN AND CITIZEN (1789)

Why It's Important: Written during the French Revolution, this document outlined basic human rights such as "Men are born and remain free and equal in rights" and marked the beginning of the modern focus on civil liberties. One of its authors, the Marquis de Lafayette, asked for Thomas Jefferson's advice while writing it.

13 BILL OF RIGHTS (1791)

Why It's Important: Following in the footsteps of the Magna Carta and the English Bill of Rights, the first 10 amendments to the U.S. Constitution set limits on governmental power and became a benchmark for modern democracy. Future president James Madison wrote it after several states called for more protection of individual freedom. He originally added the Bill of Rights to the Constitution, but Congress didn't have the authority to change the original wording, so the Bill of Rights became a list of amendments.

14 GENEVA CONVENTIONS (1860s)

Why It's Important: The list of Geneva Conventions has made the world a more humane place by protecting people during wartime—especially civilians, the sick and wounded, and prisoners of war. The first of the four treaties was proposed by Swiss activist Henry Dunant after witnessing the horrors of war in 1859—which led to the formation of the Red Cross. More treaties were added (the last in 2005) to establish international humanitarian standards to be maintained during armed conflict.

15 UNIVERSAL DECLARATION OF HUMAN RIGHTS (1948)

Why It's Important: Following World War II, the members of the United Nations swore to never allow similar atrocities to happen again. The 58 member states drafted this declaration to establish universal, fundamental human rights. It begins with "All human beings are born equal in dignity and rights. They are endowed with reason and conscience and should act towards one another in a spirit of brotherhood." (Unfortunately, not everyone has gotten the memo.)

10 THINGS YOU'RE DOING WRONG WITH FOOD

According to the Internet.

1 USING YOUR HANDS TO SQUEEZE LEMONS
You'll get more juice if you squeeze the lemon between a pair of tongs. You can also microwave it for a few seconds to make it softer.

2 PEELING A BANANA FROM THE TOP DOWN
Learn from the monkeys: Pinch the bottom of the banana and peel it open. Then you won't have to pick off those banana "strings."

3 USING A SNAGGLE-TOOTH SPOON TO EAT A GRAPEFRUIT
Sure, it's called a "grapefruit spoon," but you'll get much more grapefruit if you just cut off the peel first and then slice the grapefruit into segments.

4 PUTTING LETTUCE ON TOP OF YOUR TACO
If you line the bottom of the taco shell with a lettuce leaf, it'll keep the ingredients from spilling out when you bite into it.

5 SCOOPING ICE CREAM
Don't scoop it. Use a knife, and cut ice cream slices instead.

6 DIPPING THE BOTTOM OF THE SUSHI
When you dip the rice side into soy sauce, the rice becomes wet and starts to separate. To keep it all together, flip the sushi upside down and dip from the top.

7 USING A FORK TO PULL MUSSELS OUT OF THEIR SHELLS

Why dirty a fork when you can use an already-emptied shell as tongs to pull the next one out?

8 CORING YOUR APPLES

Little-known fact: The core of an apple is edible. (The seeds are too, but they have a small amount of hydrogen cyanide. They won't hurt you unless you eat a lot of them, but feel free to spit them out.)

9 NOT MAXIMIZING THE TRUE POTENTIAL OF YOUR KETCHUP CUP

Frustrated that you can't cram more fries into those tiny fast-food ketchup cups? They're designed to fan out into a bowl. All you have to do is tug at the top rim until it opens up.

10 SHAKING A TIC TAC INTO YOUR HAND

If you've ever tried to shake a Tic Tac out of the container, you know it can be quite a chore. That's because you're doing it wrong. See that oval shape on the lid? That's a Tic Tac dispenser. Turn the container upside down, put your fingers on the lid, pull back on the box, and one Tic Tac will come out.

---

16 THINGS FANS CAN'T BRING TO FOO FIGHTERS CONCERTS

According to the band's tour rider.

1 Pro audio/video equipment	9 Chains or spiked bracelets
2 Weapons	10 Garden gnomes
3 Glass	11 Wallet chains
4 Light sabers	12 Backpacks
5 Cans	13 Waist packs
6 Plastic bottles	14 Tridents
7 Fireworks	15 Food
8 Alcoholic beverages	16 Laser pens

An astronaut's space suit weighs around 280 pounds.

11 PUN STARS

1 GROUCHO MARX, American comedy legend
• "I know, heifer cow is better than none, but this is no time for puns."
• "One morning I shot an elephant in my pajamas. How he got in my pajamas, I don't know."
• "If you want to see a comic strip, you should see me in the shower."
• *And this exchange from* A Night at the Opera:
Policeman: "A hermit, eh? Then why's your table set for four?"
Groucho: "That's nothing. My alarm clock is set for eight."

2 OSCAR WILDE, Irish writer
• According to legend, Wilde once bragged, "I can make a pun on any subject."
    So someone challenged him: "The queen!"
    "Ah," said Wilde, "but the queen is not a subject."
• Even on his deathbed, while miserable and destitute in a cheap hotel room in Paris, Wilde quipped, "This wallpaper and I are fighting a duel to the death. Either it goes...or I do." (The wallpaper won.)

3 PETER SERAFINOWICZ, British comedian
• "I finally got around to reading that Stephen Hawking book. It's about time."
• "I'm still angry at my parents for not buying me expensive rollerblades. Cheapskates."
• "Nothing is as effective as homeopathy."

4 GEORGE CARLIN, American comedian
- "One tequila, two tequila, three tequila...floor."
- "Atheism is a non-prophet organization."
- "The safest place in an earthquake is a stationary store."

5 DOROTHY PARKER, American satirist
- "You can lead a horticulture, but you can't make her think."
- "I'd rather have a bottle in front of me than a frontal lobotomy."
- "If all the girls who attended the Yale prom were laid end to end, I wouldn't be a bit surprised."
- "I wish I could drink like a lady / I can take one or two at the most / Three and I'm under the table / Four and I'm under the host."

6 VICTOR BORGE, Danish musical comedian
- "When an opera star sings her head off, she usually improves her appearance."
- "This concerto was written in four flats because Rachmaninoff had to move four times while he wrote it."
- "Many years ago in Denmark we had inflation, and you are familiar with that problem. In inflation, we have numbers rising. Prices go up. Anything that has to do with money goes up...except the language. See, we have hidden numbers in words like 'wonderful,' 'before,' 'create,' 'tenderly.' All these numbers can be inflated to meet the economy, you know, by rising to the occasion. I suggest we add one to each of these numbers to be prepared. For example, 'wonderful' would be 'two-derful.' 'Before' would be 'be-five.' 'Create,' 'cre-nine.' 'Tenderly' should be 'eleven-derly.' A 'lieutenant' would be a 'lieu-eleven-ant.' A sentence like, 'I ate a tenderloin with my fork' would be 'I nine an elevenderloin with my five-k.' And so on and so fifth."

7 CHRIS BERMAN, American sports analyst

Berman's shtick—making corny puns out of the names of sports stars. For example:

- MLB player Scott "Supercalifragillisticexpialo" Brosius
- NFL player Eric "Sleeping With" Bienemy
- NFL player Jake "Daylight Come And Me Wan'" Delhomme
- MLB player Albert "Winnie the" Pujols

8 GEORGE TAKEI, American actor

From Takei's popular product reviews on Amazon.com:

- *On the "Accoutrements Horse Head Mask":* "I purchased this mane-ly for anonymity, but instead it was a night-mare that saddled me with un-bridled panic."
- *On "Bacon-Shaped Adhesive Bandages":* "Not to pork fun at an injury, but nothing strips the pain away like meating friends out dressed like this."
- *On "Deer Rear with Bottle Opener":* "Deer friends: Looking for the perfect 'hunting lodge' accessory? No ifs, ands, or butts, this is a staggering find."

9 DOUGLAS ADAMS, British satirist

- "You can tune a guitar, but you can't tuna fish. Unless, of course, you play bass."

Two excerpts from The Hitchhiker's Guide to the Galaxy:

- "I am so amazingly cool," said Zaphod Beeblebrox, "you could keep a side of meat in me for a month. I am so hip I have difficulty seeing over my pelvis."
- "No, don't move," Ford added as Arthur began to uncurl himself, "you'd better be prepared for the jump into hyperspace. It's unpleasantly like being drunk."

    "What's so unpleasant about being drunk?"

    "Ask a glass of water."

10 LEWIS CARROLL, British author

From Alice's Adventures in Wonderland:

• "And how many hours a day did you do lessons?" said Alice, in a hurry to change the subject.

"Ten hours the first day," said the Mock Turtle, "nine the next, and so on."

"What a curious plan!" exclaimed Alice.

"That's the reason they're called lessons," the Gryphon remarked: "because they lessen from day to day."

• "We called him Tortoise, because he taught us," said the Mock Turtle angrily.

• "You see the earth takes twenty-four hours to turn round on its axis," said Alice.

"Talking of axes," said the Duchess, "chop off her head!"

11 ROBIN WILLIAMS, American comedian and actor

• "Carpe per diem: seize the check."

• "I thought lacrosse was what you find in la church."

• "I can see it now: Osama bin Laden goes up to the pearly gates where George Washington comes out, starts beating him and is then joined by 70 other members of the Continental Congress. Osama will say, 'Hey, wait! Where are my 71 virgins?' And George will reply, 'It's 71 Virginians, you asshole!'"

• "Freud: If it's not one thing, it's your mother."

AND 1 PARTY-POOPER

"The contribution made to the comic from the realm of the unconscious is always either exposing or obscene; aggressive or hostile; cynical, critical, or blasphemous; or skeptical. Every joke contains an element of seriousness; a joke is never just a joke."

—Sigmund Freud

20 LAST THINGS THAT EVER HAPPENED

*All good things must come to an end, just like this book...
and these things.*

1 The last year that Sony made Betamax VCRs—which battled VHS for market share in the 1980s—was 2002.

2 Last time a gallon of gasoline cost less than $1: March 1999. The U.S. average was 97 cents.

3 Last song that Elvis Presley performed in public: Simon & Garfunkel's "Bridge Over Troubled Water."

4 The last time Saturday morning cartoons aired on network TV: September 27, 2014, when CW ran *Yu-Gi-Oh! Zexal*.

5 Last state to abolish flogging as a legal punishment: Delaware...in 1972.

6 Napoleon's last descendant: Jerome Napoleon Bonaparte, who died in 1945 after tripping over his dog's leash.

7 Jimmy Stewart's last film role: the voice of a dog named Wylie Burp in *An American Tail: Fievel Goes West* (1991).

8 Ethel Merman's last film: *Airplane!* (1980). She played a shell-shocked soldier who believed he was...Ethel Merman.

9 The last time you could see six of the Seven Ancient Wonders: 224 BC (It was never possible to see all seven.)

10 The last U.S. Cavalry horse was named Chief. He died in 1968 at age 36.

11 The last time Frank Sinatra appeared on TV: 1989. He played himself on an episode of *Who's the Boss?*

12 Last two European countries to let women vote: Switzerland (1971) and Liechtenstein (1984).

13 Last cow to graze at the White House: Pauline Wayne, a Holstein who belonged to President Taft (1909–1913).

14 Derek Jeter's last game at Yankee Stadium: September 25, 2014. He drove in the winning run.

15 Last word spoken by Oxford professor Joseph Wright, who edited the *English Dialect Dictionary*: "Dictionary."

16 Nirvana's last show was in Munich, Germany, on March 1, 1994. Lead singer Kurt Cobain died on April 8.

17 The last Tasmanian tiger was named Benjamin. He died in Australia's Hobart Zoo in 1936.

18 Last U.S. president with a beard: Benjamin Harrison, who left office in 1893.

19 Last American veteran of World War I: Frank W. Buckles, who lived to be 110 years old. He died in 2011. His advice for a long life: "When you start to die, don't."

20 Last Blockbuster Video rental, rented just before closing time in Hawaii on November 9, 2013: *This Is the End*.

Record for longest game of Monopoly played in a treehouse: 286 hours.

MORE UNCLE JOHN'S THAN YOU CAN SHAKE A STICK AT!

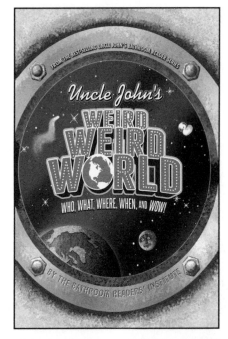

Log onto our online store at *www.bathroomreader.com* for dozens more great titles in the Bathroom Reader line. You'll find puzzle books, regional-interest books, big books, little books, and e-books! Great reading no matter where you are!

THE LAST PAGE

Tanks for reading! Now that you've completed our book of lists, here are seven fun things you can do next.

1 Make your own to-do list: Name the first 10 things you would do if you won a million dollars.

2 Stop a random person on the sidewalk and share your favorite fact from this book.

3 Think of a list you'd like to see in our next edition and tell us on Facebook at *UncleJohnsBathroomReader*.

4 Go to our online store at *www.BathroomReader.com* and order more great books from our series.

5 Tweet yourself to daily facts and fun on Twitter. We're *@Bathroom_Reader*.

6 Walk in to a fancy hotel lobby and switch the "Men" and "Women" placards on the restroom doors.

7 Follow Uncle John's advice: Never stop learning, and when the going gets tough... *Go with the Flow!*